D1209220

JUBAL EARLY

JUBAL EARLY

Robert E. Lee's "Bad Old Man"

Benjamin Franklin Cooling III

ROWMAN & LITTLEFIELD
Lanham • Boulder • New York • London

Published by Rowman & Littlefield
A wholly owned subsidiary of The Rowman & Littlefield Publishing Group,
Inc.
4501 Forbes Boulevard, Suite 200, Lanham, Maryland 20706
www.rowman.com

16 Carlisle Street, London W1D 3BT, United Kingdom

British Library Cataloguing in Publication Information Available

Library of Congress Cataloging-in-Publication Data

Cooling, Benjamin Franklin, III, 1938-
Jubal Early : Robert E. Lee's "bad old man" / Benjamin Franklin Cooling III.
pages cm
Includes bibliographical references and index.
ISBN 978-0-8108-8913-2 (hardcover : alk. paper) -- ISBN 978-0-8108-8914-9 (ebook)
1. Early, Jubal Anderson, 1816-1894. 2. Generals--Confederate States of America--Biography. 3.
United States--History--Civil War, 1861-1865--Biography. 4. United States--History--Civil War,
1861-1865--Campaigns. 5. Confederate States of America. Army--Biography. I. Title.
E467.1.E13C66 2014
355.0092--dc23/p>
[B]
2014015338

♾™ The paper used in this publication meets the minimum requirements of
American National Standard for Information Sciences Permanence of Paper
for Printed Library Materials, ANSI/NISO Z39.48-1992.

Printed in the United States of America

In memory of
Major General Joseph Brown, USAF
Commandant, Industrial College of the Armed Forces
National Defense University, 2010–2013

A son of VMI and acolyte of "Stonewall" Jackson who
would have appreciated "Old Jube" as
Jackson's successor

CONTENTS

ACKNOWLEDGMENTS

The most immediate aid and counsel came from Walton B. Owen, Gail Stephens, Fred L. Ray, Ted Alexander, as well as Bennett Graff, and Martin Gordon of Rowman and Littlefield Publishing Group. But, ultimately we are all indebted to the post-holing and insightful work that has come before in capturing Jubal Anderson Early for posterity. An earlier corps of historians, such as Millard K. Bushong, Douglas Southall Freeman, Thomas A. Lewis, Edward J. Stackpole, Frank Vandiver, and Jeffrey Wert, have been joined by a new cohort led by William C. Davis, Richard R. Duncan, Gary Gallagher, Charles C. Osborne, Scott C. Patchan, Thomas E. Schott, and Gary C. Walker, as well as Daniel T. Davis and Phillip S. Greenwalt—all of whom have contributed to the body of knowledge as reflected in the present book.

PREFACE

What do we really need to know about Jubal Anderson Early after 150 years? What is important about "Old Jube" at this time of the Civil War sesquicentennial? Called by Robert E. Lee his "bad old man," Early has had his biographies, including Millard K. Bushong's *Old Jube: A Biography of General Jubal A. Early* (1955) and Charles C. Osborne's *Jubal: The Life and Times of General Jubal A. Early, C.S.A.* (1992). Gary Gallagher and Thomas E. Schott have written on aspects of the man and his place in history (see bibliography). More recently this pair in particular has scrutinized Early as a Whig-Unionist who was reluctant to secede from the Union but wedded to his state's destiny and became a virulent—nay, rabid—Yankee-hater and exponent of "Lost Cause" apologia.

So what are the remaining, gnawing questions about this preeminent Confederate general who perhaps came closest to ending the war on Confederate terms in 1864 yet within two months essentially lost that war for the South? Why pay attention after a century and one-half to a politically incorrect figure in American history who came closest of anyone to taking Washington in the most crucial election year of the period; to capturing, killing, wounding, or even dismissing Abraham Lincoln from the White House and perchance changing the course of American history; even rendering emancipation moot? Perhaps the answer lies in the blunt phrase "but who didn't!"

At this point, Jubal Early may be said to have been the following:

- Reasonably successful country/small-town lawyer

- West Point–trained/citizen solder and Confederate general officer
- Memoirist, Confederate apologist, influential war veteran
- Submissionist, renegade, controversialist
- Arthritic, crabbed survivor of an era

We know of Jubal Early's role from Bull Run to Appomattox, or do we? How can we explain his rise from mere regimental to corps and independent army commander? Was he a professional soldier because he went to West Point, or was his prewar duality of soldier and lawyer simply replicating any number of citizen soldiers who at one time or another volunteered to serve community and government under contract and then return Cincinnatus-like to their native plows? Was he the first or merely among the very few of Lee's lieutenants who came to embrace if not fully understand the implications of what modern historians term a "hard" or "destructive" war? And, as a subordinate at all levels, was he merely a good fighter or some latent master of command, some risk-taking strategist or miracle worker who—by mid-1864—was about all Lee had left in the generals' cabinet? Was Early the tenacious combatant in the image of Stonewall Jackson, with distinct tactical, operational, even strategic abilities, but compromised by weaknesses in reconnaissance, use of cavalry, and irresolution at pivotal moments between mediocrity and brilliance? Did Early blink before the forts of Washington in July of that year when he could have ended the Civil War on Confederate terms? And was his relative obscurity in the pantheon of rebel leaders what baffled Union civilian and military leaders, allowing him to reach even that cusp of success virtually unnoticed in the first place?

One of the earlier deans of Civil War military studies, T. Harry Williams, controversially posited that the "most distinguishing feature of Southern generalship is that it did not grow." Robert E. Lee and other generals were "pretty much the same men in 1865 that they had been in 1861."[1] With that, Williams set in motion the next generation of argument that so mesmerizes Civil War students today. Was this true of a general like Jubal Early? If so—and there is certainly room to conclude that he fit Williams's paradigm—then how do we explain some things? What was his quirk of personality, style, and character that enabled this war chieftain to defy his own demise and enabled his Army of the Valley District, subsequent Shenandoah Valley disasters in the fall notwithstanding, to gain Lee and the Confederacy perhaps six months of additional life? Or was Early always a forlorn hope, a sacrificial lamb, Lee's convenient tool, like any loyal subordinate? What did his men think of him? How well regarded or not was Old Jube in the eyes of his opponents? Did he maneuver Confederate competitors out of positions of trust and rank? And, most important, how did this reluctant secessionist from Virginia's Piedmont become the preeminent spokesman for postwar's so-called "Lost Cause"? Even then, was there something more behind the unrepentant, unreconstructed Jubal Early—a driving force to redeem himself in the eyes of Marse Robert and the prostrated South that blamed him for defeat? And what did this hard-swearing, hard-drinking, fusty, nineteenth-century American leave as a portrait to posterity?

This is not a complete biography. It does propose a critical, focused analysis of a legend and a reality for our times. Here was a man at least two Civil War historians have voted as the general they most wanted to sit down with and converse over a campfire.[2] More in the style of Gary Gallagher's focused essay approach or even more particularly Paul Ashdown and Edward Caudill on another controversial Confederate hero/villain, Nathan Bedford Forrest[3] —but not necessarily psychohistory— this sesquicentennial search for Jubal Early really stems from when I first encountered him. For years, eminent Civil War historian Frank Vandiver's 1960 book (it sold for $4.95) *Jubal's Raid* guided my study. My own trilogy on Early's quest to take Washington unveiled a fascinating "soldier's soldier," a welcome antidote to Lost Cause hagiography and saccharine Virginia dynasty worship. Yet, his Old Dominion origins, his devotion to patron Robert E. Lee, and his own part in the Confederates' redemptive crusade offer curious contradictions. More important, perhaps America's own contradictions today regarding war offer a prism for examining and better understanding the rougher, more pragmatic great captains of the Civil War period like Jubal Early.

In 1957, Hollywood adapted a book by psychiatrists Corbett H. Thigpen and Harvey M. Cleckley into the widely acclaimed film *The Three Faces of Eve*. Joanne Woodward, who won an Academy Award for Best Actress, played the starring role as "Eve White/Eve Black," in real life Chris Costner Sizemore, who was afflicted with multiple personality disorder. Without suggesting Jubal Early was mentally distressed (although one might wonder toward the end of his life) or possessed of three separate and distinct personalities rolled into one, the book and film title suggest an approach to explaining this capable, unlikeable, controversial, yet indispensable figure for understanding the Civil War and its mythic postwar implications. Jubal presented three faces (if not personalities) paralleling three phases in his life—antebellum, bellum, and postbellum personalities. Just as Eve suffered a traumatic event that led to her "splitting off" into distinctly different personalities, one might see this in Jubal Early. The death of his mother, Mexico-spawning arthritis, absence of conventional marriage, personal conflict over Virginia's secession, trauma of the battlefield, infamy of defeat, and relief from command, as well as postwar poverty and Yankee triumphalism all come to mind. This "moment" is hard to either discern or document precisely. It may well have been subliminal atonement for failing so utterly before the gates of Washington! Or, it may have been David Hunter's "hard" devastating war against civilians—their homes, their provender, their way of life—in the Shenandoah Valley that triggered a psychological tipping point (or at least one of them). Quite likely Early's abject failure in what today would be cited as "responsibility to protect" (or government's responsibility to protect its citizens from crimes against humanity) in the valley preyed subliminally upon the ailing general. Outwardly he blamed the enemy. Perhaps inwardly he blamed himself, carrying that burden to his grave. Still, we can merely employ the "Three Faces of Jube" device for reexploring this Confederate general and his meaning for us today. Undoubtedly, some answers went to the grave with Jubal Anderson Early in 1894.

I

MOLDING A PIEDMONT SOLDIER, LAWYER/RELUCTANT SECESSIONIST

What was it about the Piedmont and southwestern Virginia that could yield up a rough-hewn Jubal Anderson Early? Scarcely of the lineage that produced Robert E. Lee, Early's origins were closer to those of Stonewall Jackson, falling perhaps in between these two Confederate deities. Yet Early was hardly a hardscrabble Abraham Lincoln or even a West Tennessean, slave-dealing Nathan Bedford Forrest either. In fact, he was a product of what might be termed *Piedmont privilege*—a middle-class, slave-owning family, with both parents accustomed to providing stability and local prominence (for the time and place). He was decently schooled, possessed of sufficient intellect, and came from hardy Anglo-Scottish roots. Born November 3, 1816, in the Red Valley section of Franklin County, some 18 miles north of the county seat Rocky Mount, his name reflected parents Joab and Ruth Hairston Earlys' propensity toward biblical appellation. His slave-owning father served the community as sheriff, colonel of militia, and sometime state legislator. His mother's family was accustomed to the slave-holding society of Pittsylvania County. Young Jubal came naturally by many of his later qualities. These included position and authority, military and civilian service, and dedication to a Southern culture of neighborhood community and allegiance to the Old Dominion. He would apparently own just one slave in his lifetime, yet he vehemently embraced the institution and its stranglehold on region and nation. Was this a product of his youth? We can merely speculate how his boyhood influenced his future role in American history.

Early's own sparse autobiography is not particularly helpful. Charles Osborne, his most comprehensive biographer, hints that subsequent "extreme vulnerability" and "over-developed regard for what other people thought of him" might have young roots. His emotional energy required inward and fierce denial and thus hid a softer side. Early's "profound pessimism" and inability to enjoy others' company beyond family could well have explained a certain disciplined or stoic approach spawned in preadolescent years. Lacking profound proof, most Early watchers have moved quickly to more fertile fields. Still, at least the skeleton of Early's formative years can be instructive. Perhaps the loss of his mother at a crucial stage lends a clue, although modern analyst Thomas E. Schott, like most of us, searches vainly for "some traumatic event" in Early's childhood that might illustrate his "'exclusive and re-pellant' characteristics in maturity."[1]

Early himself seemed most struck by the death of his mother in 1832, a pivotal event in any teenager's passage. She was a "most estim-able lady," he recalled, whose death not only caused deepest sorrow to her family but occasioned "universal regret in the whole circle of her acquaintances." Aside from that cryptic passage, Early admits little. In a male-dominated world, he would not have done so. Instead, he also noted that up to that time he had "enjoyed the benefit of the best schools" in the region, singling out the "usual instruction in the dead languages and elementary mathematics." Thanks to his prosperous planter father and local congressman Nathaniel H. Claiborne, young Early received an appointment to West Point, perhaps as much because the county had never sent anyone to the military academy as for one preceptor's glowing comment on his "peculiar aptitude" for science and "extraordinary mathematical genius." It was this Early who matriculated on the Hudson. Upon passing probation, he joined the class of 1837 along with Braxton Bragg, John C. Pemberton, Arnold Elzey, and William H. T. Walker of future Confederate acclaim, as well as Joseph Hooker, John Sedgwick, and William H. French, who remained loyal to national government and flag. These were hardly an exceptional band of brothers by any stretch. Nonetheless, future Civil War generals P. G. T. Beauregard, Richard Ewell, Edward "Allegheny" Johnson, Irwin

McDowell, and George Gordon Meade were also Early's contemporaries at the military academy.

Proclaiming later that "there was nothing worthy of particular note" in his career at West Point, Early admitted that he "was not a very exemplary soldier" and never held any sort of rank in the corps of cadets. Moreover, impatient of success and unbending in comportment, he admittedly had "very little taste for scrubbing brass, and cared very little for the advancement to be obtained by the exercise of that most useful art." Additionally, he was "never a very good student" was "sometimes quite remiss." Still, he managed a respectable standing of sixth in military and civil engineering and graduated 18 in a class of 50. Correspondence in the Jubal Early papers at the Library of Congress suggests family concern at the time about his dedication, perseverance, and aversion to privation and hardship. He certainly found it difficult to develop close friendships, as shown by verbal and physical sparring with future Civil War generals like Joseph Hooker and Lewis Armistead. Hooker and Early jabbed about the treatment of slaves, while a mess hall altercation with Armistead may have underscored Early's pugnacity but also led to Armistead's dismissal from the academy. Jubal's father, brother, and sister held high hopes for the budding soldier and tried to bolster his morale with news of familiar life back home, like raising tobacco.[2]

More memorable in these years, perhaps, was Early's serious flirtation with leaving school to fight for Texas's freedom against Mexican oppression. It also suggested an adventuresome streak. A century later, retired general Edward Stackpole's observation remains apt: "Blunt in speech, [Early] was ready for a fight at the drop of a hat and he didn't always wait for the fall." Dissuaded from doing so by father Joab, Early's correspondence with his parent may tell something about his embrace of cause and his ideals, lofty goals, and pugnacity (thinks Osborne). Harboring no illusions of becoming a Napoleon or even Simon Bolivar, Early still told his father of the ennobling obligation to help Texans throw off the Mexican yoke (citing, of course, America's own experience against the British). That he would be in on the ground floor of a great new endeavor suggested another youthful Early fancy—an independent Texas—and with winning Texans' confidence by fighting for their cause, he might circumvent all the impediments of class and seniority in his native land. He called it a "start in the world," something that Joab prized and young Jubal earnestly cultivated to secure parental support and approval. In any event, the scheme died, Early graduated West Point, gained a lieutenancy of artillery, and went off to fight Seminoles in Florida, as was the duty of academy graduates.[3]

Gary Gallagher sees something deeper surfacing from the youth's soul during his Mexican infatuation. Drawing similarities between states' rights under Mexican and American constitutions, whereby weak central government was counteracted by independent state and local authorities, Early was impressed by Mexico's soldiers and the president's authoritarian use of power. Words like *usurpation, tyranny, despotism*, and *overturned constitution* attached themselves to the name of Santa Anna in Early's view. An "implicit compact" between American immigrants and Mexico's central government relating to Texas's free constitution had been violated, he advanced. If this association of political philosophy and compromise of honor and rights might be seen so early in youth, might they have further maturing in the cauldron of what was yet to come for an adolescent America? Gallagher apparently thinks so, but the trend of Jubal Early's life was really not so clear at this point.[4]

There was another thread that surfaced from Early's West Point years. Apparently expressing doubts of happiness and pecuniary advance via an army career, Early listened to brother Samuel's counsel to uphold the statutory one-year obligation for service of graduates and then return to civilian pursuits, possibly law, medicine, or engineering. Thus, the idea of an alternative life had already begun to mature in Jubal's mind. Campaigning against the Seminoles brought little fame, and Early referred to his experience and honing of skills as a junior subaltern as simply hearing "some bullets whistling among the trees," none coming close, and seeing no Seminoles. Determined to return home and take up law, Early wistfully noted in his autobiography that, while transiting back to Virginia via Louisville, he received notice of promotion and might have withheld his letter of resignation if the notice had found him earlier. Too late (perhaps the first of more missed opportunities that would condition much of a later military experience), the purposeful young veteran kept to course. He may have been further chastened by a jilting young Philadelphia socialite, Lavinia, who possibly proved more influential to his future as a confirmed bachelor than any second thoughts about the army career.[5]

Early began law study with prominent Rocky Mount attorney Norborne F. Taliaferro in the autumn of 1830. Two years later, he gained his license to practice. At the same time, Early joined the Whig Party and was sent to the general assembly in Richmond as the youngest member of that body for the term 1841–1842. There, he soon learned the wiles of politics. His old mentor, Democrat Taliaferro, ousted him, although he ensured that Early succeeded him as prosecuting attorney for Franklin and Floyd counties, appointments that he maintained as a successful barrister until reorganization of the state government in 1851. Early never identified as a popular politician, losing several attempts to return to Richmond. Yet, he remained a loyal Whig. As Early himself described these years, "I continued the practice of law in my own and the adjoining counties, with very fair success until the breaking out of the war between the United States and Mexico, consequent to the annexation of Texas." For 20 years, the Mexican War aside, Jubal Early plied his profession over mostly wills and small debt adjudication as well as public brawling, while acquiring a reputation as a capable, honest, and colorless country lawyer. The conflict with Mexico arrived fortuitously to relieve the tedium of the docket. Rural Virginia never quite satiated Early's disdain for convention or zest for life.[6]

Was Early's desire to proffer his services to the Old Dominion in America's clash with Mexico so very complicated? True, as a Whig he supported national party leader but antiwar Henry Clay's opposition to Texan annexation to the United States. Yet recall his stance over Texan independence while at West Point. Mexican affront to Texas was in his blood. Early himself expressed the anomaly while declaring "when the war ensued, I felt it to be my duty to sustain the government in that war and to enter the military service if a fitting opportunity offered." Gallagher attaches the term *patriotic submission* to Early's name, a streak he sees always present later for explaining the man and his political beliefs. Indeed, when Washington called upon the commonwealth for a volunteer regiment, Major Jubal Early went back to the national colors. Military life might be like the practice of law, prosaic and mundane, yet in wartime, action, excitement, and opportunity could present themselves. If they had not done so in Florida, they might do so in Mexico, although perhaps not as Early anticipated. The Virginians arrived late to Zachary Taylor's scene of operations in northern Mexico. Their role was anything but combat glory. The Virginia regiment, said Early, "had no opportunity of reaping laurels during the war, but I can say that it had not sullied the flag of the State, which constituted the regimental colors, by disorderly conduct or acts of depredation on private property, and non-combatants."[7]

So what *did* service in the Mexican War do for Jubal Early? We know from his memoirs that he was enamored with meeting Jefferson Davis, future Confederate president, and commanding the First Mississippi volunteers in Mexico. "I was struck with his soldierly bearing, and he did me the honor of complimenting the order and regularity of my camp," Early would recall. We learn that the role Early's Virginians played in a now-quiet sector of the war was more logistical and occupational, for he had "no opportunity of seeing active service." He served as an inspector general on brigade staff, and as earlier in Florida, Early provided more organizational oversight for "breaking in the regiment at the beginning and I [actually] commanded the regiment for a much longer time than any other field officer." His immediate superiors were Colonel John F. Hamtramck and Lieutenant Colonel Thomas B. Randolph, who were both West Pointers but surely represented the looser aspects of the volunteer militia system upon which America based her military policy at the time. By all accounts, they seemed somewhat dysfunctional in their roles. This enabled Major Early, however, to further hone leadership qualities invaluable to this same system of what may be termed the "citizen soldier."[8]

Yet, Major Early on various occasions displayed qualities of initiative and risk taking. When he pressed regimental commander Hamtramck to allow him to undertake a risky scouting mission with fifty volunteers against his superior's wishes, Early received the retort, "Jubal, I can testify you are an Early who is never late, but I fear you will soon be known as the late Early." Nevertheless, the young major survived and successfully completed his mission. Early also succeeded at military governance of the town of Monterey. He claimed that both American officers and Mexican civilians conceded that "better order reigned in the city during the time I commanded there, than ever existed before, and the good conduct of my men won for them universal praise." Certainly Early's concern for the command's health, camp hygiene, and persistent drilling of the men won Hamtramck's amazement. "Our improvement astonishes even our own officers and soldiers here," Early noted upon retuning from sick leave in June 1847. On the other hand,

Early's own admission as a "rather strict disciplinarian" denied him favor among the troops in the early days of their association. By the time they were mustered out of service at Fortress Monroe the following July, however, he was the "most popular officer in the regiment" and had the satisfaction of "receiving from a great many of the men the assurance that they had misjudged me in the beginning and were now convinced that I had been their best friend all the time."[9]

The other result of his Mexican experience was a lifelong affliction with arthritis or rheumatism. The dews and damps of a northern Mexico winter produced a noticeable stoop that would forever mark Jubal Early's appearance. The angular, slim, six-footer with a square jaw and piercing dark eyes would progressively give way to a distinctively unsoldierly stoop by the time of the Civil War. The condition even led to a three-month sick leave, during which Early recuperated with his father and brother, who had removed to the Kanawha Valley in western Virginia. Just how incapacitating pain and stiffness proved at this point remained hidden by one notable event. Returning from leave aboard the Ohio River steamboat *Blue Ridge*, Early experienced a boiler explosion tragedy that claimed 14 lives. It also occasioned one of those rare glimpses of a humorous streak in the man: "After getting over the first effects of the slight injury received [from a piece of boiler iron protruding through the deck of his stateroom], I experienced a decided improvement in my rheumatism, though I would not advise blowing up in a western steamboat as an infallible remedy." Perhaps the rheumatism never lessened Early's sense of humor.[10]

The thirty-two-year-old Mexican War veteran once again left army service by the end of summer 1848. Seasoned, wiser, if bent from the arthritis and presenting a grizzled appearance far beyond his years, "Major" Early (as he was widely known) resumed his law career and displayed a decidedly maverick disdain of social conventions in Rocky Mount. That he was restless and unhappy with his choice to return to civilian life seemed evident in correspondence with old army friend L. Woods. Moreover, Early now took up living with a Julia McNealey, who—in the quaint phrase of his biographer Charles Osborne—was "as close to being Jubal Early's wife as anybody ever came." Until her own marriage in 1871, she bore Early four offspring out of wedlock, whom he embraced as his own, including one Jubal L. Early. But was it the death of his mother, the experience with Lavinia, or just rough-hewn male domination that would always make it difficult for Jubal Early to relate to the opposite sex in a compassionate manner?[11]

Whether unconventional (even by rural standards of the day), controversial among Rock Mount elite, indicative of rebelliousness, arrogant self-confidence from wartime seasoning, or just assertiveness accompanying most young men in their thirties—or something uniquely Jubal Early—the McNealey arrangement apparently did not affect his community standing as a competent, honest lawyer. A successfully contested inheritance case in distant Lowndes County, Mississippi, added to his laurels and self-confidence. Possessed of typical white attitudes toward blacks and slavery, Early nonetheless took on cases involving that sector as well as divorce. An ardent proponent of the South's slave system, Early apparently owned just one slave in his life. When Osborne styles Early's "imaginative ability" with regard to human need, perhaps he suggests that Early even in midlife was a character. If through negligent business discipline in fee collection for his services; obliviousness toward acquaintances passing him on the street because of "preoccupation of my mind"; a cavalier, "rather spasmodic" practice of the law; or procrastination in preparation, Early admitted that his legal career was "never very lucrative." Yet, he also contended his practice had become very considerable. By the end of the 1850s, a distinctive Jubal Early was about to become even more controversial.[12]

Early had reentered politics only to suffer repeated defeats attempting to represent Franklin County in the Virginia Constitutional Convention of 1850–1851 and regain his former state assembly seat two years later. But he did win commonwealth attorney rank under a new state constitution. His abortive campaign to secure the convention seat had shown a quality that would soon resurface. He claimed, "I opposed firmly and unflinchingly all the radical changes, miscalled reforms, which were proposed," and consequently was defeated, along with fellow candidates so inclined. Early seemed a contradiction: a maverick yet wedded to stability and conservatism. Unconventional and contrarian by word and action, he would always seem fixed to the past, not the future. Avowedly, that future was hardly clear in the 1850s when many Americans seemed wedded to the status quo. Early admitted to a "very limited degree the capacity for popular speaking" and, together with a neither popular nor captivating manner, felt his forte lay not with argument before a jury but "on questions of law before the court, especially in cases of appeal." A test of his self-effacement soon came with Virginia's secession convention in 1861. Ironically, Early would devote no space in his autobiography to this portion of his life. Yet, it also suggested unconventionality in the man's makeup as well as convictions of personal honor, disciplined loyalty to state, Whig conservatism, and liberty and property protected by the 1789 federal constitution. [13]

The Union was rent by the election of a minority candidate, Republican Abraham Lincoln, as president in late 1860. Immediately or soon thereafter, Southern states either voted for secession or called for state conventions to consider the issue. Yet, the Old Dominion, like much of the upper South, seemed confused. In mid-February, 145,697 white male Virginia voters elected 152 delegates to a secession convention. Only about one-third favored immediate separation, however. Delegates Jubal Early and Peter Saunders were not among them. The Franklin County representatives reflected upcountry lineage and attitudes. They were Unionists, determined to wait and see what the Lincoln administration might do in response to the initial epidemic of Deep South secession. But was secession only a matter of time given Virginia's precarious location tied to the region south of the Potomac and Ohio rivers or economic links to slavery? Major Jubal Early with his particular allegiance to constitutional Union, stability, and Virginia appeared cloaked with local approval. Having canvassed heavily against secession in his home county, much rode with Early on the train to Richmond. He was conservative, Unionist, and for the constitution as it stood at the moment. He was also a most loyal Virginian. [14]

The talented body that lawyer/soldier Jubal Early joined seemed inclined toward moderation despite pressure from special lobbyists sent from South Carolina, Georgia, and Mississippi to urge Virginia's immediate secession. Tidewater separationists at the Richmond meeting fretted about national government reinforcement of coastal forts on Virginia soil and coercion of the populace by their guns. But orator Early twice in February used his military acumen to dampen such fears. He noted long-standing garrison duties, war plans, and defensive measures at places like Fortress Monroe—hardly unique to the crisis of the moment. Characteristically, Early bluntly declared that the only threat of forts' guns were to those irrational enough to "run their heads into the mouth of one of them." [15]

Whether or not Early's words and demeanor illustrated Osborne's phrase "logic, humor, and common sense," they certainly reflected his practicality. Nothing done by Washington up to that point had provided tinder for the secessionist firebox. Incendiary orations in the Richmond Mechanics Hall did, however. Verbiage reached a crescendo when Lincoln's inaugural speech of March 4 (termed "enigmatical" by Early and Unionist colleagues but a threat and augury of war by their opponents) merged with the question of slavery, repeal of the slave trade prohibition, and extension of slavery into the territories. Early soon engaged in heated debate with secessionist John Goode. Wrath and impatience simmered beneath Early's measured surface as he cautioned for allowing the new president to faithfully execute the laws in all the states that would ensure "peace and protection for our property," meaning slaves. Temporary sanity returned when Goode and Early patched their differences, but time was fast running out on parliamentary conciliatory and procedural methods both in Richmond and Washington to avert further disunion. By April 12, the Virginia convention had a delegation in Washington to meet with Lincoln. That day, Jubal Early again took to the convention floor. Once more he embraced the practical, the pragmatic, the logical, and couched this time on the question touching Southern pocketbooks. [16]

Early now raised the economic issue of the impact of continued impasse and possible secession upon tobacco production in the Old Dominion. It was a simple question of markets and capital—Northern markets and Northern capital. Tobacco consumption "depends on the number of mouths to be supplied," and the North held the trump card—"there is more tobacco consumed there." Slaveholders and nonslaveholders alike were affected. Exit Virginia, and the federal government would use a protective tariff to stimulate tobacco production across lower Ohio, Indiana, and Illinois, thereby excluding Virginia products from this larger market. Financial ruin would result for Old Dominion growers and manufacturers. Early also showed economic acumen by citing recent drought in the state, causing importation of Tennessee corn via the youthful Virginia and Tennessee Railroad link through his home region. He advanced the attraction of upper-South interstate trade with the Ohio Valley as cause for his home state to remain in the Union. He also raised the specter of a Confederate army transiting Virginia to get at the Northern foe, thus compromising Early's twin talismans of the legitimacy of two governments: one national in Washington and one state in Richmond. [17]

The Virginia convention rebuffed secession in a ballot on April 4 by a two-to-one margin, much to Early's delight. But events elsewhere now intervened. Firebrand secessionists won the day in Charleston, South Carolina, where they attacked federal property. Fort Sumter was defended as Lincoln told the Richmond delegation that it would be. Early rose with heavy heart (he claimed) on April 13 to deplore the desecration to the old flag and his affinity for old army mate and fort commander Robert Anderson (possessing Virginia blood of an officer of the Revolution who fought for the very liberty now threatened by South Carolina's precipitous actions). Early deplored a very real danger that "placed a gulf" between the so-called Confederate states and Virginia, upon whose soil war and invading armies now threatened to trod. A cruel twist intruded when he closed his peroration: "If there be any Virginians who advise or encourage the idea of marching an army from the Confederate States through our borders to Washington, they mistake the tone and temper of our people." He trusted that the issue might never come, "but when it does come, mark it, that the invasion of our soil will be promptly resisted." He vowed, "The spirit of manhood has not deserted the sons of Virginia."

Early still resisted secession in the subsequent April 17 balloting, which voted down secession, 88 to 55. Departing the Union would occasion "such a war as this country has never seen," he told colleagues. Yet Lincoln's executive actions in the wake of Fort Sumter gave him pause. Lincoln's call for 75,000 militia from the states to enforce laws of the land and suppress rebellion reeked of Santa Anna's usurpation of authority in Texas to the Virginian. It seemed an attack on states' prerogative to Early, suggests Gallagher. Early doubted the legality of the militia call without the president first issuing a warning. That failing, he asked, did Lincoln have the right to call on the military to aid civil authority? Obviously, it was all in interpretation of the constitution and the law. Early also thought it odd that Lincoln would recall Congress only by Independence Day—months away. It seemed, said this frustrated Constitutional Unionist (called by opponents the "Terrapin from Franklin County" because of his slowness to embrace the inevitable), that the Lincoln regime had "lost all prudence, discretion, and good sense." When Virginia's Ordinance of Secession finally passed on April

25, Jubal Early, the loyal Virginian, finally submitted to the ultimate authority of states' rights. It was not the move that Early had anticipated, but once taken, it was a popular back home overnight. Moreover, Governor James Letcher two days before had nominated Robert E. Lee to lead Virginia forces. Whether or not the Old Dominion had the "right of secession or revolution," Early informed fellow delegates, he wished to see his state triumphant. Lee was the proper leader to do so. By the end of the month, Early signed a ratified secession ordinance, tendered his services to Letcher, and as a Virginia colonel began organizing volunteers in Lynchburg.[18]

Gallagher poses the inherent contradiction of Jubal Early at this point. How could Early's professed prewar love of the Union seem heartfelt when years later his "unrepentant pro-Confederate invective became legendary"? Gallagher suggests the Early of the secession winter was consistent with negotiating political shoals of the moment yet one who saw seeds of Virginia (hence Confederate) loyalty emerging as unshakable due to constitutional trampling actions by Abraham Lincoln in the spring. Early's model was Robert E. Lee. Early voted "even against hope," he said, that war might be prevented. He claimed to have found it "exceedingly difficult to surrender the attachment of a lifetime to that Union" that he had been accustomed to viewing in the words of fellow Virginian George Washington as the "palladium of the political safety and prosperity of the country." On several occasions during the resulting war, Early, seemingly always a reluctant secessionist, flung the deed back in the faces of more ardent separatists like erstwhile 1860 presidential candidate and subsequent military subordinate John C. Breckinridge, as well as one sometime secessionist delegate in the convention, Jeremiah Morton. Yet such actions would occur when the cause was faltering, not in May 1861.[19]

Gallagher contends that "Early's devotion to the nation was genuine, an outgrowth of his belief that the Constitution safeguarded the liberty of white citizens to have a voice in their own governance and to amass and enjoy property." Thus, his "political submission" (Gallagher's phrase) to the Union was really conditional. Embracing states' rights, slavery, honor, structure, and stability, Jubal Early, like so many Southerners, had watched the unfolding saga of slave liberation in his own state at Harpers Ferry in 1859. Abolitionism as represented in John Brown's raid troubled the established order, boded ill for the future, and suggested a Northern radical revolution that threatened person and property. The ingredients of racism and Confederate nationalism lay waiting to break forth from the breast of so ardent a state supremacist as Jubal Early from 1859 onward. But two years later, adhering to a wait-and-see policy about the threat to the South and its way of politics, economics, and society posed by the popular election of the minority party and its standard-bearer—Republican Abraham Lincoln—Early's decision was tipped by Fort Sumter and the national call to arms to suppress insurrection. Early and Virginia were too physically close to the new regime in Washington to now await intentions, actions, and conclusions. Virginia when it seceded provided a frontier between nations but also the invasion route to suppress other sister states departing in peace. So Gallagher can conclude Lincoln's actions beginning on April 15 violated Early's concept of the constitutional compact between the United States and Virginia—to which he always had turned for protection of property and civil order. Hence, "he felt duty bound to stand by his state and accompany it into the Confederacy." The irony was that thousands of Americans both north and south of the Potomac and Ohio rivers felt likewise in some manner—the other side had violated the sacred pact of the founding fathers. That was why American youth seemed willing to go to war about it![20]

So that spring, as perhaps for decades, Early's loyalty lay preeminently with Virginia. It was much the same for his future chieftain, Robert E. Lee. Any concept of "nation" to these men was a backdrop, a transcendent concept not fully matured in the nineteenth-century world in which they lived. It had been put to the test by actions taken in the name of the United States. Early, as lawyer-soldier, could merely declare, "As we are now engaged in this contest, all my wishes, all my desires and all the energies of my hand and heart will be given to the cause of my state. Whether we have the right of secession or revolution, I want to see my state triumphant." With that he offered his sword and services to Governor John Letcher and received, in turn, the appointment of colonel in the Virginia militia. Typically, Jubal Early pronounced strongly that his state's approval of the secession ordinance "wrung from me bitter tears of grief." Were these hypocritical expressions to salve conscience? Many erstwhile Rebel leaders expressed similar sentiments. Early, however, would never look back. Devoted to a Union that was now past, he staked his life and fortune on Virginia's course in some new union with uncertain future. Would it reflect some manifestation of national unification so endemic of budding movements elsewhere or mere confederation, ironically embedded in trappings of the old—caste and class and slavery? Early was no political philosopher and hardly a man of nuance and subtlety. His test like that of Virginia and the Confederacy would come in the fiery trial of war.[21]

What can we say of Jubal Anderson Early to this point? The notion of duty, honor, country instilled at West Point or "my country right or wrong, but right or wrong, my country" seems to have conflicted with affinity to home state, legalism, and property in his mind. Hardly part of the Old Regular Army's band of brothers (many of whom, admittedly, also followed the paths of their states of origin), his allegiance lay less with brief years in uniform than with his civilian calling, a Virginia of law as a bulwark of societal stability, tradition, loyalty, and, of course, slavery. Constitutional compact between state and nation, sense of honor and "dignity" of his state and its society, a certain code based on protection of property and civil order explain Jubal Early's approach. Still, from demerits at the academy to obstinacy at being railroaded toward secession, Early showed a streak of the contrarian, of being his own man and deciding things his way. Finding oneself is the province of the young, and whether flaunting a common-law wife or choosing the law over Mars, Early set his mark at this time. Psychologically, perhaps, he was not only announcing his individuality but personally determining a conceptual capacity or extent of an ability to think about and organize his experiences to a particular point. He had been in a minority all his life, he declared with reference his Whig Party politics. "I have been standing up against currents that few men of my humble capacity could withstand," he continued, "in defence of the rights of the minority." Slaves not included, of course, but he remained convinced that such rights could be asserted not by force or violence but under the constitution and according to the laws. When the antebellum national regime proved incapable of doing so by choice as witnessed in Lincoln's actions, then Jubal Early felt no remorse about following his state under a new banner that would do so. Functioning more tactically, Early had not as yet faced strategic complexity or the need to rise to that stratum of thinking. But it would come—in the cauldron of what Abraham Lincoln styled a "People's War." Ironically, the courses chosen by Lincoln and Early would ultimately cross again—this time on the battle-field. [22]

2

PROVING HIMSELF

First Manassas to Second Fredericksburg

Biographers of Jubal Early as well as his own memoirs provide a detailed account of the crucial early war years that shaped the future general's experience. That experience in camp and field embraced preparing his Lynchburg units for combat and shipping them to the Virginia front. Then, battles from First Manassas to Williamsburg (where he was wounded) and Malvern Hill in defense of Richmond, thence to Cedar Run (Mountain), Bristow Station, Groveton, Second Manassas, and Chantilly in a return to northern Virginia further shaped him. Early's experience came in command of organizations larger than a mere company and regiment. He began to assume a dramatis persona of his own with the invasion of Maryland (Harpers Ferry and Sharpsburg). The period of the Confederate zenith at Fredericksburg, Chancellorsville, and Salem Church showed strengths and weaknesses in Early's abilities.

By war's midpoint in the spring and summer of 1863, Early had proven himself to superiors and subordinates alike at brigade and divisional command. A protégé and something of a mirror of his superior, equally idiosyncratic corps commander "Stonewall" Jackson, Early rose in rank and responsibilities—perhaps slower than he wished—from one- to two-star rank only by April 1863, which earned his typically acerbic comment that it had taken so long as to appear "they were picking up the scraps now." But he was known at headquarters and

Richmond. A tried and proven fighter and makeweight on the battle-field, no slog through the litany of those years seems necessary. Answers to questions about the man sparkle from his conduct, character, and performance that will distinctly bear on the second and more important half of Early's war in the eastern theater.[1]

Early began the Civil War essentially where he had left off in Mexico and Florida. The care and feeding of troops provided focus for the Virginia colonel. Sent to Lynchburg by the governor to raise three regiments, he took command of one—the Twenty-Fourth Infantry—and transitioned it to Confederate service. He soon developed a fundamental mistrust of War Department bureaucrats and railroad officials who promised much in the delivery of supplies to mustering volunteers and then transporting them to the front. Of course, everyone was unprepared for the demands of modern, large-scale industrializing warfare. Together they would learn hard lessons about inadequate firearms, mismatched uniform clothing, poor diet, and sanitation in camp and field. Much of that came together in their first battle, on the plains at Manassas, a scant thirty miles from the enemy capital at Washington. Supply and transportation issues surfaced in that campaign. In fact, the railroad held the key to that initial confrontation between amateurs, although the country lawyer-soldier probably did not realize it at the time. Army reinforcement that helped win the battle for the Confederacy remained peripheral to his narrow tactical experience at the moment. Still, First Manassas (Bull Run) appropriately reflected application of old and new resources for war: Early's infantry marching and fighting on foot, then injection of fresh reinforcement of that manpower onto a Napoleonic-style battlefield brought there by strategic use of a new technology— the railroad. It would not be Early's sole experience in that regard.[2]

Railroads were not unfamiliar to the Rocky Mount lawyer, and Early came to appreciate their importance as the war progressed. Moreover, even while preoccupied with troop musters and administration at Lynchburg, he also served as an intelligence conduit to Richmond. Prophetically, that experience involved the invaluable Virginia and Tennessee Railroad that connected eastern and western parts of the youthful Confederate States of America. Vital logistically to the military as much as commercially to civilians, this tenuous rail link was a strategic target. Early dutifully conveyed information to higher authorities of a rumored Federal raid on the railroad by as many as 10,000 men, including 1,200 horsemen, through Fayette County to Lewisburg in the western part of the state. Reports of insurrection along the line were similarly rife, wired Early on the fourth of June. This caught the attention of President Jefferson Davis. Response indicated the name *Early* was becoming known in Richmond.[3]

Early's contributions became even more familiar because of First Manassas. His brigade served as reserve support in the July 18 fighting near Blackburn's Ford as well as the main action to the west on Chinn Ridge and Henry House Hill three days later. Commanding the Northern force was Irwin McDowell, whom Early admired from West Point days. Early now built new ties to such men as Arnold Elzey, who eventually worked for him later in the conflict. His arduous march to reinforce the left of army commander P. G. T. Beauregard's line late on the crucial afternoon of the main battle saved the Louisiana general's victory and helped precipitate the Yankee rout. Intelligence historian Edwin Fishel declared it to be one of two "knockout blows" that cost McDowell the battle (the other being railroad-conveyed Edmund Kirby Smith's brigade arriving from the Shenandoah Valley, which marched to the sound of the guns in the nick of time). Beauregard never forgot Early's role, which would effect a postwar reunion advantageous to both aging warriors. Early also renewed his acquaintance with President Davis, who arrived to oversee post-battle recovery. Here was another chit for future reference when needed. Moreover, Early now carried a reputation. He deplored stragglers and was as hard bitten as he was hard hitting in the spirit of counterattacks and seizing the initiative. So much of what we know was colored by Early's strong opinion about everything, including positing McDowell as the last of the gentlemanly fighters in a war that would eventually savage combatant and noncombatant participants. However, the period yields few conclusions about Early, except that his old West Point pugnacity had resurfaced and that his soldiers had begun to style him "Old Jube."[4]

Early penned a lengthy and detailed after-action report that read more like a lawyer's brief. It provided all the detail needed to show superiors the vital role he and his brigade had played in this first major battle of the war. Moreover, Early slipped in a comment at the end that suggested a question of priorities. Noting that lack of reconnaissance hindered pursuit of the enemy after the combat, he recorded, "On the next day we found a great many articles that the enemy had abandoned in their flight, showing that no expense or trouble had been spared in equipping their army." Such information could have reached headquarters from countless other sources, but the ever-prickly Franklin-Countian wanted to tweak higher authority. To Early, Richmond bureaucrats had shortchanged his mustering units regarding arms, clothing, and equipment the month before at Lynchburg. That Confederate mobilization had been a haphazard, ersatz affair at the expense of his men, something Early wanted clearly known at the capital. Was focus a problem for Early? Or were logistical matters just as important to him as those of combat—the two went hand in hand for a sharp-eyed soldier like Early.[5]

Still, as the short war turned prolonged and two armies faced one another near Washington, Early's uniqueness began to blossom in the winter and spring of 1861 to 1862. He ensured that his men voted on November 5 in the Confederate national elections for a provisional government. Later, unhappiness with his officers' wives in winter encampments, the impedimenta of needless baggage, and continued displeasure with unsupportive railroad officials earned Early a reputation as crusty and opinionated. His high-pitched voice led to more apocryphal tales as a Virginian spoilsport, oblivious to the fact that the army was a coalition from numerous states and required a leadership example for amalgamation. Interruption of a ceremony held for Marylanders in the Rebel army as well as dead heroes Barnard Bee, Frances Bartow, and C. F. Fisher from elsewhere pointed to Early's overzealous expression of Virginia patriotic parochialism—and maybe a proclivity for drink. But the latter derives from observer Samuel Ferguson's memoir, and we need more definitive evidence of Jubal's quirks. Indeed, more secure evidence of Early's developing character emerges from an official document in his personal papers. Discipline—personal and corporate—was everything to the new brigadier (promoted August 13 for his singular actions the month before at Manassas).[6]

Jubal Early had little patience for foraging and freebootery by soldiers at the expense of Virginia citizenry. General Orders Number 7 from his Fourth Division headquarters on March 15, 1862, during Confederate withdrawal from northern Virginia provides an overlooked example of words and attitudes that always marked Jubal Early. They may even yield a clue to later animosity that he displayed for the enemy's disregard of any code of conduct. Early wanted his general order read by company commanders and also published on dress parade to each regiment. The reason was apparently the "disorder and impression which have marked and disgraced the march from Bull Run to the Rappahannock." The amount of straggling from the ranks was "such as to present the appearance of a disastrous route [*sic*]," and Early had observed that it was not confined to the men alone. Early's disdain went to his commissioned subordinates of all grades: "If they straggle from their proper positions under the childish practice of getting something good to eat, how can they expect the private soldiers to observe order and regularity on the march[?]"[7]

Early further launched into a discussion of civil-military relations. "This Army," he observed, "has been called together for the purpose of defending the houses of the people of this Confederate States from desecration of ruthless marauders, yet complain[t]s come up from all quarters of outrages, thefts and robberies committed by stragglers from this army upon citizens as loyal as any in the limits of the Confederacy." To take a horse from the field or stable of a citizen "without his account for the private use of an officer or soldier is nothing less than larceny," he preached. This and all other kinds of theft would be dealt with by Articles of War and otherwise the laws of Virginia. Moreover,

> burning of rails and destruction of all private property when not absolutely necessary for the public service must be prevented and all officers are required to exact themselves to the interest to prevent deserters and all honest soldiers who do not desire to share an infamous reputation with the marauders and thieves who unfortunately have found their way into this Army, are entitled to give their cheerful aid in suppressing the disgraceful outrages which are being perpetrated.

Clearly then, it was the young undisciplined amateur soldiery of both sides who had begun unbridled transgressions against the civilian populace. Jubal Early would never overcome his aversion to such actions, although later he vented his wrath mainly against the enemy in that regard.[8]

What followed next involved Union general George B. McClellan's abortive campaign to capture Richmond. Here, Robert E. Lee emerged from the shadows as master of the eastern theater. Here, too, lay the beginnings of a dream team with Thomas Jonathan "Stonewall" Jackson and James Longstreet as Lee's trusted lieutenants. Additionally, Jubal Early would progressively display martial valor and emerge as a star at the next level. He would take a wound leading an "impetuous assault" (Early's superior Longstreet called it) on an annoying enemy battery in front of Fort Magruder at Williamsburg. The event kept him absent from most of the ensuing Seven Days battles. His typically lengthy after-action report written from recuperation at Lynchburg on June 9 cited incurring a "very severe wound," that he "became so weak from loss of blood and suffered such excruciating pain," and that he had withdrawn from command on the field. But Early's passion for action and worry that the wound might damage his future in the army made him insufferable during recuperation. Would Richmond officials pigeonhole Early, or would taking the case directly to the army commander ensure his return to rightful command? This was his quandary. Moreover, was this the beginning of a familiarity between the two Virginians that might hold great promise?[9]

Restored to a temporary brigade command the very day Malvern Hill ended Lee's attempts to destroy McClellan's defeated army, Early and his men saw little action. Soon an apparently ambitious and aggrieved Early personally wrote Lee about a lack of what he considered a suitable assignment. The patient army commander, still sorting out suitable subordinates, soothingly stroked the brigadier that his time would come for proper assignment and that his service thus far spoke creditably as an officer "of intelligence and capacity." Meanwhile, wearing the Williamsburg wound as a badge of distinction and appreciation from a grateful nation, said Lee, Early would have ample time to continue to prove himself. His superiors Richard S. Ewell and Jackson would see to that. Indeed, Early would not prove wanting. His placement in the center of Jackson's line at Cedar Run (or Cedar Mountain) on August 9 ensured a stalwart defense that eventually yielded victory over Nathanial Banks. Later, as the Confederates stole a flank march around John Pope's Army of Virginia, rain and high water isolated Early's adventurous bridgehead at Warrenton Springs on the Rappahannock. Fog of war and ineptitude of Federal pressure averted disaster. Jackson reported "in this critical situation, the skill and presence of mind of General Early was favorably displayed."[10]

Under Ewell's divisional command, Early swept on to additional feats of reliability at Bristoe Station and Groveton (where Ewell himself went down with a deadly wound) and Second Manassas—once again anchoring Confederate positions and providing counterattack strength when needed at the crucial moment. A case might be made that two August days at Second Manassas were truly Lee's greatest battle— thanks in part to Pope's continued bungling but more especially to a superb battle plan on the second day that pivoted Longstreet's corps off Jackson's defensive base like a scythe sweeping a field of grain. Early, with Jackson, positioned along the unfinished railroad running from Groveton to Sudley Church, undertook assigned roles proficiently, and accomplished them with precision. Early and his men also sprang to the challenge of plugging a hole in the wavering Rebel line there and again on September 1 during the thunderstorm melee at Chantilly, closer to Washington. Early boasted in his after-action report how his unit had "never been broken or compelled to fall back or left one of its dead to be buried by the enemy." It had invariably driven that enemy "or slept upon the ground on which it has fought in every action" excepting Bristoe Station (before Second Manassas), where it had withdrawn per Jackson's plan. Historian Joseph Harsh declares that Early and his bri- gade "played a game of bluff to delay the enemy at Bristoe," and Early relished that role only a little less than a good fight. Now, he, like the rest of Lee's army, was ready for new horizons.[11]

Opportunity came with invasion of Union territory north of the Po- tomac. Actually, although not known at the time, the Chantilly affair that took the lives of two promising Union major generals, Isaac Ingalls Stevens and Philip Kearny, and constituted a drawn battle had cost Lee even more. His chance to destroy Pope's retreating army after Second Manassas and perhaps march with little difficulty into Washington had been stymied. Manassas and Chantilly had so bloodied and worn Lee's legions that their offensive punch had been blunted. They needed rest, victualing, and rearming. The latter might come from Yankee booty left on the field; the former required disengagement and recuperation. To the ever-restless Lee, the crucial strategic moment in the second year of the war and the allure of liberating people of the Southern, slaveholding Old Line State of Maryland beckoned alluringly. So Early and the Army of Northern Virginia (as it had come to be styled) turned north. Bivouac near Big Spring outside Leesburg before crossing the Potomac and encampment subsequently near Monocacy Junction southeast of Frederick would become familiar locales to him and his men, both in

1862 and two years later. Insufficiencies of the Confederate supply and commissary system rode along with the Southern expedition and worried generals like Early. The tattered garb of the foot soldiers garnered little citizen support for their cause, and the resort to a diet of fruit, green corn, and unsalted beef meant diarrhea that probably impacted far more on the subsequent events than either participants or historians have willingly admitted. Lee ordered strict discipline against looting and required payment for subsisting on the Marylanders' economy. While flour and salt were issued at Frederick, Confederate paper never appealed to merchants. Arguably, Lee took the wrong path into Maryland anyway—secessionist support lay in counties to the east, close to Baltimore and Washington, not western Maryland, through which Lee's army would traipse.[12]

A rejuvenated Union Army of the Potomac under restored commander George B. McClellan eventually forced a showdown. What turned out to be the bloodiest single-day's fight of the war took place to the west in Washington, not Frederick, county. The famous "Lost Order" (also associated with the Monocacy interlude), Jackson's capture of Harpers Ferry (the strategic importance of which would figure equally in Early's later 1864 transit of the area), and Lee's somewhat reckless dispersal of his army in the face of the resurgent foe courted disaster outside the little town of Sharpsburg. Early's role predictably emerged as staving off tactical defeat. But first, it may have been Early's men, coursing Frederick streets en route to the Antietam rendezvous with fate, who caused John Greenleaf Whittier's patriotic ode to dame Barbara Fritchie. Or maybe it was the subsequent visit through Middletown to the west. In any event, the Rebel soldiery (ostensibly, a one-legged straggler traveling with them) encountered two six- and ten-year-old girls waving a small Union flag while monotonously voicing "Hurrah for the Stars and Stripes." One bedraggled soldier threatened to yank the emblem from the child's hand only to have Early intervene and suggest to the man that he was a fool because "she could do no harm with her 'candy flag.'" But in the end, it was Early and the slugfest north of Sharpsburg around Dunkard Church at Antietam that made his mark in Maryland.[13]

At Sharpsburg (or Antietam, as Northerners styled the battle), Early and his brigade (subsequently he took over the division with the wounding of Andrew Lawton, who had succeeded Ewell after Groveton) dove straight into the morning's carnage. Bloody combat ate voraciously at Jackson's command, battered by Union attacks coming south on the Hagerstown road. It was Early once more who seized the initiative and plugged the defensive line north of the little whitewashed church. It was Early who brought another old West Point comrade, Union general John Sedgwick's attack to a standstill in the West Woods. Little wonder that Early was prominently mentioned in the dispatches for attacking "with great resolution the large force opposed to him" (said Lee) and "great vigor and gallantry the column on his right and front" (added Jackson). For such service, Jackson accorded him the place of honor as rear guard, covering eventual retreat from the battlefield. Early probably expected promotion; his actions had been energetic and his losses minimal, and after all, he more than anyone had saved the day in the morning fight. Lee suggested permanent advance to Ewell's divisional command should the latter not return, or Edward "Allegheny" Johnson (Early's equal in rank) similarly remain hors d'combat. The War Department failed to act, and Early was left only temporarily commanding Ewell's division with no advance in rank. The Maryland experience would figure prominently in his memoirs. Meanwhile, the contending armies returned to maneuvering in central Virginia.[14]

The march back south of the Rappahannock and Rapidan rivers produced its share of Early stories. The most famous was his retort to corps commander Jackson's sharp query of why "he saw so many stragglers in rear of your division today." Never to be outdone, Early had replied that, while most of the stragglers belonged to other commanders, the principal reason that the "Lieutenant General commanding saw so many stragglers in rear of my division today is probably because he rode in rear of my division." And when Early and his staff got to Orange Courthouse and ventured by invitation to "Montpelier," former president James Madison's ample plantation, expecting a bounteous feast from its present owner, they were vastly disappointed. Lengthy wait and scanty fare led to much grumbling among the group. Ill-prepared biscuits, horrid coffee, and five eggs to share between the seven of them led to Early's silent disapproval. He stomped from the room at meal's end uttering oaths and the ungracious vow, "I'll be damned if I ain't going home and get something to eat." Perhaps the house's new owner, who never appeared in person, was sending a message of dissatisfaction about the transiting army's ravages upon the civilian economy, loyalty to one side or the other notwithstanding.[15]

Union and Confederate armies took positions opposite one another at Fredericksburg by early December. McClellan had departed command once again. His senior subordinate, Ambrose Burnside, took command and spread a formidable array of men and guns on Stafford Heights and southward, which faced Lee's host similarly posted across the Rappahannock behind and below the city, all the way to Hamilton's Crossing on the railroad to Richmond. How to cross the intervening river was Burnside's problem. Shelling out sharpshooters in the town so as to effect a bridgehead soon caused massive damage and eviction of the civilian populace, much to Lee's personal distaste. "These people delight to destroy the weak and those who can make no defense. It just suits them," was Lee's condemnation. Subsequent looting of the abandoned colonial-era city houses further enflamed Confederate sensibilities. Early surely learned of these travesties even though he was positioned in reserve with Jackson toward Hamilton's Crossing, and they may account for his subsequent venom toward foemen in blue. Eventually, the Federals crossed the river, and Burnside directed almost suicidal attacks against Lee's high-ground positions on Mayre's Heights. Subordinates like Sedgwick similarly mounted other attacks against Jackson with more success. Early once again intervened in a breakthrough of Jackson's position and prevented disaster. This time it was as division, not brigade, commander, but the result was the same. Said Early, "The enemy was very seriously punished for this attack"; actually, the initial success was about the only moment of Federal glory at Fredericksburg. For his part, Early learned that maneuvering a division was more complicated than that of a brigade.[16]

Yet it seems from another tale that all Early really may have gleaned from Fredericksburg was when he, Lee, and cavalryman Wade Hampton watched Burnside's withdrawal two days after the battle. Early commented that he wished all the enemy dead. The army commander rejoined that he merely wished they would go home and mind their own business. But once Lee rode out of earshot, Early snarled, "I not only wish them all dead but I wish them all in Hell." Quite likely, Jubal Early did harbor such sentiments whether the story was true or not. As he advanced in rank and command and his reputation and demeanor became better known to the troops, by 1863 Early was famous as much for raspy comment as intrepid action at crucial moments. During Sedg-wick's breakthrough at A. P. Hill's expense, "That gallant old warrior, General Early, to whom I had sent," stated the beleaguered Hill, "came crashing through the woods at the double-quick" to rout the enemy, much as he had done on previous occasions. The appreciative Rebels rallied, shouting "Here comes old Jubal, let old Jubal straighten that fence, Jubal's boys are always getting Hill out of trouble." Indeed that seemed to be the case at Second Manassas, Sharpsburg, and now Fred-ericksburg. The ever-pugnacious Early was all business, not a bad pro-fessional quality to show to an army of amateurs.[17]

Indeed, later that winter, Early uncovered a lighter side when the snowball antics of a Port Royal encampment brought a twinkle to his eye. But he was mostly devoid of sentimentality. And Early was never one to allow insubordination within his command. Constantly berating his Louisiana troops of Harry Hays's brigade about plundering in the countryside, he called their hand on a desired transfer elsewhere that January. "Who do you think would have such a damned pack of thieves," he confronted their officers finally. If they could find any commander in the army who was such a damned fool as to take them, they could go ahead and transfer, he chirped. Colonel Leroy Stafford of the Ninth Louisiana suddenly broke out laughing, and the confronta-tion evaporated in the absurdity of the whole business. The "Louisiana Tigers," as rough and unruly as their new major general—for Early finally got his second star on January 19, 1863—stayed with Early's command to the bitter end two years later. By spring, yet another cam-paign season opened, and Early and the Tigers would need one another again. Early became involved once more with actions of former West Point comrades. There was Joseph Hooker, with whom he had experi-enced that confrontation over slavery, and John Sedgwick crossed Ear-ly's path for yet a third time in nine months, more seriously since the two were unwittingly paired independently by their superiors. Both would be charged with doing something about the city of and terrain at Fredericksburg as Hooker attempted to outflank Lee to the west. Hooker wanted Sedgwick to attack the heights; Lee wanted Early to defend them. The mission, to paraphrase Charles Osborne, came down to underwriting the very existence of the Army of Northern Virginia. By implication that, too, meant the enemy Army of the Potomac.[18]

Hooker envisioned a "Cannae on the Rappahannock" (Osborne's phrase) as he led the main part of his army upriver and around Lee's left flank. Sedgwick was to batter his way past the Fredericksburg obstacle, hence the Confederate right flank. Lee countered against the main thrust; Hooker blinked and became bogged down in the impenetrable wilderness around Chancellorsville to the west of Fredericksburg. It was left for Early (with a scant 10,500 men and 56 guns) and Sedgwick (with perhaps four times the infantry and double the artillery) to battle it out for the heights and roads leading south and west out of the city, which could affect events elsewhere. Strengths and responsibilities would fluctuate as army commanders drained resources from the pair. Fate and fortunes of battle, the fog of war, commander foibles, and the response by the men in the ranks all determined the early May result. Lee's orders to Early were clear to a point: Maintain his position against the odds but, if overpowered, then retire down Telegraph Road toward Guiney's Station to protect lines of communication and supply routes in the rear of Lee's army. If the enemy withdrew or moved to rejoin Hooker, then Early should leave a token observation force on Mayre's Heights and himself march to join Lee's embattled force. Over the course of several days, all of this came into play, giving Early (in eminent historian Douglas Southall Freeman's incomparable phrase) the "right to swear." Yet Lee in his accustomed, quiet manner recorded afterward, "Major General Early performed the important and responsible duty intrusted to him in a manner which reflected credit upon himself and his command."[19]

Were these really damning words of faint praise? Did Early perform as Lee must have expected he would do as the division commander "best qualified to guard the heights and to protect the rear." Again, Freeman observed almost caustically, "To this post of military trust, in less than two years, had risen the former Commonwealth's Attorney of Franklin County, Virginia!" The sequence of errors thanks to conflicting verbal instructions from Lee's headquarters led to a premature withdrawal from the Fredericksburg defenses on May 1 and much marching and countermarching, probably to the vocal ire of Jubal Early. The culprit proved to be misinterpretation of those orders by staff officer R. H. Chilton, conveyed to Early on May 1. Early obeyed, but the situation straightened out before any real harm was done. Early's defenders returned in time to continue their deception of Sedgwick's Federals. Yet all the shifting of troops, independent withdrawal of the majority of artillery support by his gunner-in-chief William Pendleton, and subsequent malpositioning when returning from the shuffle left Early more vulnerable than before. The deception worked up to a point. Sedgwick's own irresolution, inconclusive intelligence of the enemy, and only marginally better communications with Union army headquarters at Chancellorsville gained time for Early.[20]

Early did not use that time well. Charged with defending a line from the Rappahannock upstream from Fredericksburg to Deep Run below, he continued to believe that any Federal attack would come between Deep Run and Hazel Run, against hills and valleys rather than supposedly impregnable Mayre's Heights. Most of the artillery that had left under Pendleton's instructions now returned, so Early had forty-eight cannon to compensate for gaps in his infantry line. Eventually, Hooker's preemptory order to advance forced Sedgwick to take action, and he sent his superior force storming up the Heights about dawn on May 3. It was too much for Early's meager defenders spread out for three miles along the old Confederate positions of December. William Barksdale's 900 Mississippians defending the stone wall location (infamous from the first battle's bloodbath) particularly collapsed. A temporary truce had uncovered their weakness to the enemy—unbeknownst to Early. Perhaps the stone wall had worked all too well in December; it did not in May, although Federal casualties were high the second time also. In the end, Early's defense collapsed, and no doubt Second Fredericksburg was a Confederate defeat. Early had failed in his mission. He lost 700 men and four cannon. Lee merely told him how he regretted the loss of the town.[21]

Still, Early escaped, retiring two miles down Telegraph Road (per Lee's instructions about protecting the line of communications) and regrouped. Sedgwick did not pursue, for his mission was to aid Hooker as quickly as possible. Early eventually fused his left with reinforcements sent by Lee when Sedgwick marched straight out Plank Road to Chancellorsville. Together, with Lafayette McLaws and Cadimus Wilcox (part of Early's original defense on the north end), they stopped Sedgwick's advance at Salem Church. Early prepared for his customary counterthrust. Lee expected it, in effect, assuming Early together with the others could "demolish" and "destroy" Sedgwick, as Lee told Early in a 7 p.m. dispatch on May 3. The Federals were ahead of both Lee and Early by this time. A beaten Hooker and a chastened Sedgwick simply withdrew across the upper fords of the Rappahannock. Early reoccupied his Fredericksburg lines, yet he had failed in what he was supposed to do—prevent their capture in the first place. Only by chance had Second Fredericksburg been redeemed by Salem Church, thus permitting Lee to administer what some historians regard as his finest battle. [22]

It would be left to old-soldier carping as to culpability for Second Fredericksburg. Lawyer Early was much briefer than usual in his after-action report of May 7, but then defeat never warrants verbosity. First Corps commander James Longstreet (absent with his command on an independent mission in southern Virginia) would later castigate Early for dereliction by withdrawing south on Telegraph Road (actually as Lee intended) rather than immediately retiring out Plank Road to help Lee at Chancellorsville. For Early's part, soon after the battle, he stirred a controversy with Barksdale over states' honor of whether Virginians or Mississippians had retrieved the lost ground on Mayre's Heights. To Osborne, "Jubal Early had scraped through." In Freeman's view, Early owed more to Wilcox than "he acknowledged then or thereafter," plus even at the time "it would have been easy to have raised many questions concerning Early's handling of the situation." Yet, he backed away, feeling Early had "kept his head" and "without excessive loss of men or ground," for in the end, Early together with Wilcox "had frustrated an essential part of the Federal plan, that of an attack by Sedgwick on the rear of Lee's army." For intelligence historian Edwin Fishel, to the extent Early's deceptive efforts had accomplished anything, "they did not delay Sedgwick's advance." That had been determined by Hooker's preemptory order. Others would suggest Early focused on the wrong part of his defensive line, let Pendleton send off too much needed artillery, or simply was not ready for independent responsibilities. In Freeman's final analysis, however, "Jubal Early had shown himself resourceful, unafraid, and manifestly capable of acting on his own." [23]

Controversy and the blame game, somewhat muted at the time, would accompany Early from Second Fredericksburg onward. Perhaps it came with ascension in command and responsibility, especially independent mission. Possibly it was inevitable given Jackson's mortal wound at Chancellorsville and comparisons made by future remorseful generations of Southerners seeking redemption for that demigod's loss. Yet, who can dispute Freeman's incomparable assessment to begin his second volume of *Lee's Lieutenants*? "On occasion," advanced this historian, Early "snarls so raspingly that he seems to raise the question whether he is acting division commander or still at heart the Commonwealth's Attorney of Franklin County, Virginia." Showing development as a soldier, stubbornness in combat seemed more apparent than impetuosity, and if Early knew or cared about the "art of ingratiation," he would have been a hero in Freeman's view. He concluded that, as an "executor," Early's record from Cedar Mountain to Salem Church is "second only to that of Jackson himself." This from the same pen of the man who had declared of Early's earlier service "that he was able, many believed, and that he was coldly brave, all who saw him on the field admitted." Yet at that point, of what he would become as a commander, "none cared," and when he had been promoted to brigadier from colonel, suggested Freeman, "there was probably scant enthusiasm."[24]

3

SEARCHING FOR STONEWALL'S GHOST

Special Orders 146 issued from the Army of Northern Virginia head-quarters on May 30, 1863, reorganized Robert E. Lee's army yet again. In the wake of Thomas Jonathan Jackson's death, Richard Stoddert Ewell assumed command of the old Second Corps. Jubal Early's division, along with those of Edward "Allegheny" Johnson and Robert Rodes, went with him. Early's division counted 7,226 officers and men, he said later. The search for Stonewall's ghost—his successor—had begun. The troops called Ewell "Old Bald Head," for he was quite that, but Jubal Early wasn't far behind; receding hairlines on both of them meant that turmoil and sorrows of the previous month were taking their toll. Ewell was also crippled now, hoisted into and strapped to the saddle—hardly the way to energetically command infantry in a foot soldiers' war. Ewell's stump pain, like Early's arthritic discomfort, may have factored into their manner and decisions more than anyone yet has admitted. Looking back, generations think their Civil War predecessors were—or should have been—iron men. They were not. In any event, Ewell's corps totaled 34,000 men as a new invasion of the North beckoned. The two generals liked and respected one another. How they might fare under these new conditions remained anyone's guess.[1]

The next period in Jubal Early's life and career involved his command of mainly a division, yet that could be deceptive. High points for this period would include battles like Second Winchester, Gettysburg, Rappahannock Bridge, and Mine Run. After that, however, an independent assignment to the Shenandoah Valley and western Virginia suggested that Early might be something more to Lee. The next May and June, from the Wilderness to Cold Harbor, indicators suggested that despite some faux pas, Early had become one of Lee's obvious protégés. He was entrusted with temporary corps command when A. P. Hill became too ill to function properly. Then he moved again temporarily to Second Corps command as Ewell's fragility became too obvious, and to a hard-pressed army commander when Longstreet went down in friendly fire in an uncanny repetition of Jackson's mortal wounding the year before. Lee now needed a more secure command structure to withstand the relentless pressure of Federal offensives. In the meantime, Early's role in the Gettysburg campaign as well as each of those battles and his independent winter action against Federal raider William Averell in southwestern and western Virginia explain much about this evolving senior Confederate field leader.[2]

"Nothing of consequence occurred in our front during the month of May," Early declared in his postwar memoirs. Indeed, the high point came later when Ewell's corps trooped north using the Shenandoah and Great valleys into Maryland and Pennsylvania. A striking victory over Robert Milroy at Winchester and nearby Stephenson's Depot—featuring Ewell's brilliant maneuvers and Early's shock-tactic attacks—helped turn a simple defeat into a debacle for the Federals. What was memorable to both sides was perhaps Milroy's personnel loss of nearly 50 percent but more so the huge amount of materiel that fell to the Confederates—200,000 rounds of small arms ammunition, four twenty-pounder Parrott, 17 three-inch rifled cannon, and two twenty-four-pounder howitzers. The overconfident Milroy still had the presence of mind to dispatch 111 wagons of quartermaster stores to safety, so the victorious Rebels gained the means to fight, if not to eat, on their second Northern invasion. Lee wanted more foraging and less fighting anyway. Early and his men would soon be doing both, with the former overshadowed ultimately by the meeting of two armies at Gettysburg.

Early exaggerated the extent of the booty, downplayed the defective ammunition (which lessened its value) captured from Milroy, and claimed the pillaging afterward was by stragglers and camp-followers. Nonetheless, Winchester stoked the spirits of Lee's army, and local sympathizers suggested the Ewell–Early team worthy successors to Jackson's old methods and delivery. Ewell made Early commander of the Department of Winchester "while in the vicinity" (comprising the entire valley "south as far as Woodstock and north as far as the lines of the army"). Early was to suppress plundering, "or our discipline is gone; the prospect of victory which has hitherto marked our course will be lost, and we will become, like our enemies, a band of robbers, without the spirit to win victories." Would Ewell's prognosis hold once the Confederates crossed the Potomac? Of course, Washington authorities and Northern citizens panicked as usual. The nation's capital, Maryland, and the Keystone State of the old Union seemed endangered.[3]

The ensuing Pennsylvania invasion that culminated at Gettysburg, like so much operational Civil War history, hardly bears detailed recounting. Suffice to say that Ewell's corps, with Early, Rodes, and Johnson as infantry and Albert Jenkins riding point with his cavalry, formed the tip of a vast raid, and they enjoyed the absence of serious opposition. Whether policing up stray African Americans in their path (regardless of their status as runaway refugees or free people but potentially useful as impressed labor down South) or foraging actions that fretted Lee's prohibition, war now came in earnest to the civilian North. That extraction of people, crops, and livestock as well as military supplies for the good of the Confederate army was fact. So, too, was Early's wanton destruction of radical Republican congressman Thaddeus Stevens's Caledonia Iron Works and "ransoming" of little Gettysburg when, operating independently of Ewell's main force, Early moved through en route to try to capture the Susquehanna railroad bridge at Wrightsville. Of course, requisitioning civilians for goods with payment in Confederate script was established policy from the previous year's Maryland foray. Ewell's sparing of U.S. government property at Carlisle Barracks may have been more nostalgic than pragmatic and suggests selective adherence to Lee's orders and a quite understandable Rebel urge to make Pennsylvanian farmers and townsfolk howl! Historian and newsman Wilbur Nye later dissected what could be portrayed as the march of Southern vandals northward (if history had not taken the more docile view of errant knights), commenting (particularly in reference to black impressments and reenslavement), "It is hardly credible that troops or commanders were unaware of the situation." As far as Stevens's property was concerned, Gettysburg campaign historian Edward Coddington suggests that "Early's conduct in burning the furnace, saw mill, two forges, and a rolling mill at Caledonia was rank insubordination." In light of the obvious contradictions of sparing Carlisle Barracks but burning the Caledonia Iron Works, indiscriminately dragooning black refugees, asking tribute from Gettysburg and York citizenry or token payment, or simply stealing private property (provisions, clothing, etc.), an interesting double standard appears to emerge from the Ewell–Early incursion. Set against rabid Southern complaints—especially the next year from Early himself—about Yankee depredations in wartime that would become a staple of Lost Cause litany rationalized by Early after the war, rank hypocrisy now seems to attach to Jubal Early the soldier.[4]

Early's actions at Caledonia cost Stevens his $65,000 investment in property, $10,000 worth of provisions from the company store, 40 horses and mules, large quantities of corn and grain in the mills, $4,000 worth of bar iron, up to 80 tons of grass, large quantities of fence rails, and the rendering destitute of the works' employees. Some 22 years later, Early would explain this as retaliation for "various deeds of barbarity perpetrated by Federal troops in some of the southern states" and against Stevens in particular for a "most vindictive spirit toward the people of the South." Those words reflected the post-1863 turn of warfare and a harsh postwar Reconstruction in which Stevens appeared just as Early claimed. But in his 1866 memoirs, the general suggested more blandly how supplies were taken from the country people "under a regular system ordered by General Lee" with redeemable certificates given. "There was no marauding, or indiscriminate plundering," all such acts were "expressly forbidden and prohibited expressly." As for Thaddeus Stevens's property, Early observed that tit-for-tat destruction for Yankee depredations "in those parts of the Southern States to which [the enemy] had been able to penetrate" was somehow different. Stevens's works supplied war material to the Union war effort in contrast to Yankees preying upon innocent Southern homes and "destroying a vast deal of private property which could be employed in no way in supporting the war on our part." Early took responsibility for Caledonia. "This I did on my own responsibility, as neither General Lee nor General Ewell knew I would encounter these works," Early bragged.[5]

Given Early's remarks after First Fredericksburg, can one doubt that a vindictive, "hard," or "destructive" war streak had now surfaced in Old Jube? Punishment of Yankees seems evident. As he marched eastward on the turnpike to Wrightsville and independent of a tight leash from either corps or army headquarters, Early showed similar tendencies at Gettysburg. Reaching town, he assembled civilian authorities, demanded large amounts of provisions (7,000 pounds of bacon, 1,200 pounds of sugar, 1,000 pounds of salt) as well as 1,000 pairs of shoes and 500 hats or, as an alternative, $10,000 in cash. Town officials pleaded poverty, but merchants opened their doors to supply some items. Two thousand rations were found in boxcars on a railroad (distributed to Gordon's brigade, after which the cars were burned), and at least some of Early's men got riotously drunk. Merchants who had not sent off their merchandise for safekeeping experienced pillaging. Early's quartermaster came and left town with "every horseshoe and keg of nails that could be found in the borough." Still, on the whole, Early left town having netted little of his request. York, Pennsylvania, was next, where he "then levied a contribution on the town for 100,000 dollars in money, 2,000 pairs of shoes, 1,000 hats, 1,000 pairs of socks, and three day's rations of all kinds for my troops." In both locales, Early promised no harm if his demands were met. If not, then he would turn loose his men to sack and destroy. A York committee of citizens rounded up 1,500 pairs of shoes and $28,600 cash. Apparently Early kept his word; the goods went to needy rankers, the money to buy cattle from local farmers quite willing to sell for hard money rather than Confederate promissory notes. Early later showed too much bravado in claiming that he had marched to the banks of the Susquehanna "without resistance, the performance of the militia force at Gettysburg and Wrightsville amounting to no resistance at all, but being merely a source of amusement to my troops." That said, ironically, the Confederates did not capture the Wrightsville bridge that could have opened a door to even more bounteous provender in Lancaster County and beyond.[6]

Union militia burned the bridge even as John B. Gordon's brigade attempted its capture. Perhaps Early devoted too much time to personally negotiating ransom at York rather than pushing on to Wrightsville. He would do this again the following year in Maryland on the road to Washington. Once more, he would lose invaluable time, another bridge, and a chance at immortality. Now, he spent his energies touring York to see which properties could be put to the torch, while Gordon's infantry slogged on in the heat. Early intended to help Ewell accomplish a double envelopment of the Pennsylvania state capital by getting to the east shore of the Susquehanna, he claimed. That required speed, not dawdling while ransoming towns. Ewell thought Lee wanted him to capture Harrisburg (he moved straight for that objective through Carlisle), while Early ambitiously sought to both aid the effort and extract tribute. At the least, he sought to bring back much-needed horses from the east shore where Unionist owners had rushed them. Troop movements by the Army of the Potomac quickly shut down all adventurous activities attached to Lee's widespread columns. Just as the previous autumn when George B. McClellan resurged more quickly than Lee anticipated, Joseph Hooker and subsequently George Meade unhinged whatever Lee had in mind for central Pennsylvania. Again, Lee wanted to draw his enemy away from Washington's defenses as well as secure supplies. Again, he succeeded on both counts. Yet again, decisive battle ultimately beckoned—this time at that little hamlet lately ransomed by Jubal Early.[7]

All roads now led to Gettysburg. Early's division was soon on one of them. Controversy would arise anew, this time more seriously after the war, when the Gettysburg story became enveloped in old soldier recriminations; fanciful "what ifs" and "might have beens" that involved Lee, Longstreet, Ewell, and Early; and the whole idea that the Confederacy lost the war at this tiny south-central Pennsylvania crossroads. The crux of Early's role (and that of Ewell, too) centers on the first two days of the contest. On July 1, 1863, Ewell's Second Corps descended from the north, encountering Oliver Otis Howard's XI Corps just north of the county almshouse. A. P. Hill's Third Corps came in from the west of town against John Reynolds (subsequently Abner Doubleday's I Corps). Ewell pummeled Howard, with Early once more effectively outflanking their opponents. Whether the Yankees ran as they had at Chancellorsville or simply withdrew, hotly pursued by the Confederates, victory on the north side of Gettysburg nonetheless belonged to the men in gray. What happened next in the fatigue and confusion of late afternoon, the clogged streets of Gettysburg, and command indecision contributed much to the story regarding this pivotal moment. The spotlight focused on Ewell and his subordinates, mainly Early. Douglas Southall Freeman appropriately entitled this chapter in the third volume of his *Lee's Lieutenants* "Ewell Cannot Make a Decision." And that was about it. But Early did not help, so one must wonder, were either of them ready to administer a final coup d'grace to the beaten Federals that fateful day?[8]

It was all a matter of timing. No doubt Howard's men were beaten; no doubt they rallied with I Corps survivors and Winfield Scott Hancock's arriving reinforcements atop "formidable" (Ewell's words) Cemetery Hill on the southern edge of town. Linked by a short saddle with nearby Culp's Hill, Union artillery as well as infantry offered a porcupine defense against further Rebel attack. However, men in the ranks awaited their generals' pleasure, as generals study not just terrain but also indications of enemy intention, information, and intelligence from subordinates and scouts—and direction from supreme command—before acting (that is, if they are unsure of themselves and the enemy). The Confederate generals hesitated in the late afternoon of July 1 for a variety of reasons, not the least of which included battle- and march-weary troops, casualties, the town's complex of back alleys and cut-up house lots, and perhaps, most of all, groups of milling prisoners in the public square waiting to be processed. Ewell claimed afterward that he could not bring artillery to bear on the new Federal position, and all his available troops "were jaded by twelve hours marching and fighting." Early seemed more optimistic. He pressed Ewell and Hill—in fact, all about him who would listen at some point—for continued battle. Ewell apparently was not ready. He and Early rode forward to study the enemy position. The Federal guns looked intimidating. Early could not be sure of the location and intent of key components of his dispersed command. Ewell wanted direction. What were Robert E. Lee's intentions? He had not arrived yet on the field. While noted for giving subordinates discretion (a "positive weakness" declared Freeman), Lee was averse to bringing on a general engagement. He had sent such instructions forward. The crucial moment slipped away for destroying a defeated enemy. Between 4:00 p.m. and darkness, initiative evaporated on the successful Southern side.[9]

Did Ewell take counsel of his fears, his stump of a leg bothering him? Was he basically irresolute after convalescence, a recent marriage, or some newfound casualty aversion? Early seemed to fluctuate until, flushed with victory, he counseled taking Culp's Hill and enfilading those damned Yankees around the Evergreen Cemetery gate. Ewell waited. He had been told more recently to carry the hill "if he found it practicable, but to avoid a general engagement until the arrival of the other divisions of the army," which were ordered forward quickly. Such words and tone—"if he found it practicable"—would echo the next year for Early before Washington. On July 1, 1863, when the army commander finally appeared in the gathering dusk at Ewell's temporary command post at the almshouse, the moment of decision for that day was long gone. Rodes was there, Johnson was not, Early was sent for, and a war council convened. Lee was briefed on the situation, and according to Freeman, everyone realized the moment for further attack that evening had slipped away. Attack at dawn? Lee queried. Early presumptuously injected himself into the deliberations, supposedly asserting the Round Tops, south of town on the Confederate right flank, afforded the proper objective, yet the whiff of the defensive was in the air, much to Lee's amazement. This was the first time anyone had seen their commander since leaving Virginia. They labored under the impression that he wished to draw the enemy to him for another Fredericksburg, so Ewell and his subordinates anticipated the old Lee of June in Virginia, not the army commander who, a month later in Pennsylvania, suddenly wanted to attack and destroy his opponent. The meeting broke up, having agreed upon an immediate assault from the army's right flank. Ewell's corps would remain in place, demonstrate, and if opportune, launch its own attack against Culp's Hill and occupy that ground. Lee set up headquarters just west of town and had a further meeting with Ewell. The plan did not change. Overnight, rumors of Federal endangerment of Ewell's left flank via Culp's Hill caused trepidations about precipitous actions in the morning.[10]

Were Lee's leadership and faulty command methods expecting too much from subordinates (historian Michael Palmer's point)? Had Lee become apprehensive of Ewell's ability to decide and act (Freeman's impression)? Were Ewell and Early correct that "Cemetery Hill was not assailable from the town," or could the enemy's unpredictability of standing firm and fighting (just when Confederate overconfidence about their opponent had become virtual gospel) prove true? Just what constituted the "lost opportunity" at Gettysburg? Would it have mattered anyway when a possible alternative involved maneuvering an enemy out of his position or attacking Meade's preferred Pipe Creek defensive position on Parr's Ridge far to the south? Excepting Fredericksburg, Lee embraced the offensive—strategic as well as tactical—to effect a decision, an Austerlitz or Cannae, the annihilation confrontation. Was the absence at Gettysburg of the venerable Jackson a psychological weight expressed so vehemently by young staffer A. S. "Sandie" Pendleton at the moment of hesitation on July 1: "Oh, for the presence and inspiration of 'Old Jack' for just one hour!" Certainly Jubal Early rather than Dick Ewell had the temperament conducive to the army commander's desires, but of course, he, too, was part of the bittersweet tactical hesitation that day. More confident than Ewell in the afternoon that the defeated Federals might be dislodged, by evening he, too, felt opportunity lay with Culp's not Cemetery Hill. His own and Rodes's exhausted divisions were all Ewell had at hand for any assault until Johnson's men arrived, so crucial time had passed.[11]

Early's memory of events was decidedly opaque in his autobiography. Perhaps the victory might have been made more decisive, he opined, "by a prompt advance" of all the Confederate units upon Cemetery Hill, "but a common superior did not happen to be present" and so the opportunity was lost. He made no mention of his subsequent forceful advocacy in Lee's council, thus leaving it to others, like his biographers Millard Bushong and Charles Osborne, to paint more speculative portraits of his performance and mindset that day. Osborne suggests that Early's flip from attack advocacy to the "voice of prudence" may never be explained. On the other hand, scholars like Kenneth P. Williams and Edwin Fishel have suggested the strength of the Union position under Hancock's and Howard's management by 4:00 p.m. wisely caused Ewell pause. The definitive historian of Gettysburg, Edward Coddington, laboriously dissected the issue of Cemetery and Culp's hills on July 1 and concluded that all the later ink and hand-wringing by Confederate participants and apologists did not refute one conclusion. Early was "cocksure" to the point of fault, Ewell was prudent but unappreciative of fleeting time while awaiting Lee's directive, and Lee himself had to bear the most responsibility for the failure that day. Lee's unwillingness to gamble on all-out assault that would lock his still-dispersed army into a general engagement set the tone of subordinates' actions. A second day of confrontation proved necessary.[12]

Then, too, how are we now to consider Jubal Early's postwar Lost Cause pillorying of Longstreet for causing Lee's defeat at Gettysburg? Was all that to hide his own role in the July 1 missed opportunity? To some analysts today, he totally fabricated the notion that the evening conference between Lee, Ewell, Rodes, and himself advanced the notion of a coordinated dawn attack involving Ewell and company on the left and Longstreet on the right. In practice, however, events took over on the second day. Plans were good, coordination woeful, performance fell short. Timing, again, was the crucial factor, uncertainty of terrain most certainly a factor also. Whether Longstreet procrastinated because he defied Lee's battle plan (as Early and his Lost Cause cohorts charged later) or merely expended time reconnoitering his assignment (perfectly understandable absent Stuart's cavalry to properly develop the extent of the opponent's position) will continue to provide grist for pro-Confederate apologists. The Army of Northern Virginia came just as close to cracking the reinforced, tightly compressed, superior interior lines of George Gordon Meade on July 2. Longstreet shattered Sickles's corps and broke through the lower end of the Yankee line. However, exploitation of victory was no more in the cards on the second day at Gettysburg than it had been on the first.

If Longstreet could not exploit victory, Ewell never heard the sounds of artillery in order to begin his own work on the north end, and counterbattery fire from Cemetery Hill suppressed his own guns. Johnson's division mishandled taking Culp's Hill, and only by late afternoon were Early's brigades hurtling forward against East Cemetery Hill. Early claimed success, and indeed, he breached Federal defenses in places. But Rodes failed to support him, as merely 75 to 100 prisoners and four stands of colors provided only a Pyrrhic success, a brief moment of glory, and subsequent rationalization of still another elusive result. Coddington thought that if Rodes, Early, and Johnson had moved together before dark, the "story of the Confederate offensive on July 2 might have had a different ending." Coordinated attack from two directions would have rendered Cemetery Hill vulnerable. Coddington concluded that such coordination was unheard of in the Civil War anyway, and its possibility that day "should be relegated to the realm of pure speculation." More instructive, perhaps, was Freeman's later excoriation of Ewell and Early for leadership deficiencies that afternoon. Ewell's role was "semi-passive," and his employment of artillery was "inefficient." Liaison between corps and division commanders, and even among the latter themselves, was wanting. Early had little knowledge of the condition of his troops and, in fact, did not "seem to have been as much disposed as he had been on the 1st to seek to impose his will." Of course, it would be the disaster of the third day that filled history books and Lost Cause legends. Early and Ewell played little roles in that. [13]

Then, it was back to Virginia for Lee and his army. Early later reminisced that, despite various opinions as to the utility of the Pennsylvania campaign and its result, "undoubtedly we did not accomplish all that we desired, but I cannot regard the campaign in the light of a failure." Putting a typical face on things, he concluded that, without the move north to Pennsylvania, they would only have had to fight perhaps costlier battles that summer—in Virginia—"although the enemy might have been repulsed." Nevertheless, the fact was they were back on home turf where they had started. Confederate losses would manifestly affect Lee's future plans and freedom of action. Granted (as Early claimed), they had taken the conflict out of war-stricken central Virginia, lived off the Yankees for half a summer, and kept the Army of the Potomac from the doorsteps of Richmond. The transfer of the contending armies "to the upper waters of the Rappahannock and the Rapidan was a decided advantage to us," claimed Early after the war. Once more, Early displayed his typical narrow understanding of the conflict. His prism was that of an eastern army subordinate and son of the Virginia Commonwealth: "We remained in camp during the month of August, and the forepart of September, resting our men from their late fatigues, and recruiting our strength by the return of the sick and wounded who had recovered."[14]

Surprisingly, Early failed to note in his memoirs that it was his West Point classmate John C. Pemberton who surrendered the Vicksburg bastion on the Mississippi, truly changing the war's direction that July. Simultaneous with the Gettysburg defeat, Vicksburg was strategically the more pivotal of the two Confederate catastrophes. Moreover, Early also neglected to note that strategic pressure from the western theater drew Longstreet's corps from Lee and, subsequently, the XI and XII Corps from Meade for the Chickamauga–Chattanooga operations. It is little wonder that neither side was capable of doing much in the Old Dominion. However, three episodes involving Early did occur in the fall, and they reflected his part in the Confederacy's changed fortunes. First, in October, Lee sparred with Meade back and forth on the line of the Orange and Alexandria Railroad. An affair at Bristoe Station with A. P. Hill's costly frontal attack against Federals posted behind the railroad embankment only tangentially touched Early's division. A more sinister blunder at Rappahannock Bridge in November and subsequent Mine Run campaign south of the Rapidan at the end of that month accomplished little for either side. Early and Lee were both chastened by the absence of a decisive battle. A more seasoned Federal enemy, of sound mind and body for planning and execution, was back. Any alibis to the contrary, the first two actions although minor in nature were sobering; the third was more a result of trying to continue campaigning when bitter winter cold suggested winter encampments provided better answers.

Of Rappahannock Bridge, Freeman perhaps overstated that it was a "disaster unlike any experienced by the troops in all their marching and fighting," with every "rank and grade from headquarters to guardhouse" humiliated. Yet Early bore some responsibility for the loss of perhaps 1,200 to 1,600 officers and men, including some four colonels and three lieutenant colonels of Harry Hays's Louisiana brigade, caught off guard on the north side of the river bridgehead by John Sedgwick's alert, well-planned, and well-executed attack. Malpositioning of earthworks on the wrong side of the river, acoustical shadows, and onset of darkness all contributed, Early reported about the sudden reverse. He also hinted that, after all, even Lee had acquiesced to the siting of the defense. Early quickly turned to his division's accomplishments at Gettysburg as offsetting what is the "first disaster that has befallen this division since I have had the honor to command it." At times, Early not only passed responsibility but also glossed over hard truths.[15]

Early temporarily led the Third Corps, due to Ewell's sudden sick leave, for what he termed a "skirmishing at Mine Run." The armies once again encountered one another in the complex backwash near the Wilderness just as winter set in. What struck the temporary corps commander was not combat in such circumstance but rather "wanton barbarity" of the enemy upon the local civilian economy. A small tanyard near Locust Grove (within sight of Meade's headquarters, claimed Early), "used solely for the purpose of tanning hides on shares to furnish shoes to the women and children of the neighborhood," had been burned, hides taken from vats and cut to pieces, and the owner's house burned. Smokehouses had been vandalized, "helpless women plundered of every mouthful of provisions," the most common country carts and farming implements destroyed, and a number of other outrages committed, "which could have been perpetrated only by a cowardly foe, stung with mortification at this ridiculous termination of so pretentious an expedition," said Early in his after-action report. He embellished the details in his autobiography, claiming to have personally viewed the "houses of a number of citizens ransacked and the furniture destroyed," pianos "hacked to pieces with axes," libraries of books and private papers scattered over the ground. Women and children would have no shoes that winter, and people across the locale were "deprived of the means of properly cultivating their crops next season," not to speak of losing "what little source of amusement, recreation or mental employment there was left to them." "Can it be doubted that this was calculated to break the spirit of the 'rebellion'?" he asked. Just as quickly, Early answered, "Meade's expedition to Mine Run accomplished this much if no more."[16]

Early's biographer Charles Osborne decided that he was "beginning to forge an unbreakable connection between what he saw as the Yankee's uncivilized behavior and their craven ineptitude." Rage now blinded him "to his own illogic," although the pattern from Fredericksburg to Thaddeus Stevens's ironworks, ransoming Pennsylvania towns and then Mine Run, seems apparent for developing Early's rage. No doubt Early was unaware of any official Union policy that from the previous year had been steadily transitioning "soft glove" or "rose water" toleration of Southern citizen resistance to what historians have come to term *hard war* or *destructive war policy*. Union general John Pope had brought such practice east with him from Missouri the previous summer, thereby prompting immediate and vehement protest to Washington by Lee and Jefferson Davis. Disloyal and occupied Tennessee as well as loyal but occupied Kentucky witnessed such formal and informal transition in policy by Union field armies and occupation forces largely because of indiscriminant blurring of civilians with partisan rangers and guerrillas. So, as Osborne advances, that Union military harshness against civilians in Rebel territory "would become more and more a part of a deliberate, rationalized military policy." Early became more incensed as it did so, while admitting no cause from his side's perspective. Early's transition to virulent Yankee hating seemingly matured in the twelve months between December 1862 and December 1863.[17]

Special Orders 308 of December 15, 1863, now sent Early on a separate mission. He repaired to Staunton, Virginia, to "assume command of the troops there and in the Valley of Virginia, and make the best disposition of the same to resist the advance of the enemy." Here was his first truly independent assignment, directed by Lee and without any intermediate commander. Did this reflect the commanding general's increasing confidence that here was a man for the Shenandoah, the rougher land of southwestern Virginia, who might rally the countryside and local defensemen as well as any Confederate troops defending the locale? It would free Early from the tedium and damps of winter encampment. He would not grace the premises in his unique garb of "striped woolen skull cap" pulled down around his ears, leggings held to knee-top with white tape and a Virginia cloth overcoat reaching to his heels. This was Old Jube's counter to his arthritis; for everyone else, it was comic theater. Unfortunately, the interlude would also surface more of Early's quirks. Comfortable dealing with infantry and artillery, he would now encounter the foibles of the mounted arm. These would not be J. E. B. Stuart's regulars, but irregulars—half militia, half partisan/guerrillas who manned the frontiers of the home front in the valley and beyond. And a formidable Union raiding force was about to test the mettle of Early and this temporary command. [18]

As it turned out, Early's independent winter—like that of Longstreet in East Tennessee after his abortive December attack on Knoxville—proved of marginal result. His initial baptism came in trying to intercept Federal brigadier W. W. Averell's December raid through the Allegheny Mountains to break the Virginia and Tennessee Railroad. The Federal cavalrymen got to Salem, Virginia; captured and destroyed quantities of supplies; and tore up rails and bridges before evaporating from whence they had come. The Salem commissariat listed losses of 50,000 pounds of salted pork, 143 barrels of flour, 2,400 pounds of rice, 1,900 pounds of sugar, 225 pounds of candles, 70 pounds of soap, 150 bushels of wheat, 21 barrels of lard, and 130 bushels of corn—all much needed for Longstreet's beleaguered force wintering in upper East Tennessee. Soon, Confederate pursuit, plagued by bad intelligence, wretched weather, and an elusive quarry, escaped Early's snare. Old Jube wrote what Freeman termed a "sour report" and fell to griping about the quality and performance of local cavalry detachments under John Imboden. He wasn't kind either to Tom Rosser's regular cavalry in the lower Shenandoah. Freeman went to great lengths to describe Early's inability to move beyond perceived transgressions of others. To be sure, Early never ceased grousing about Imboden and took his case all the way to Lee. Wisely, the latter merely mediated the two disputatious but vital field commanders. Snarling and sneering had become Early's forte, according to Freeman. The general failed to appreciate that there was a difference between private and public utterance—for the good of the service. His apparent dyspepsia was partially salved the following month by operations in Hampshire and Hardy counties of what had become Unionist West Virginia. Fitzhugh Lee and Rosser engineered Early's successful retrieval of supplies and establishment of loyalties in that mountainous region. Perhaps arthritis, perhaps a lack of notable success, bruised his ego; still Early did not have a pleasant winter even if his official reports hid the fact. [19]

After the Moorfield raid, Early slipped off ostensibly to attend to personal business and crush dissidence in his home county before returning to the main army at Orange, Virginia, at the end of February. He returned in higher fettle. (Could an interlude with Julia McNealey have soothed the savage brow?) At any rate, he now sported a new uniform and black-plumed beaver hat that apparently impressed the staid Robert E. Lee. But Early also returned to find an ailing Ewell as well as the latter's suspicious and protective new wife, the Nashville widow Lucinda Brown, and her son serving on Ewell's staff. That pair sensed Early's hand at intrigue when Richmond and Lee began to question the regular corps commander's continued ability for field service. Impressions that Early was angling for Ewell's command fretted the air of winter encampments along the Rapidan River. This climate surrounded some mysterious transgression by Early that occasioned his temporary arrest by Ewell for conduct "subversive of good order and military discipline." Lee proclaimed it Early's fault. Freeman thought, "Whatever the details, outwardly they made no difference in the relations of Early and Ewell." Yet Freeman also decided that the incident neither lowered Early's own self-opinion nor dampened his ambition or continued intolerance of the faults of others, like reserve cavalryman John Imboden. Just how would Freeman's conclusions play in the 1864 campaigns? [20]

The war in the east now took a defining turn. Ulysses S. Grant came east from his victorious rise to fame in the trans-Appalachian theater and assumed overall direction of Union armies. He chose to travel with Meade's Army of the Potomac rather than preside from politically charged Washington. Pitched combat with Lee was inevitable, and it soon occurred in the Wilderness and at Spotsylvania Court House in early May. If Confederates discovered their opponents to be basically the same as before in combat, they also discovered that the newcomer heading them did not retreat. Early probably noticed little change at the time; his contemporary reports say little. He played his customary operational role as division commander executing crucial offensive moves at crucial moments to bring tactical victory. Yet on the second day at the Wilderness, not unlike his performance at Gettysburg, Early's usual aggressiveness turned pallid when a golden opportunity presented itself. Brigade commander John B. Gordon fairly pleaded to allow a flanking attack on the exposed Yankee right flank. Here was a second Chancellorsville beckoning. But Early feared what he could not see—possible enemy reserves that would destroy Gordon. Avoiding risk, disposed to a pessimistic view, and unusually cautious, both Early and corps commander Ewell dithered all day. Apparently Lee's unhappiness with such inaction eventually sent Gordon's men in, and the result was unqualified success but, again, in the waning hours of the day when exploitation was impossible.

Millard Bushong claims, "With Lee assuming responsibility for the offensive, Ewell and Early supported it with all their resources." Early relied on rumor, Gordon on facts gleaned from scouts—no apparent Federal reserves, hence the possibility of unbridled success. Early and Ewell procrastinated, Lee eventually pointed more toward Ewell's deficiencies (after Gettysburg, the senior commander had increasing misgivings about a maimed veteran leading a corps in the field), and Gordon's success came too late to have operational effect. It may have been that the Wilderness was a "grim standoff," in the words of Charles Osborne, where "Lee had succeeded in neutralizing the power of Grant's mighty army," although at heavy cost. Grant now began his relentless side-slipping drive southward, both armies entrenching daily. Moreover, the war moved ever closer to Richmond.[21]

There was nothing remarkable about Early's actions after the Wilderness and at Spotsylvania. His reports to Lee and his actions on the North Anna River and beyond reflected the new parry and counterparry of the Overland campaign's unrelenting shift of operations to the left, headed for the James River. Lee now had little alternative but to react and keep between the Federals and his own line of communication to Richmond. Manpower losses were staggering for both sides. Grant and Meade could afford them more than Lee. Consequently, his freedom of action became much restricted. Grant and Meade might draw upon reserves from Washington's defenses and new Northern levies. On the other hand, Lee could maintain a one-to-three (defense-to-offense ratio) offset if he remained strictly on the defensive. This fact was soon borne out by Grant's ill-timed attack at Cold Harbor on June 3. But Early, too, proved equally guilty of attack fever. Placed temporarily in charge of the Second Corps for an ailing Ewell (as of May 2), Lee gave him discretion to pitch into advancing Federals in the area north of the Chickahominy and the 1862 battles for Richmond. Together with another rising young star and aggressive fighter, Stephen Ramseur, Early got caught delivering a costly assault at Bethesda Church that day. Frankly, Civil War generals (like their successors a half century later in Flanders during World War I) remained too prone to seek quick resolution when modernizing firepower had rendered obsolete frontal assaults and the bravado of open-field confrontations. Earthen field fortifications combined with rifle-musketry and field artillery proved the case at Cold Harbor and Bethesda Church. A perplexed Early, looking for some opening, told Lee on June 6, "I find the enemy has everywhere the most intricate system of breast-works, facing every way and making a perfect labyrinth, and that it is almost a matter of impossibility to strike him on the right flank, as he always has a fortified position for it to rest on."[22]

At some point after North Anna, Early later claimed that Lee had made the offhanded remark to him that "we must destroy this Army of Grant's before he gets to the James River." If Grant reached there and got across (much as McClellan had wanted to do at the conclusion of the Seven Days but whose own failures had quashed that scheme by Washington), "it will become a siege, and then it will be a mere question of time." That proved the case, presaged by all the overland bloodshed that had gone before. Grant, with Meade's army, hooked left and southward again after Cold Harbor. Federal arms crossed low down on the James by mid-June. Maneuver would soon give way to a stagnating new campaign for Richmond–Petersburg, attended by miles of entrenchments and more periodic ill-timed and ill-executed assaults with the aim to stifle and capture Confederate logistical lifelines. Both Lee and Grant would search vainly for some way out of what became an impasse and a way to end the conflict.

Jubal Early would become involved in some new and unanticipated ways. To date, he had shown a competence, reliability, and a trustworthy and aggressive nature endearing to the offensive-minded Lee. Yet Lee also had the impression (as Freeman phrased it, drawing on a conversation between Lee and one of his staffers, Moxley Sorrel, at the conclusion of the Wilderness) that Early's irascible, idiosyncratic temperament would raise jibes and sarcasms if elevated to command of the First Corps (in the wake of Longstreet's wounding). And the army commander was surely aware of the undercurrent of unhappiness in the Ewell household about this ambitious subordinate. Early also displayed a disturbingly slipshod disregard for proper reconnaissance, an abiding dislike of the cavalry, and a fanatical—even virulent—desire to punish enemy transgressions against Virginia civilians, all of which could cloud good judgment. On the other hand, tight command and control by Lee within the confines now taken by static warfare suggested that Early was a good candidate if opportunity arose.[23]

By early summer, Early had become Lee's "go to" general in times of command crisis. Due to A. P. Hill's ill health, he assumed command of the Third Corps on May 8 and, by the twenty-ninth of the month, switched to temporary command of the Second Corps when Hill returned and Ewell was shuffled off to "have the benefit of rest and medical treatment" (in Lee's words). The "end of the old organization" of the Army of Northern Virginia, as Freeman styled it, came at a price. The Ewell–Early partnership dissolved on a sour note. Ewell was perhaps egged on by his wife and her son, who mistrusted Old Jube's actions and angling for corps command (that today escapes clear definition). Lee's increasing misgivings about Ewell's capacity after Gettysburg and the flat nature of attritional loss of alternatives (Longstreet recuperating, J. E. B. Stuart killed at Yellow Tavern, A. P. Hill constantly ill, and Ewell no longer effective) narrowed Lee's options. Given changing fortunes elsewhere in Virginia that impacted his situation at Richmond–Petersburg, Lee ordered Early with the Second Corps on June 12 to relieve Union pressure in the Shenandoah Valley. This move—back to independence of action and freedom of movement—offered Early a golden opportunity. He had become the sainted Stonewall's perceived successor. On the other hand, the move also severed forever his direct connection with the Army of Northern Virginia. It remained to be seen if Lee's choice was sound.[24]

4

JUBAL'S MOMENT OF TRUTH

The Washington Campaign

Confederate president Jefferson Davis wrote Jubal Early two days before Christmas 1878. "Did I ever tell you," the former chief executive asked, "when [Jackson] was no more that in the selection of a Genl. to be sent to the Valley, Genl. Lee and I agreed that Early was the living man who like Jackson could be relied on to carry out the purpose entrusted to him without asking for additional instructions?" It was not so simple in 1864, and Early may have wondered at that time why his selection. His consultations with Lee held something more in mind than merely defending the Shenandoah, however vital that was to the Army of Northern Virginia's future. Early was the most logical man for a larger task, a task worthy of Jackson himself. By record and temperament, Early had proven himself to his commander. He was truly Lee's "bad old man," and if the war had taken on a relentless tone by Federal design, then Lee needed a person of similar temperament to counter it. So Early and his Second Corps would become Lee's instrument of counterthrust. Yet up to a point, Early was in only temporary corps command. He was junior to at least Major General John C. Breckinridge, and that Kentucky scion may even have had better claim to the new task assigned to Early.[1]

In early June, Lee still seemed to be in a quandary about the valley. The region was not only Lee's exposed left flank but also his granary. Several commanders had failed to hold back the Federal tide. True,

Breckinridge had beaten Major General Franz Sigel's presumptuous advance up the valley at New Market on May 15. At that moment, Grant and Meade battled Lee at Spotsylvania Court House, and in distant north Georgia, Major General William T. Sherman was pushing General Joseph E. Johnston ever closer to Atlanta. Still, neither Atlanta nor Richmond were threatened directly. Breckinridge and New Market provided a ray of hope for beleaguered Confederates, and much talk circulated about him as the next Stonewall Jackson. Indeed, the tall, soldierly Kentucky aristocrat showed that he could move fast, execute well, and function in independent authority. True, Breckinridge's victory came against a second-rate opponent. Three weeks later, Brigadier General W. E. "Grumble" Jones's hastily gathered emergency force was badly beaten at Piedmont by a much superior and better organized Federal army under Major General David Hunter. The situation became dire once again. Jones was killed, his defenders scattered, while Hunter's men now seemed more draconian in design. Grant had instructed Sigel and Hunter both to travel light and live off the country. Hapless civilians caught in the path of this renewed Yankee invasion became pawns in the military struggle. Moreover, not only was the upper (southern) part of the valley now exposed for the first time, but well-established logistical facilities like depots and railroads were also threatened. If Piedmont boosted Northern spirits just as President Abraham Lincoln was renominated for a second term at the Baltimore convention in June, the battle posed a major crisis psychologically and economically for Lee and the Virginia front.[2]

Meanwhile, Breckinridge and his men had been recalled to help an increasingly distressed Army of Northern Virginia. It was not directly part of the Army of Northern Virginia but attached and therefore under Lee's command. Only the advent of Hunter, the disarray of Confederates in the valley after Piedmont, and possibly new Federal cavalry raids from West Virginia against rail and depot facilities led Lee to reluctantly dispatch Breckinridge back to where "he can do a great deal personally in rallying the troops & the People," he explained to Davis on June 6. And so the shuttle began anew, a race to get in position with a polyglot force numbering perhaps 9,000 men before the Federals. Even Lee realized this number and quality would be inadequate to cope with possibly double the numbers Hunter and others brought with them to wreak havoc and sow destruction. It was at that point that Lee took a desperate gamble. He would detach Early and Second Corps to join with Breckinridge to defend Lynchburg and then clear the Shenandoah of the enemy for good. Despite depleting the defenders containing Grant and Meade, Lee assured Davis that the gamble was worth the risk.[3]

Short- and long-range strategic goals were never in conflict. Lee ultimately needed to relieve the omnipresent Union pressure against Richmond. Defending the valley was merely a first step. Lee certainly recognized the allure of a time-honored way to achieve his larger goal of enemy rollback. He had done this before. Subordinate James Longstreet had urged him to return to such counterthrust even before Grant's juggernaut started in motion. Using the valley as the way to invade Northern territory for a third time added a new twist. Feinting at Pennsylvania while chopping up the Baltimore and Ohio Railroad in western Maryland always had an allure, as did destroying any Federal opposition en route. Memories of Winchester the previous summer and Harpers Ferry before that were always with senior leaders of the Army of Northern Virginia. So, too, were bittersweet reminders about Sharpsburg and Gettysburg. This time, Lee wanted to tackle Washington and its defenses directly. If weakly garrisoned, the nation's capital might be captured. He simply needed the means. That was where Early came in.[4]

Lee explained his immediate problem to President Davis on June 11: "I acknowledge the advantage of expelling [the enemy] from the Valley," however the "only difficulty with me is the means." It would take a corps, he said, even if it risked Richmond in the process. Directly assaulting Grant and Meade seemed fruitless, and so Lee chose Early and the Second Corps as his instrument. Was this convenience? Early was part of the inner Army of Northern Virginia circle, a fellow Virginian, a proven fighter. Still, why not rely on a reinforced Breckinridge and keep Early defending Richmond? Whatever the reason, Lee's verbal directive to Old Jube, when the two met at Lee's headquarters near the old battlefield of Gaines Mill on June 11, set the expeditionary force's departure for the following day. At his customary consultation with Davis that day, Lee hinted, "If the movement of Early meets with your approval, I am sure it is the best that can be made, though I know how difficult it is with my limited knowledge to perceive what is best." He may still have harbored reservations. Grant and Meade were in motion once again, headed for the south side of the James, and Lee needed all the defenders he could muster. Yet Lee informed Davis at 6:50 p.m. on June 15 how Early was now on the mountain road to Charlottesville with 15 days' rations. Still, "if you [Davis] think it better to recall him," said Lee, please send a messenger to overtake him quickly. "I do not know that the necessity for his presence today is greater than it was yesterday," opined Lee. "His troops would make us more secure here, but success in the Valley would relieve our difficulties that at present press heavily upon us." He said nothing about Washington.[5]

Early kept both Lee and Breckinridge appraised of his progress. He had hoped to cut through Brown's or Swift Run Gap in the Blue Ridge and knife into Hunter's rear before proceeding with Lee's invasion scheme. At least that was Early's remembrance for posterity. Dispatches at the time said nothing. The fact was that Hunter and the Federals had moved far ahead and now directly threatened Lynchburg. So Early had to tackle his old nemesis—railroad officials—to get his corps forward first to that city in two segments. His dispatch to Breckinridge in that regard from Charlottesville at 12:30 p.m. on June 16 showed Early's old grit when it came to railroaders. "Everything depends upon promptness, energy, and dispatch," he said. "If they fail take the most summary measures and impress everything that is necessary in the way of men or means to insure the object." Early had the authority to direct the Kentuckian, he told Breckinridge, "and I will take the responsibility of what you may find it necessary to do." He boomed, "I will hold all railroad agents and employees responsible with their lives for hearty cooperation with us." In a 2:30 p.m. add-on, Early warned not to "trust too much to the energy of the superintendent. I have had to deal with him before." Imploring Breckinridge to stay in close communication, Early promised to do likewise. He was concerned for Hunter's precise whereabouts: "Be certain that Hunter's main force is east of the mountains else the most important part of the duty assigned me will be thwarted." That was Target Washington, and from the start, Early never lost sight of his primary goal as assigned by Lee.[6]

Early was soon in his old Piedmont stomping grounds. His dispatches fairly glowed with enthusiasm. Wade Hampton had defeated and driven off enemy cavalry at Trevelyan Station in Virginia, Nathan Bedford Forrest "gained considerable victory in Southwest [Tennessee and northern Mississippi]," while Breckinridge's kinsman John Hunt

Morgan was reported doing good work on a raid into their Bluegrass State. But the ailing Breckinridge had his hands full at Lynchburg, including his own incapacitation. Another convalescent general, North Carolinian Daniel Harvey Hill, stepped in to help rally local defenders just outside the important logistical center. This scratch force confronted Hunter's threat by June 17. Somehow two brigades, plus Virginia Military Institute cadets, manned the fortifications until Early's vanguard arrived about 1:00 p.m. that day. Early was not enamored of Hill, but he needed "another commander than the senior brigadier," he wired Braxton Bragg, Davis's senior military adviser. Whatever Early's problem, he, Breckinridge, and various subordinates effectively stymied Hunter's overstretched invasion force, now spooked by the rumored arrival of Jackson's former corps. Early also displayed his customary disgust with irregular cavalry—whom he termed derisively "buttermilk rangers" after their reputed valor in searching for food and booty rather than reliability as disciplined fighters. No matter, Early's 13,000 Confederates reached parity with Hunter and aggressively confronted this hesitant opponent. In a dramatic scenario, ironically replicating what Early himself would display the next month before Washington, Hunter drew back, his desultory probes easily repulsed by defenders. Soon, the invaders took to full retreat. Lynchburg was safe.[7]

Lynchburg was saved, observed historian Douglas Southall Freeman, and the Southside Railroad as well, for Early had ended the third diversion of Grant's campaign against Lee. Nonetheless, Freeman pointedly concluded, Early "had not destroyed Hunter," and Lee showed his regrets in a dispatch to President Davis on June 26. Hunter was still dangerous in Lee's view, for rumors abounded that his formerly discredited foe from Second Manassas, John Pope, was being brought back to work with Hunter. By this time, though, Lee was working an additional assignment for Early's Maryland invasion, so he simply sent Early word on June 18: "Strike as quick as you can, and, if circumstances authorize, carry out the original plan, or move upon Petersburg without delay." Lee's fatal discretionary phrase "if circumstances authorize" bedeviled the Confederate effort now as it had in previous years. But Hunter obliged both men. Irresolute and worried for his overextended line of communications (the thought of a return march through one hundred miles of his self-devastated valley might be an error), Hunter outraced Early and Breckinridge to Salem and then made the fateful decision (coaxed by division commander George Crook) to retire westward into West Virginia's Union-held Kanawha Valley en route to the Potomac via the Ohio River. Not anticipating the resultant hardships and time requirements of this march, Hunter effectively absented his army from the theater of operations for a good month. Early told Richmond on June 22 how he had lost contact with Hunter but had rested a day and how tomorrow he would "move in accordance with original instructions." Later he recounted that his command had marched 60 miles in three days over rough roads in pursuit and had secured no rest since leaving Gaines Mill. A shroud of secrecy would now descend upon events in the Shenandoah. Lee and Early wanted it that way.[8]

Early remembered later how a series of telegrams from Lee left it to his decision whether to return to the army or carry out the original plan (regarding Washington) after Lynchburg and disposing of Hunter's army "as I might deem most expedient in which I found myself." Actually, Lee sounded rather desperate at that point. He had not yet received Early's report of the Lynchburg victory (written the following day). Early now was determined about the course of action. At this time and for the foreseeable future, Early knew what he wanted to do. He had achieved success. He had Lee's original instructions in mind. After chasing Hunter for a day or so, he moved midway down the Shenandoah to Staunton. Here, he would concentrate his wagon and artillery trains and "prepare the men for the long march before them," ostensibly all the way to Washington. "My men have stood the marching very well," he would write Lee on June 28, "but the teams are getting fagged as we have to rely on grass entirely." He had "reduced the transportation considerably," he reported, "and hope to be able to get along until we can get some forage." He noted provisions "to last until we get were [*sic*] some can be attained." Indeed, if anything, the march from Lynchburg to Staunton had been a victory march to a roadway lined with adoring civilians liberated from Yankee wrath. They showered the ragged warriors with food and drink, cheers and affection. To cap it off, Early encamped and fashioned what he soon styled the "Army of the Valley District" after Stonewall Jackson's original appellation.[9]

The Staunton interlude was crucial. What was to be done about Breckinridge and the command structure? Despite the happiness of Early's men, what about their shoeless feet, tattered uniforms, the food and forage problem (the fifteen-days' provisions from the Army of Northern Virginia were running out), the ammunition resupply, and broken equipment? Moreover, the polyglot force of veterans, militia, home guard, and irregulars that had saved Lynchburg would never do for a hard-hitting, fast-moving offensive expedition. What, as Early recorded immediately after the war, was to be done with a Second Corps numbering a little over 8,000 muskets where "divisions were not stronger than brigades ought to have been nor brigades than regiments"? What about resiliency through "active and arduous service in the field for forty days," engagement in all the great battles from the Wilderness to Cold Harbor, the particularly heavy loss at Spotsylvania (including an entire division and its commander, Major General Edward Johnson), and only one of twelve brigadiers still commanding his own brigade? He added "constant exposure to the weather, a limited supply of provisions, and two weeks' service in the swamps north of the Chickahominy" as telling "on the health of the men." Was Early subtly underscoring his own personal battle fatigue by June 1864 when he wrote these thoughts a year later looking back from the frigid self-exile in Canada?[10]

No matter. Early used Staunton to wisely reshape as well as recondition. Breckinridge agreed to stay on—as Early's deputy in charge of a "corps" more befitting his position and seniority (at least in principle). He took charge over John B. Gordon's division and Arnold Elzey's old command (Elzey being too infirm to keep up, so John B. Echols replaced him). Stephen D. Ramseur's and Robert Rodes's divisions would continue as they were, but Robert Ransom was tasked with bringing order out of the cavalry chaos, and Brigadier General Armistead Long reshaped Early's artillery, numbering 36 to 40 guns (some rifled, most smoothbore). The army would comprise 67 infantry regiments and six additional fragmentary battalions; 11 regiments and nine cavalry battalions; three battalions of artillery from Second Corps and Breckinridge, respectively; and perhaps three horse artillery batteries of ten guns. Horses for the artillery were always in short supply, and Lee would pen an illuminating letter to Davis on July 5 about the overall horse problem for the Confederacy. This was not unique to Early and Second Corps, but the expedition into Maryland would surely have securing horses in mind.[11]

Furthermore, Early ordered the wagon transport stripped to the barest numbers, and a grumbling officer corps and enlisted force strictly allotted what each man could carry on his person. The supply wagons would haul five-days' rations, and the men carried two additional days in their knapsacks. Wagons were left behind to bring up shoes when available. Although controversial, reservists were sent home to mind farms and crops and guard against any random incursions of enemy raiders. This earned a rebuke from Secretary of War James Seddon that Early had exceeded his authority, for they belonged to Brigadier General J. L. Kemper, who was commanding reserve forces from Richmond "by special order from the President" and only temporarily reported to Early (or more strictly to Breckinridge). Seddon lamely demanded that such discharges from duty in the future emit only "through the commanders specially assigned to command the reserves." Early probably both swore and chuckled at such bureaucratic rigidity if he ever learned of it. Circumstances in the field—protection of the home front and nonessentiality for his own campaign needs—dictated action not protocol. Early never was much for protocol![12]

Then, before departing Staunton, Early sat at his field desk and penned one of the most important dispatches of the campaign. Directed toward Lee, it provided a clear dissection of Early's thinking at the time—not post hoc in either an after-action report or postwar remembrance. It would be the first of one or two critical expostulations of Early's intent and subsequent actions at the time, not to be overlooked by historians and students of the general and this campaign. Responding to Lee's own dispatch of June 26—received by Early "at this place on same day"—he proceeded to lay out his campaign plan. First, he dismissed Hunter as now retiring to Greenbrier, destroying his wagons along the way. How much further he might retire in that direction, Early could only conjecture. But to have followed him and perhaps dispersed his force would have rendered his own army "unfit for any further operations for some time and my teams would have all been broken down," said Early. He had decided against it but rather chose "to turn down the valley and proceed according to your instructions to threaten Washington and if I find an opportunity—to take it." These words clearly reflected Lee's verbal instructions to Early on June 12. Two weeks later, Early hearkened back to Lee's own words: "I think the circumstances form this movement." The word *circumstances* would surface several more times in their communications as the campaign progressed.[13]

Early continued to explain his course of action talking about "but a small [enemy] force in the Lower Valley comprised almost entirely of 100 days men" only estimated to number from 1,000 or 2,000 to 5,000, "and I hear there is nothing at Washington but the same kind of men and not in larger force." Here lay the crux of success for Early and his men—and a quandary. He planned to use a portion of his cavalry "to destroy the bridges on the Baltimore and Ohio Railroad" and to send the main army to dispose of the enemy occupying Winchester and "get possession of Harpers Ferry and cross over at that point, if I find no great obstacle in the way." When once in Maryland, he would send a "select body of the cavalry to cut the railroads between Washington and Harrisburg and Baltimore and Philadelphia, while I am moving on Washington." All that drained resources and ate up precious time to reach Washington unannounced. Even here, it seemed Early was aware of another mission from Lee: "I shall also make an effort to release our prisoners at Point Lookout." Truthfully, this was a half-hatched scheme at senior government levels, sanctioned by Lee but unfortunately compromised by a leakage of a planned joint land- and water-borne operation that never congealed properly for implementation. This additional mission, however, would directly affect Early's success. Early created his own success—"How much of this I may be able to accomplish will depend on circumstances, but no effort of mine shall be spared to accomplish all and I hope at least to obtain relief for you from the pressure against you." He closed by noting how the "telegraph line is now open to New Market and I will keep up communication with you." He thought he might travel even more quickly through Loudoun County on the Virginia side of the Potomac en route to his target of Washington, but he awaited more definite information in that regard. While unspoken, Early obviously expected local partisan ranger chief John Mosby (whose fiefdom included Loudon) to provide such information.

Of course, Lee had not seen Early's latest when, from Petersburg, he wrote Davis, who was 30 miles away in Richmond, on June 26. Together both of them were 100 miles away from Early's departure point, a distinct disadvantage for strategic direction in changing circumstances. Lee sounded disappointed that Hunter had escaped while "not much punished except by the demoralization of his troops and the loss of some artillery." "Black Dave," as Hunter was called, was still dangerous if he remained in the valley and, if reorganized and reequipped, could "repeat his expedition," thus necessitating Early's staying in the valley. Yet Lee told the president, "I think it better that Early should "move down the Valley, if he can obtain provisions, which would draw Hunter after him, and may enable him to strike Pope [Lee still thought he was returning from exile in Minnesota] before that general might effect a junction with Hunter." Lee thought he could hold the defenses against Grant—not disposed to attack and strictly on the defensive. But "if circumstances favor," noted Lee, "I should also recommend [Early] crossing the Potomac." Frankly, Lee was mostly concerned about procuring supplies for his army and the prospect of successfully freeing Point Lookout prisoners, which could yield a division or even corps-size contingent back to his army: "Great benefit might be drawn from [this scheme] if it can be accomplished." It would require only a small party "as the whole would have to be transported secretly across the Potomac where it is very broad." The means remained to be procured. He envisioned Marylanders operating on Maryland soil under a "bold, intelligent, ardent and true" leader as "everything in an expedition of the kind would depend upon the leader." Obviously, only Maryland native son Bradley Johnson, with Early, fit that profile.[14]

Lee warmed further regarding the Point Lookout scheme, as he "understood that most of the Point Lookout garrison was composed of negroes" who would offer little opposition to the Confederate raiders. Even command of such troops "would be poor and feeble," so a "stubborn resistance, therefore, may not reasonably be expected." Taking a company of Maryland artillery armed as infantry, the dismounted cavalry, and their infantry organization, "as many men would be supplied as transportation could be procured for." By throwing them suddenly on the beach with some concert of action among the prisoners, Lee thought the "guard might be overpowered, the prisoners liberated and organized, and marched immediately on the route to Washington." The artillery company could operate captured Point Lookout cannon, the dismounted cavalry with the released prisoners of that army "could mount themselves on the march," and together with the infantry would form a "respectable force." Under an able leader, such a body of men, "although they might be able without assistance to capture Washington,

could march around it and cross the upper Potomac where fordable."
He doubted such a crossing could occur any lower than possibly Alexandria; provisions "would have to be collected in the country through
which they pass" (ostensibly no problem for strongly secessionist southern Maryland) or tidewater Virginia. River operations "must be confided to an able naval officer," namely dual-hatted army colonel/navy
captain John Taylor Wood (the president's nephew). "The subject is
one worthy of consideration," Lee concluded, "and can only be matured
by reflection," but the "sooner it is put into execution the better, if it be
deemed practice able."

Lee added two thoughts; the one directly related to the whole campaign's success. As nearly as he could learn, "all the troops in the control
of the United States are being sent to Grant, and little or no opposition
could be made by those at Washington." His reading of Northern newspapers, intelligence gathered in the field, and perhaps anything sent
through the cordon of Washington's fortress system from resident secessionists may have led to that conclusion. And it was fairly accurate
for the moment. But the situation was fluid, intelligence imprecise, and
speed of action imperative. Lee finished his missive to Davis with a
second cryptic remark: "With relation to the project of Marshal Kane, if
the matter can be kept secret, which I fear is impossible, should General Early cross the Potomac, he might be sent to join him." Here lay the
dying embers of unshakable faith that Marylanders would rise and overthrow Yankee rule. Wooing Marylanders to the Confederacy had driven
strategy and passion from the war's beginnings. Exiled George Proctor
Kane, ardent secessionist and marshal of the Baltimore police at the
time of Lincoln's surreptitious passage of that city for Washington in
1861, unceasingly badgered the Davis administration with schemes for
dislocating the Union war effort and including heavy recruitment
among the Old Line State's reputedly oppressed citizenry for Confederate service. That may have explained the notion of joining Early's
column, or it may have been part of what future assassin John Wilkes
Booth had earlier briefed Confederate officials, including Kane, about
kidnapping Lincoln—again not entirely divorced from Early's taking
Washington.[15]

Although never entirely clear as to precise numbers, Early's rejuvenated expeditionary force marched out smartly from Staunton camps at
3:00 a.m. on June 28. Perhaps 15,000 to 20,000 "foot cavalry" (Early

later thought the official head count taken at Staunton showed maybe 12,000 to 14,000) now headed for the Potomac. We cannot be absolutely sure about Civil War statistics, especially Confederate numbers. The lower Shenandoah Valley lay open to their advance. Citizenry again flocked to see them pass. By July 4, Yankee Independence Day, the Army of the Valley District would be poised to cross onto Maryland soil before moving east toward the Yankee capital. As intended, Federal authorities hardly sensed Early's coming. Scattered tales of Rebel host on the upper Potomac received scant credence in Washington much less at Grant's City Point headquarters near Petersburg. Early's campaign was succeeding brilliantly. But the best of intentions soon became governed by evolving "circumstances."[16]

Early remembered in his autobiography how Lee's original written orders had covered dealing with Hunter, "then to move down the Valley, cross the Potomac near Leesburg in Loudon County, or at or above Harper's Ferry, as I might find practicable, and threaten Washington City." It was only in retrospect that Early could tell the *Baltimore Gazette* in December 1874, "I will add that General Lee did not expect that I would be able to capture Washington with my small force; his orders were simply to threaten that city, and my only chances of capturing it depended upon its being found without any garrison." The object of the movement, claimed Early, was to "cause the withdrawal of a large part of Grant's army from the vicinity of Richmond and the eventual abandonment of the siege." True enough, but a decade after the event, Early would opine, "General Lee, I have no doubt, would have been gratified if I could have taken Washington, but when I suggested to him I would take it if I could, he remarked that it would hardly be possible to do so." All the elements in these accounts hold an aspect of truth given variance in hearing, remembrance, perception, and expectations. No matter; in late June 1864, whatever the intended successful outcome, Early's operation depended upon speed of delivery. Delays, dalliance, deviation, and diversion would not accomplish the ultimate goal for meaningful result, yet virtually from the time he left Staunton, Early became subject to the changing fortunes of war.[17]

Lee assured Davis on June 29 that Early's "general plan of action is in conformity to my original instructions and conversations with him before his departure." He now emphasized, however, that "I still think it is our policy to draw the attention of the enemy to his own territory."

Grant would be forced "to attack me, or weaken his forces." Hunter would be obliged "to cross the Potomac or expose himself to attack." Lee anticipated good results from either of those events. Even General Joseph E. Johnston's success in north Georgia, as announced in the newspapers, besides its own good effect, "will favor Early's effort." If united with a release of Point Lookout prisoners, Lee reiterated, "the advantages would be great" (although finding the proper overall leader for the scheme continued to bother Lee). "There will be time to shape Early's course or terminate it when he reaches the Potomac, as circumstances" (again that overstressed word) would dictate. Early could not be withdrawn from the valley without inviting a return of Hunter's expedition, Lee continued to believe, but "to retain [Early] there inactive would not be advantageous." And, "as before stated, my greatest present anxiety is to secure regular and constant supplies." Although presently the Petersburg situation was doing well, "I must look to the future." [18]

Perhaps Early's communiqué to Lee from New Market at 9:00 on the morning of June 30 would encourage his chief. Early sounded in high spirits, his men in fine condition, and "their health greatly improved." They would have no difficulty with supplies, as the wheat and grass crops in the valley from Salem north are "very fine and abundant" but a little damaged by Hunter. The reserve contingents were securing those crops. He apprehended little danger from Hunter, while explaining to Lee how repairs to the telegraph line extended to Liberty or even Salem. Still, he was moving more quickly away from that communication umbilical with Lee than it could be repaired. In a somewhat jocular tone, Early assured Lee, "If you can continue to threaten Grant, I hope to be able to do something for your relief and the success of our cause shortly." He promised, "I shall lose no time," which proved true until he reached the lower valley. Then, a contingent of Confederate scouts under Captain George W. Booth, adjutant in Colonel Bradley Johnson's Maryland cavalry, encountered the first Federal opposition outside Winchester. The pleasant march northward to adoring roadside bystanders now turned serious, although nobody yet thought the Yankees had the slightest inkling of Early's real mission. Early still had a cushion of several days, but he must not dawdle. [19]

A turn of events now disrupted Early's timetable. He claimed later that his original intention had been to advance directly on Washington south of the Potomac through Loudon County. This route would have placed him squarely confronting the more formidable forts on the southern side of the city, so one might well question his recall. Perhaps a meeting with either Mosby or his commissary officer more accurately thwarted that idea. Surely Mosby did not want an entire army traipsing through his relatively quiet domain. Such passage would requisition supplies from the relatively comfortable burgher-farmers. Or perhaps Early's additional contention was correct. His provisions depleted, he would have had to spend precious time stopping to thresh and mill wheat, "as neither bread nor flour could otherwise be obtained." No matter; at the time, the army continued down the Valley Turnpike toward Potomac crossings. Then, another of Lee's dispatches, ostensibly penned on July 3, reached Early at Winchester. Lee wanted the expedition to remain in the lower valley "until everything was in readiness to cross the Potomac." He especially desired destruction of the Baltimore and Ohio Railroad to deny the Union government shifting reinforcements, especially Hunter returning to threaten Early's rear. Early obligingly sent much of his irregular cavalry over North Mountain and to Duffield's Station, six miles west of Harpers Ferry, to render inoperative the rail line. But by 1:00 a.m. on June 29, B&O president John Garrett wired Secretary of War Edwin Stanton that something more serious seemed to be brewing on the upper Potomac than mere guerrilla raids against his property. Washington and Grant continued to scoff at the idea. Intelligence held all of Lee's forces still in the Richmond–Petersburg lines. Garrett retorted, "I am satisfied the operations and designs of the enemy in the Valley demand the greatest vigilance and attention."[20]

A railroad president and his operatives plus local but discredited Union commanders Franz Sigel, Max Weber, and Julius Stahel held the key to uncovering Early's invasion. Washington discounted anything useful from panicky third-rate, foreign-born reserve commanders, yet from these two sources—one civilian and one military—would come the first information that should have proven Early's undoing. The outnumbered Federals destroyed or evacuated supply dumps at Martinsburg and Harpers Ferry and conducted a fighting withdrawal back to Harpers Ferry. Probably some ran; others were orderly in crossing the Potomac, destroying the bridges and leaving the town itself to the enemy. Possibly 5,000 to 6,000 Federals took refuge not on Bolivar Heights as in 1862 but heavily fortified Maryland Heights and stayed there. True, Early might have continued north from Martinsburg to Williamsport crossings as he had done the previous summer to spread panic and fog of war as to his intentions by threatening Pennsylvania once more. Rumors abounded that this was precisely Early's destination, but of course, that was not the plan. Early's chosen trajectory lay through Harpers Ferry to reach the highway and railroad directly to Frederick, from which he could then quickly descend on Washington. Sigel's move thwarted that notion. Early had little choice but to find crossings upriver and then decide what to do about the Maryland Heights impediment. Yankee artillery on Maryland Heights bluffed his response, as Early explained in answer to Lee's July 3 letter, four days later from Sharpsburg. [21]

No doubt, Sigel and company significantly dislocated Early's march on Washington. Here lay the real delay that would bedevil Early for the next week or so. Early told Lee that feeble opposition had attended his move to Martinsburg and Harpers Ferry. He admitted that Federal actions at Harpers Ferry denied passage, so he had turned to the Boteler's Ford crossing that Lee's army had used retiring from Antietam two years before. Although he hoped the enemy might evacuate Maryland Heights, he had sent Breckinridge and Gordon to dislodge them, while Rodes moved to Rohersville. Sigel and the "4 or 5000 in all mostly heavy Artillery and 100 days men" did not oblige. Early explained that "Maryland Heights are so thoroughly fortified and defended by so many and such heavy guns (one or two being 100 Pds Parrot [sic]) that I will not attempt to carry them though I am satisfied I could do so, but it would be with such loss as would cripple us to count for doing anything else." He intended withdrawing that night and crossing South Mountain by Boonsboro to Frederick City. "I then move on Washington," he promised. Early did not tell Lee that circumvention of Maryland Heights easily cost a day's march or more.

Early once again assured Lee, "I think there is no suspicion of a move against Washington but my movement is thought to be a raid on the Baltimore and Ohio railroad and to get horses." Aware of reinforcements coming from Washington or Baltimore to relieve Sigel, he boasted, "If this force leaves its fortifications I can soon dispose of it." To date, Early's losses had been "very slight" while a "large amount of forage and provisions and other stores were abandoned [by the enemy] at Martinsburg and Harpers Ferry. In fact, he claimed, "I cannot use or dispose of all the forage. I hasten my movement towards Washington," suggesting that, once he had moved forward to Martinsburg, backtracking to go through Loudon seemed impracticable. His present course "will materially aid the project mentioned in your note" (presumably the Point Lookout raid). He closed with, "I hope you will soon hear good news from me through Northern papers." Early promised to send a courier back to Lee through Loudon when, as he put it, "I get to the Monocacy."

Nonetheless, Early was losing his race with time. He did not know this to be fact, of course. He was carrying out various aspects of Lee's direction. However, his men devoted themselves to enjoying the oysters, champagne, and mayhem to honor their enemy's July 4 holiday. Any repeat of the 1862 capture of Harpers Ferry itself with the invaluable bridges across the Potomac now evaporated quickly. In fact, Early's July 3 orders to Breckinridge seemed mostly bent on requisitioning supplies from civilians and government stores at Martinsburg, not moving his stretched marching columns quickly to cross at Harpers Ferry. True, eventual detour via Boteler's Ford was again accompanied by bands playing "Maryland, My Maryland," as they had in 1862, but ominously the stony bottom cut into unshod feet this time, and few Marylanders showed enthusiasm for their coming. Western Maryland wasn't Rebel in sympathy generally and especially after three years of Union military presence. Early intended an orderly invasion just as two years before. He ordered strict enforcement of orders against foraging and plunder "else disgrace and disaster will overtake us." Any requisitioning and confiscation was to be officially sanctioned and conducted by his commissariat officers. This would be governmental levying for supplies, paid for in Confederate specie. Of course, Maryland sellers had long since dismissed that currency as having any value. Early would also impose government-sanctioned levies upon towns through which his army would pass in western Maryland. Was Early merely reverting to his earlier version of economic warfare? Was he simply retaliating for Hunter's actions in the valley? Or were sizable requisitions imposed upon Hagerstown, Middletown, and eventually Frederick Early's way to overlook foraging that accompanied at least the outliers of his main marching columns? Ironically, John McCausland bungled his assignment to extract $200,000 out of Hagerstown by mistakenly computing only 10 percent of that amount. His rough riders did better ransacking downtown businesses for clothing and supplies, including trinkets for lady folk back home.[22]

So far, matters seemed to be progressing according to Lee's desires. Both generals may well have intended a touch of psychological operations to unhinge enemy garrison commanders, politicians, citizenry, and especially newspapers like the *New York Herald*, all of whom would spread chaos and uncertainty in advance of the invasion. Such incursions always spread fear in the countryside, and Pennsylvania governor Andrew Curtain and Department of the Susquehanna commander Major General Darius Couch called out the militia to handle what was still judged a cavalry raid at best. The more Early moved, the greater his success, although this was hardly the primary intent. Still, the national government could not be sure who the Rebels were, what they were doing, or where precisely they were going. And if Washington uncovered the Point Lookout raid (and it may have been compromised by commonplace knowledge on Richmond streets by this point and passed to spies), the War Department simply accelerated an ongoing transfer of the prisoners to the Elmira POW camp in upstate New York, for instance. Grant remained blissfully and firmly committed to the words of his 5:00 p.m. dispatch to Washington on July 3: "Early's corps is now here [Petersburg]. There are no troops that can now be threatening Hunter's department, except the remnant of the force W. E. Jones had and possibly Breckinridge." Local signal corps and other headquarters personnel at Harpers Ferry knew better but blithely wrote home about an "annual stampede" or "skedaddle" at the enemy's coming. Washington dispatched Brigadier General Albion Howe and 2,800 artillerymen to help Sigel and Weber with whatever threatened them, and they, too, became immobile on Maryland Heights. Mosby's partisans broke telegraphic communications with Washington on the B&O at Point of Rocks, adding to the fog of war and disbelief. Then, suddenly, Lincoln, Stanton, and Halleck—even Grant—had to admit by July 5 that a Rebel army, not guerrillas or mere cavalry, seemed abroad in Maryland. Indeed, by this point, even deserters from Lee's army informed Union intelligence that Early and Breckinridge were invading Maryland "with a view of capturing Washington supposed to be defenseless." Obviously, this was more than merely the "annual stampede" at rumors of invasion. Sigel had succeeded inadvertently (but brilliantly) in slowing Early's passage. Still, Sigel's actions alone could not uncover Early's goal. That would depend more on Garrett and others.[23]

Frankly, between claiming to capture "considerable stores, which had been abandoned at Harpers Ferry, destroying railroad bridges from Back Creek through Martinsburg, ripping up track eastward to Duffield's depot" five miles from Harpers Ferry and the "aqueduct of the Chesapeake and Canal over Antietam Creek, and the locks and canalboats," Early's expedition at this point almost seemed more designed for a Confederate version of strategic destruction or hard war. Moving the main force circuitously through Sharpsburg (where Early apparently took time showing his staff the old battlefield), Early avoided Maryland Heights entirely, using instead Boonsborough and Fox's and Crampton's Gaps to move eastward. He claimed to have "entered Frederick City on the morning of the 9th [July], driving the enemy's cavalry through the city," but it was that cavalry that further tipped Early's hand. By this point, the enemy might not know where he was headed, but they might make educated guesses. And, ironically, Early suddenly captured the attention of the highest official in the land—President Lincoln himself.[24]

Abraham Lincoln always had some hidden hand in Union military affairs. Confident of the team running the war, by 1864 he often kept in the background. This often meant that he was marginally informed by the high command, itself embarrassed by the fog of war, Grant's inattentiveness, and sheer incredulity that anything so sinister could be headed toward the nation's capital. Lincoln always read War Department telegraph messages and on July 5 specifically queried his friend John Garrett about what was going on. Frankly, the president had reason to be concerned. It was a national election year, even in wartime. He had been renominated for a second term in June on what was styled a national Union ticket (of Republicans and War Democrats). His cabinet—that "team of rivals" in Doris Kearns Goodwin's term—and Washington politics fretted him. Salmon P. Chase, a perennial thorn, if extremely able treasury secretary, had finally been eased out of the cabinet at the end of June. Then, Lincoln had refused to sign a harsh reconstruction bill that had passed Congress in the waning hours of July 2, causing heartburn among radical Republicans. The pivotal state of Kentucky boiled over in turmoil over the potential of emancipation leading to conscription of black as well as white males, and harsh oppressive occupation tactics by local Union commanders fueled near-rebellion. Guerrillas turned the Bluegrass State into a seething cauldron bordering on secession. Lincoln resorted to suspending the writ of habeas corpus to restore order on July 6. The summer was anything but calming. Looking to significant military victories by Independence Day, the president had found none.[25]

Indeed, above all, the war was not going well anywhere for the Union that summer. Grant had closed on Richmond but not taken it or dispersed Lee's army. Casualties had soared. Sherman was still battling his way through north Georgia en route to Atlanta. He had neither captured that strategic rail center nor dispersed Joseph Johnston's defenders. The Union naval blockade still had chinks. Guerrillas, partisans, even pure banditry permeated most of the captured South, and those ever-lengthening casualty lists, posted on billboards outside telegraph and newspaper offices across the North, boded ill for citizen support. Peace advocates, like Horace Greeley, badgered the administration about a negotiated settlement with the Confederacy and renunciation of the Emancipation Proclamation. Everyone, it seemed, had wearied of war. In short, despite pleasant weekend interludes with family at the sylvan cottage on Military Asylum or Soldiers' Home grounds in suburban Washington, Lincoln had his worries, one of which now was Jubal Anderson Early, although the president neither knew the man nor his name nor for that matter what his mischief was about. He suddenly took an interest in learning more about both and just what was going on.[26]

Early moved ever closer. He stopped for the night of July 8 at the ample farmhouse of Charles Coblentz on the eastern outskirts of Middletown. He ransomed the town for $5,000. His men bivouacked nearby on Hollow Creek, while Johnson and McCausland's horsemen sparred with Lieutenant Colonel David Clendenin's nettlesome Eighth Illinois cavalry opposition further along on Catoctin Mountain. The next morning, Early and his entourage rode to Frederick, where the army commander took breakfast with slaveholder and Southern sympathizer Dr. Richard Hammond. By this point, Early had been briefed by Lee's son Robert on the go-ahead for the Point Lookout foray. He accordingly assigned Frederick native son Bradley Johnson the mission, and Johnson departed out the Libertytown road en route to Baltimore environs to rip up Union communications. Loss of this invaluable command for later would prove costly. At the same time, Early sent his logisticians to scare up town fathers and ransom Frederick as well as secure any supplies left by evacuating Federals in this logistical hub city of central Maryland. At some point that morning, he and his staff moved to the farmhouse of John Loats on the south side of the city near the old Hessian Revolutionary War barracks, later a Union hospital and close to the fairgrounds where the anticipated presentation of tribute would be rendered. The city's Mount Olivet Cemetery, resting place for Frederick citizens of note Francis Scott Key and Barbara Fritchie lay across the road.[27]

Early's demands were consistent—secure money or material goods or burn the city. If he apparently took no direct role in negotiations with a Fredrick delegation led by Mayor William G. Cole and local bankers, ordnance chief Lieutenant Colonel William Allan, commissary general Major W. J. Hawks, quartermaster John A. Harmon, and chief surgeon Dr. Hunter McGuire demanded $200,000 "in current money for the use of the army" or $50,000 in material goods at current prices. Additionally, the Confederates wanted 500 barrels of flour, 6,000 pounds of sugar, 3,000 pounds of coffee, 3,000 pounds of salt, and 20,000 pounds of bacon. The town fathers claimed this was impossible; the two sides haggled, and time passed with the sounds of battle escalating south of the city. Nobody seemed too much in a hurry. Early's young aide Lieutenant Colonel Alexander (Sandie) Pendleton happened to ride in from the unexpected fighting that broke out that day along the Monocacy River to the south in order to see how the ransom negotiations were going. Instead, he and his friends found a friendly restaurateur who supplied them with a victory meal, including champagne and ice cream. Rebel cavalrymen, meanwhile, helped themselves to Frederick store shelves. Whether Early personally entered discussions remains unclear. He had charged Breckinridge with most of the army to move south on the turnpike to Washington and brush aside rumored militia opposition expected at the Monocacy or Frederick railroad junction where road and rail bridges crossed the Monocacy. Eventually, Frederick's tribute passed like exchange between some medieval baron and his serfs. Only after agreements had been reached with civil officials would the Confederates discover they might have missed some $262,500 worth of additional government supplies stored in some seven other locations.

Actually, Early's timetable had little leeway for policing all that by this point anyway.[28]

Early intended Rodes's division to demonstrate eastward from the city at the famous Jug Bridge crossing of the old National Road to Baltimore over the Monocacy. The army's main thrust, however, would take Breckinridge with Ramseur's and Gordon's divisions of infantry, McCausland's cavalry, and Long's artillery southward on the main thoroughfare to Washington via Urbana, Hyattstown, Clarksburg, Gaithersburg, and Rockville to the District of Columbia and Georgetown. They were to move rapidly and seize the covered highway and iron truss railroad bridges at the junction. Anticipating merely more militia and desultory Yankee cavalry delays, Breckinridge ran into determined resistance from an unanticipated source. If Washington and Ulysses S. Grant were slow to react to danger, John W. Garrett was not, and he meant to protect that invaluable iron truss bridge at the Monocacy. Early had not anticipated such a turn of events.

Garrett tapped the closest military source he could find at Baltimore. Major General Lewis "Lew" Wallace, commander of the Middle Department and VIII Army Corps, at Garrett's urging took upon himself to uncover and blunt whatever enemy was transiting his department. Wallace was a veteran volunteer officer with experience under Grant in the west, but he had been shunted off to rear-echelon duties because of army politics. Now, he mustered perhaps 6,500 troops, a six-gun battery, and a 24-pound garrison gun in a blockhouse guarding Garrett's railroad bridge. Two days before, he had sent a screening force, including Clendenin, west of Frederick that uncovered Early's oncoming threat. Wallace concentrated his blocking force on the south and east banks of the river to dispute crossings from Jug Bridge to the junction just to be sure. He stopped Brigadier General James Ricketts's 2nd Division, VI Corps (finally sent by Grant and Meade to bolster forces and spirits at Harpers Ferry), and pressed them into the road-block. Early's customary weak reconnaissance and preoccupation with exacting tribute missed this new problem. Yet it was patently obvious by the evening of July 8 just where Early's main thrust was headed—the Washington road.[29]

Matters proceeded in a leisurely fashion during the morning hours of July 9. Local farmers were caught harvesting wheat and secreting livestock from the rumored ravages of the onrushing Rebel horde. Early expected Breckenridge and Ramseur to cross the Monocacy without difficulty. Breckinridge and Wallace skirmished and gingerly felt out each other's intentions. Little headway was made. Then, an overconfident McCausland found a farm ford, crossed over, and sent dismounted cavalry crashing into what proved to be the VI corps men, not militia. McCausland's decimated attackers were routed. Meanwhile, Frederick burghers prolonged their negotiations, awaiting decision on the field before yielding any bounty. That outcome took longer than Early anticipated, probably occasioning some of his colorful language, and it wasn't until early afternoon that he irritably rode off in person to find out what caused the delay.[30]

His ploy with Rodes at the Jug Bridge pinned down valuable resources needed by Wallace lower down on the river. Nonetheless, sun and mounting heat began to take their toll on Early's timetable on a July afternoon. Only by 2:00 p.m. would he personally view the ground near the railroad junction and claim later to have then "discovered" the flanking opportunity afforded by McCausland's movement (which he uncharacteristically termed "brilliantly executed"). He then "sent to Breckinridge to move rapidly with Gordon's division to McCausland's assistance and to follow up his attack." All this was done "under the personal superintendence of General Breckenridge," while Ramseur skirmished north of the river with disputatious Vermont and Maryland fighters. Wallace, Ricketts, and the overstretched defenders fought hard and valiantly at the junction all afternoon until finally overwhelmed by a combination of inadequate artillery fire support (the one battery of three-inch rifles from Baltimore soon ran short of ammunition when arrayed against Early's whole artillery corps) and the relentless push of Gordon's overlapping veterans who replaced McCausland's hapless "buttermilk rangers." Still, the contest proved very costly, as Gordon personally attested later. Wresting Wallace and Ricketts off their defense of Monocacy Bridge wrecked Gordon's division for future work and depleted Confederate artillery chests.[31]

Early allocated little space to Monocacy in both his after-action report to Lee and his postwar autobiography. Gordon and McCausland as well as Wallace's rout were mentioned in both but nothing about heavy casualties or overexpenditure of ammunition. Indeed, Monocacy would prove to be a short-term tactical victory but contributor to Early's strategic failure. Gordon observed in his postwar memoir that the battle was "short, decisive, and bloody." He claimed, "The Confederate victory was won at fearful cost and by practically a single division [obviously his own], but was complete. The way to Washington was opened for General Early's march." At the time, however, Early, Breckinridge, and the division commanders like Gordon spent the after-hours regrouping, tallying losses, and preparing POW rolls. Getting about 600 prisoners corralled (Wallace had 1,300 total casualties, although he ultimately reduced immediate estimates), their own 900 dead and wounded accounted for (the Confederate dead ultimately buried in Mount Olivet Cemetery, Federals at the national cemetery in Sharpsburg), and a possibly nine-mile-long supply and booty train across the river bogged down the victors that evening. Wallace's burning of the covered highway bridge at the height of the battle proved particularly inconvenient for Early, so the Confederates lost an additional 24 hours on the Monocacy. Most significantly, Wallace's initiative definitely uncovered Early's true goal. It finally shocked the Union high command, including the president, into facing reality. Washington was the target. As of July 9 and 10, 1864, it lay virtually naked to the enemy. Wallace wired the War Department that he had fought from 9:00 a.m. to 5:00 p.m., was overwhelmed by Early's numbers, and retreated "with a battered and half-demoralized column" back to Baltimore. He estimated Early's force "at least 20,000" but "do not seem to be pursuing." "You will have to use every exertion to save Baltimore and Washington," he warned."[32]

Wallace, from at least the evening of July 8, had doubted that Baltimore was Early's goal. Washington was too logical and Confederate activity that day led to Wallace's 8:00 p.m. telegram to Halleck noting how Breckinridge "with a strong column" was moving down the Washington pike and was within six miles of the hamlet of Urbana. Whether or not the date and time group of that telegram was accurate, Wallace nonetheless had pledged to cover the threat and had shifted his meager force accordingly. By his more loquacious formal August after-action report, Wallace could declare that his Monocacy dead (for which he proposed an epitaph on a suitable monument at the battlefield) had "died to save the National Capital, and they did save it." Such a theme would echo through the years, perpetuated especially by a Maryland judge, who as a boy witnessed the slaughter of McCausland, Clendenin, Ricketts, and Gordon from the cellar of his family home, "Clifton," on the battlefield. Judge Glenn Worthington wrote a book about it entitled

Fighting for Time or the Battle That Saved Washington and Mayhap the Union. On the night of July 9, the vital question was had Early by force of circumstances through some of his own actions (too much extortion of tribute and poor personal reconnaissance while delegating initiative to others) or tepid response by those "others" (subordinates and their commands who wasted valuable time at getting across the Monocacy) lost the footrace to Mr. Lincoln's city? Had Lee's own directive concerning the Point Lookout raid and cutting Union communications at Baltimore diverted invaluable and reliable "eyes and ears" of Johnson's cavalry that could have helped Early avoid the battle altogether? After all, Johnson was the local Frederick native who presumably knew the very way through Buckeystown to Urbana across the Monocacy at Delaplaine (Michael's) Mill. Such a route would have saved Early time, casualties, and ammunition while flanking Union arms out of their blocking position. Given Wallace's July 8 wire to Halleck, perhaps Johnson or McCausland did find that route. Its existence then fell upon deaf ears at headquarters, never made it to Early's attention in the first place, or was simply forgotten in the excitement of unfolding combat the next day. Clendenin's horsemen knew of such a detour. McCausland apparently used it to get to Urbana immediately after the battle July 9, where he again confronted Clendenin and was rebuffed. Early might have been on his way to Washington at the moment that little Glenn Worthington witnessed carnage in his front yard. But Johnson was off on his mission, and another crucial moment went wanting.[33]

Actually, as far as the war itself was concerned, July 9 proved important in two additional ways. Sherman's legions that day crossed unopposed the Chattahoochee River, the last natural barrier to taking Atlanta. Also, at 5:00 p.m. in south-side Virginia, a finally aroused Grant ordered the rest of Major General Horatio Wright's VI Corps to Washington by water. One sentence in his chief of staff's final telegram of the previous evening had finally caught Grant's attention. "It is the impression," Halleck declared, "that one-third of Lee's entire force is with Early and Breckinridge, and that Ransom has some 3,000 or 4,000 cavalry." Grant closed his own sequel reply to Halleck at 6:00 p.m. on the ninth with the thought, "If the President thinks it advisable that I should go to Washington in person I can start in an hour after receiving notice leaving everything here on the offensive." At long last, the commander in chief himself had exerted influence. Jubal Early had become not just Robert E. Lee's "bad old man." He was now Abe Lincoln's "nemesis." Yet at 5:15 p.m. that fateful afternoon, the president sent a wire of his own. To John Garrett he queried, "What have you heard about the battle at Monocacy today?" "We have nothing about it here except what you say," Lincoln admitted. Washington still seemed ill informed about the threat on its doorstep.[34]

In contrast to north Georgia, affairs in Maryland seemed quite favorable to the Confederacy. Early arranged his march order for the final sprint to Washington by placing Rodes in front, with Gordon's battered command near the rear. Unfortunately, the artillery marched in the middle, hardly an agreeable arrangement for dust clouds enveloping infantrymen following guns and caissons. He left a portion of Ramseur's men as a work party, trying once more to wreck John Garrett's railroad bridge as had been done during the prelude to Antietam. Lacking requisite gunpowder to blow the span into the river, the inept effort tried vainly to bring it down with cannon balls. Garrett's road crews had any damage repaired within the week, although Ramseur's people burned all the buildings at the junction. More importantly, perhaps, they now served as a rear guard to pursuit by Hunter's army, the first elements of which would reach Martinsburg by July 11. Lee's dispatch that day would pointedly remind Early of the danger. Ramseur, meanwhile, also served to police stragglers from Early's army, and they would be many. This final forty-mile march to the capital soon became an ordeal. Shrouded in heat and dust in a drought-stricken region, battered and weary foot cavalry still thought of what awaited them in the oasis that was Washington. But chances of ultimate success hung in the balance, reduced, unbeknownst to the soldiers and even beyond Early's control. Union reinforcements (Ricketts earlier and now the rest of VI corps) enjoyed the Union's logistical advantage of rapid transfer via what military parlance called "interior lines of communication"—the river and rail net—to save Mr. Lincoln's city. Jubal Early's own lines of communication was quite the opposite.

Early's trek began promptly at 4:00 a.m., before the heat of the sun rendered man and beast inefficient. It had come atop the hundreds of miles since Staunton, the deviation around Harpers Ferry, a previous 14-mile trek to get through Frederick on the eighth, then a major battle on the ninth. Embracing the new segment of the final march found officers pleading and demanding renewed sacrifices. Early's veterans plodded 20 more miles on Sunday, July 10. They left the heatstroked and lame along the roadsides, and whatever succor they received from residents at Urbana, Hyattstown, and Clarksburg often went more to their Yankee prisoners than for these cavaliers of Dixie. By nightfall, Early's legions bivouacked anywhere between north of Gaithersburg and Rockville. Few if any realized that a panicky Washington was still defended only by a hodgepodge array of garrison troops, hospital convalescents, civilians, and militia scratched from the wartime population as well as whatever dismounted cavalrymen and artillerists plus limited-time "100-day" units mustered to replace the trained heavy artillery gunners sent earlier as infantry cannon-fodder for "Butcher" Grant's needs. Washington remained for Early's taking, just as he and Lee had hoped. Such was the situation as the general took Sunday dinner with John De Sellum and his spinster sister at their Gaithersburg farm that evening.[35]

Early's sojourn with the De Sellums at "Summit Hall" (the house still stands) was illuminating. De Sellum was a pillar of the community, a slave-owning but loyal Marylander who apparently thought the South should be "whipped back under the Constitution, Union, and Government of the United States with the rights and privileges she had before the war." Over dinner conversation about John Brown's raid on Harpers Ferry as well as the justness of the Southern cause, one colonel named Lee stirred unrest by exclaiming heatedly that De Sellum was an abolitionist pure and simple. "It is no use to blame the devil, and do the devil's work," he announced. Early and others defused the situation, but De Sellum's Southern sympathies and slave ownership failed to save him from Early scavengers. The foraging began before Early's arrival and continued thereafter. Fences went to fires, and horses, cows, bacon, tons of hay, and barrels of corn went off with the raiders. On Monday morning, the eleventh, an irate De Sellum, feeling his hospitality violated, confronted Early before his departure. Was Early intending to give his farm up to indiscriminate plundering, his host demanded? Well, drawled Early, since De Sellum wasn't in sympathy with the Confederacy, "you can't expect favour or protection." He did write an order leaving the De Sellums two barrels of corn. De Sellum's sister secreted $3,000 beneath her skirts, and Rebel privates searching the house never found it. Later, De Sellum claimed to have hidden three

Confederate soldiers from pursuing Federals, although he sarcastically commented, "How many of Early's men I directed to the North Pole or how many left by crossing the Potomac southward I only know by the large number of abandoned muskets left around my house." Early's raiders won little sympathy for their thievery in Maryland, nor did Early for his harsh attitude, but then, that wasn't their purpose in 1864.[36]

McCausland led the Rebel van to Washington on Monday morning, July 11. Once more heat and dust dogged the march. The cavalryman probed the Tenleytown, DC, defenses south of Rockville and found them abundantly strong, at least in principle. Located by engineers on commanding heights, individual forts bristled with artillery and linked to one another by infantry entrenchments and unarmed batteries. Perhaps the glint of spyglasses mixed with signal flags gave McCausland pause. The topography and the defensive line—stretching east and west from the high perch of Fort Reno—might be far too strong for a direct assault. He conveyed that impression back to Early, enjoying a meal at the Montgomery House hotel in the county seat of Rockville. Early and his officers had passed the morning in an almost superhuman effort to get the men up and moving and organized for the day's work. They hiked through the town, as Early (perhaps acting on McCausland's intelligence or already intending an alternative next move via some as-yet-unexplained April 1864 map of Washington's defenses prepared by army cartographer Jedediah Hotchkiss and possibly based on Union engineer diagrams passed by some spy) turned them eastward, avoiding the Tenleytown fortress.

Unfortunately for Early, Fort Reno's signal station promptly reported telltale dust clouds of the marchers, alerting defenders all along the Union line to that move. In addition to signalers, Major Thomas T. Eckert, superintendent of the U.S. military telegraph had "field lines built to the forts around Washington and offices opened at Forts Lincoln, Totten, Stevens, Reno, and Corcoran at Chain Bridge and Arlington." These would be "kept open until the rebel army had retreated," Eckert told superiors later. They proved "of great service in affording a means of rapid communication between all parts of our line." Indeed, not only did the Federals enjoy interior lines strategically (water and rail for reinforcement), but Washington's defenders also now enjoyed tactically interior lines—communication and logistical advantages for discerning and responding to Early's every move. In some ways, Early was doomed before he even came within range of Washington's guns.[37]

The strung-out column of Confederates dragged eastward on the New Cut Road from Rockville, past Veir's Mill on the headwaters of Rock Creek before turning south on the Brookeville turnpike toward Washington at Leesborough and Mitchell's Crossroads. Early remembered in his memoirs that the "day was an exceedingly hot one [the thermometer at W. H. Farquar's place further out at Sandy Spring reached 94 degrees that day], and there was no air stirring." While marching, the men were "enveloped in a suffocating cloud of dust, and many of them fell by the way from exhaustion." "Our progress was therefore very much impeded," he claimed, but he "pushed on as rapidly as possible, hoping to get into the Washington fortifications before they could be manned." Early was now with Colonel George H. Smith's 62nd Virginia Mounted Infantry, 200 to 250 relatively fresh bodies having escaped the Monocacy fight. They passed a humble Grace Episcopal Church and Sligo Crossroads, where the acting commander Lieutenant Colonel David Lang brushed aside Union picket opposition. Off to the right stood two splendid country houses of Washington's elite— old newspaperman and political king-maker Francis Preston Blair's "Silver Spring" and his son, Lincoln's postmaster general, Montgomery Blair's "Falkland." Early would remember both. For the moment, however, there was no time to linger. He wanted to personally reconnoiter Union forts interdicting his passage.[38]

Early's entourage reached a vantage point where the U.S. Army would erect Walter Reed Hospital some four decades later. The time was shortly after noon. Pulling out binoculars, Early observed "that the works were but feebly manned." The works in question numbered Fort Slocum to Early's left, Fort DeRussy beyond the valley of Rock Creek to his right, and Fort Stevens directly in front of him on the Seventh Street Road. Connecting infantry trenches and unarmed field gun batteries completed what Early saw. He directed Rodes to have his men— marching by flank as the "only practicable mode of marching upon the road we were on"—to "go into line as rapidly as possible, throw out skirmishers, and move into the works if he could." Rodes's men could not, at least before "we saw a cloud of dust in the rear of the works towards Washington, and soon a column of the enemy filed into them on the right and left and skirmishers were thrown out in front, while an artillery fire was opened on us from a number of batteries." In retrospect, Early assumed this was a sign of veterans reinforcing the defenders.[39]

Early's memory may have compressed the details, but of one thing he was sure in his autobiography: "This defeated our hopes of getting possession of the works by surprise, and it became necessary to reconnoiter." Whatever was true on the early afternoon of July 11, the greatest opportunity of the war slipped from Early's grasp. It might have happened anyway. However, Rebel cavalryman John Opie and others in the ranks always thought that a "volley, a rebel yell and a vigorous charge would have given us Washington." True, a few, like Virginian John Worsham, admitted that when he viewed the "most formidable looking [line of fortifications] I ever saw," he quietly gave thanks that Early had not given the order to assault that position. But by waiting and watching, the moment when the war hung in the balance most assuredly slipped from Early's grasp. Later, veterans would declare boastfully to have seen the dome of the capital, viewed the city's church spires, and listened to town clocks striking—all questionable given the din of battle. Of one thing they could be more certain. These Southerners and even a commander like John B. Gordon never could figure out why Early denied them a chance to take the city of Washington that afternoon! Gordon wrote in his reminiscences decades later, "all the Federals encountered on this approach could not have manned any considerable portion of the defences." He concluded, "Undoubtedly we could have marched into Washington."[40]

Rodes's skirmishers and sharpshooters engaged the Union defenders. Gordon, at some point, ostensibly deployed a battery to kick up red dust around the embrasures of some fort's guns and even claimed later to have boldly ridden onto some portion of the Yankee line himself (possibly down the Blair Mill Road toward space between Forts Stevens and Slocum), although we cannot be sure which of the two days confronting Fort Stevens that he did this. But apparently Early never deployed any sizeable amount of his artillery either because of ammunition shortages or simply keeping them in reserve until time of assault. Frustrated, weary, or just simply resigned to the situation, Jubal Early simply rode back to Blair's vacant mansion "Silver Spring" and set up headquarters. He was a good mile or so from his intended point of entry at Fort Stevens. The house, "Silver Spring," in the French country style, was a sylvan paradise with shade trees, carefully tended flowering shrubs, a bubbling spring-fed water garden, and quaint statuary. It provided an alluring and deceptively accommodating invitation for weary generals and staffs seeking solace from the march. Early had few qualms about requisitioning the place from Blair's overseer, as the family had strangely decided to go on vacation upon rumors of the Rebels' approach. A well-stocked liquor cellar of wine and naval rum soon added to the stupor of waning July afternoon heat. While Confederate marksmen pinged away at the fort, scouts probed for weak spots, and Early waited. Somebody found some county maps for the general's perusal. [41]

The scene across the lines was chaos in comparison. If only Early had known! He later complained about the absence of any help from the city's secessionist-sympathizing residents. But they had either left town earlier in the war, been intimidated into acquiescence by wartime authorities, or were simply prevented by provost guards from exiting to help the invaders. Certainly Early's army had driven before it into the city a horde of country people with livestock, carriages, and wagons. So roads were jammed, and sheer confusion in the city came with mobilizing defenders, panicky officials, and lack of information other than that the Rebels were at the gates. The Lincolns had been induced to return Sunday evening from Soldiers' Home (deemed too closed to Fort Totten and that segment of the Northern defense line most threatened by the invaders, claimed Stanton). The president had answered a wire from distraught Baltimore citizens that everyone should remain cool and vigilant, as he hoped neither city would be captured. Telegrams between Washington and Grant's City Point headquarters illustrated a shaky understanding of everything, and at some point the wires would go silent thanks to Bradley Johnson, Harry Gilmor, and their raiders over near Baltimore. [42]

At one point on Sunday, Lincoln sent one of his veiled observations to his senior field commander. Grant should certainly "retain your hold where you are," said his commander in chief, "and bring the rest with you personally, and make a vigorous effort to destroy the enemy's force in this vicinity." There seemed a "fair chance to do this if the movement is prompt," he observed. But Lincoln then pulled his punch. "This is what I think," upon Grant's own suggestion, "and is not an order." And that is what Grant took it to be, an observation not an order! He had sent Ricketts and was now dispatching the rest of Wright's VI Corps and 3,000 additional troops, while a division of the XIX Corps arriving from the Gulf was also moving to help at Washington. Hunter and the Harpers Ferry contingents added to the equation in Grant's view. He felt this was more than enough reinforcement "to compete" with what he still referred to as Ewell's corps. The enemy "will never be able to get back with much of his force." So in a fashion that has disturbed modern scholars like Henry Halleck biographer Curt Anders, Grant told Lincoln bluntly, "I think on reflection, it would have a bad effect for me to leave here [Petersburg]." To Anders, what "bad effect" might Grant's leaving Petersburg's stalemate to save Washington from being sacked *possibly* had? Why, queried Anders, had Grant been so oblivious to the reality that the most important military operation in the East had shifted back once again toward Washington?[43]

Early and his officers, too, might have wondered, although continued reconnaissance gave them more immediate pause. Like at Monocacy, and disputing Early's later allegations that he faced veterans from the start at Fort Stevens, initial impression of mere militia opposition began to fade as the afternoon wore on. Dusty uniforms mingling with civilian mufti and other garb of convalescents, even sailors from the navy yard, plus the "exceedingly strong" works, heavy artillery, entangling abatis, and even felled trees rendering impassable the ravine of Rock Creek to the immediate west of Fort Stevens supposedly confirmed Early's hesitation. But the first contingents of Army of Potomac veterans marching to the front were really dismounted cavalry from Petersburg, in town to be remounted and pressed into the breach, as was an "army" of spectators, including Lincoln himself. True enough, the bloodying whiz of Rebel sniper bullets, the heavy roar of fortress artillery and desultory skirmishing marked the first afternoon's combat in Washington's suburbs. Lange's dismounted soldiery got to within 50 to 100 yards of Fort Stevens, although the initial contingents of VI Corps infantry finally arrived on the scene late in the day, and the situation remained nip and tuck until dark. A concerted Confederate attack might well have succeeded. McCausland and outriders across the front even into Virginia kept defenders pinned down in that sector. Second in command Breckinridge dreamed of perhaps returning to his sartorial seat as vice president at the Capitol. How close he ever ventured to the combat has never been established. It remains idle speculation that he or Lincoln or Early ever saw one another across the intervening battle space. Everyone, it seems, just awaited developments.[44]

Given the fact that so many Civil War attacks never developed until later in the afternoon, might the Confederates have still driven through Washington's defenses if Early had ordered such? Probably not more than 8,000 defenders squared off against Early's superior force. Or perhaps the afternoon heat and lassitude at "Silver Spring" and adjacent bivouac areas caused the Confederate host an accommodating reason for not undertaking what might have cost the attackers 1,000 or 2,000 casualties. Was Early himself even up to the task? Long campaigning might well have occasioned him to take council of his fears. The passage of time allowed Early to later develop explanations. Both in his official report and postwar memoirs, Early saw Hunter soon closing off lines of escape upriver, Darius Couch "organizing a militia force in Pennsylvania," Mosby of little apparent use in his peculiar quarter, McCausland and others discovering that Washington's heavily gunned forts were too strong for Long's twelve-pounder Napoleon smoothbore field guns. Scarcely 8,000 to 10,000 muskets (Early cited Breckinridge's infantry at no more than 2,500) still in the ranks, beset by heat, dust, and malnutrition that conveyed his army as "more of a stumbling procession" or a "strand of taffy," to quote Early biographer Charles Osborne. Early's official words spoke almost in awe of the "very strong and scientifically constructed circle of inclosed forts, connected by breast-works, with ditches, palisades, and abates in front and every approach swept by a cross-fire of artillery, including some heavy guns." Early gratuitously added to his negative list Imboden's poor destruction of the B&O west of Martinsburg and Washington secessionist failure to provide support to the expedition. An alibi list was easy to formulate in retrospect. And so it stood when dusk closed off opportunity. That evening, Early called a war council in the Blair parlor to determine the next move.[45]

Rodes, Gordon, Ramseur, and Breckinridge joined Early for toasts from Blair's whiskey and rum supply while story swapping. Light banter held the day, remembered staffer Henry Kyd Douglas afterward. Certainly the Kentuckian himself added to the bonhomie, recalling his relations and friendships with the Blairs while voicing great concern about desecration of property by looting Rebels. His greatest achievements and dearest friendships had been forged prewar in the "Silver Spring" and "Falkland" settings, he claimed. Fate had drawn him back, although Early may have cackled about such solicitude to an enemy's property in wartime. They all were aware, however, of the irony that Breckinridge might well return to the Senate chamber triumphantly should circumstances permit the next day. And that was the business at hand, announced Early finally. They could not remain stationary; they had to do something immediately, or escape over the fords upriver would soon be cut off, Early pointed out. "After interchanging views" with his subordinates and "being very reluctant to abandon the project of capturing Washington," the expeditionary commander determined to make an assault on the enemy's works at daylight next morning, "unless some information should be received before that time showing its impracticality."[46]

Division commander John B. Gordon proved less charitable in his postwar memoirs toward the high command dallying at "Silver Spring" that first evening. Contending that nary a dissenting opinion was raised in the war council as to the rashness of entering the city, the group considered in "jocular vein the propriety of putting General John C. Breckinridge at the head of the column and escorting him to the Senate chamber and seating him again in the Vice-President's chair"; sore-footed men in gray "were lazily lounging about the cool waters of Silver Spring, picking blackberries in the orchards of Postmaster-General Blair, and merrily estimating the amount of gold and greenbacks that would come into our possession when we should seize the vaults of the United States Treasury." "While we debated," Gordon recorded sourly in his memoirs, "the Federal troops were arriving from Grant's army and entering the city on the opposite side." Whether he dissented from the procrastination of merriment and good cheer at the time remains unknown. Old Man Blair's rum cellar could not have helped with decision making.[47]

In fact, if Francis Preston Blair's daughter Elizabeth Blair Lee is to be believed, the moment of opportunity was long gone by evening. Farm workers and retainers told her, when the family eventually returned after the raiders had gone, that a "perfect saturnalia" had occupied the Rebels on the premises of "Silver Spring" all day until Early and Breckinridge rode up about 5:00 in the afternoon. The rowdy, drunken revelers had cavorted in both male and female Blair clothing and went on "rummaging and robbing" until the two generals' appearance. The pair "were in a great rage with some commanding officer for stopping here," Elizabeth wrote to her naval husband (Rear Admiral Samuel Phillips Lee) at the end of July. "Gen Early said 'You have ruined our whole campaign'—if you had pushed in the Forts this morning at 8 [o'clock] we could have taken them—Now they have reinforcements from Grant & we can't take them without immense loss perhaps tis impossible."[48]

The crucial dispatch that helped alter Early's plans for the next morning arrived from Bradley Johnson sometime that evening. Still close to Baltimore and nowhere near heading toward Point Lookout, Johnson told Early that a "reliable source" held two corps coming from Grant's army and maybe the whole Army of the Potomac to follow.

On the one hand, this was just what Early's operation was mainly intended to accomplish—threaten and take Washington, draw Grant back from Petersburg, and tangentially free prisoners. On the other hand, if true, Johnson's news left Early and his Army of the Valley District in an extremely uncomfortable position. "This was news to make Early hesitate," comments Douglas Southall Freeman, and while always skeptical of scouting reports, "he could not disdain a report from an officer of Johnson's standing." So in the dead of that stifling night, couriers went to principal subordinates. Hold on any attack until Early personally could take another look at Yankee lines at daybreak. "As soon as it was light enough to see," Early recounted in his memoirs, "I rode to the front and found the parapets lined with troops." Therefore, Early claimed, he had "reluctantly to give up all hopes of capturing Washington, after I had arrived in sight of the dome of the Capitol, and given the Federal authorities a terrible fright."[49]

Early was rather certain in his July 14 report to Lee: "I became satisfied that the assault, even if successful, would be attended with such great sacrifice as would insure the destruction of my whole force before the victory could have been made available, and, if unsuccessful, would necessarily have resulted in the loss of the whole force." Therefore, at dawn on July 12, having perhaps squandered the opportunities of the previous day and "as it was evident preparations were making to cut off my retreat, and while troops were gathering around me I would find it difficult to get supplies, I determined to retire across the Potomac to this county [Loudon at Leesburg] before it became too late." He was driven to this, Early told Lee, "by the conviction that the loss of my force would have had such a depressing effect upon the country, and would so encourage the enemy as to amount to a very serious, if not fatal, disaster to our cause." Sounding a bit presumptuous perhaps, although with good reason, Early at the time seemed to sincerely believe that "if, therefore, I had met a disaster I could not have got off, and if I had succeeded in the assault, yet my force would have been so crippled that I could not have continued their active operations so necessary in an expedition like mine."[50]

So Early intended demonstrating with skirmishers and sharpshooters until he could withdraw at dark on July 12. That suited everyone on both sides, as it turned out (except, perhaps those still out on the skirmish line), but the game changed when President Lincoln appeared for a second afternoon of battle tourism. The ever-inquisitive chief executive naturally wanted to see how matters stood with repulsing the invaders at Fort Stevens. Commander of the VI Corps Major General Horatio Wright arrived with the rest of his command, took charge of the fighting, and impetuously (and, as it turned out, regrettably) invited Lincoln to view the action from the forward parapet there at Fort Stevens. The president accepted, sprang up to the fire-swept position, and was nearly shot for his trouble. He was ostensibly standing behind the parapet itself when a stray bullet hit surgeon C. C. V. Crawford of the 102nd Pennsylvania atop the work. The president had been in that very spot the day before when the action was not so brisk. The surgeon keeled over, and Mrs. Lincoln swooned when she heard about it. This was surely one of the most unappreciated "might have beens" in American history. The Confederates, most certainly Early's sharpshooters, never realized all this, for the smoke of battle hid just who stood atop the fort that hot July afternoon. Early knew nothing about it—he would have danced a jig if his boys had shot the hated tyrant Lincoln, and Old Abe would have been just another war casualty. But by this time—maybe 5:30 p.m.—Early and Breckinridge were preparing to evacuate, not fight.[51]

Moreover, this incident led to a sharp escalation of the battle by late afternoon, perhaps unexpectedly for Early, at least. He had not anticipated any counterthrust from the desultory Yankee opposition. Yet Wright got Lincoln to issue battle orders to incinerate nearby civilian houses infested with Rebel marksmen and clear the area of enemy skirmishers and sharpshooters. Artillery fire destroyed the nests, and then a pitched confrontation ensued, sufficient enough to fill two cemeteries from a so-called Battle of Fort Stevens—the real battle that actually saved Washington. Two of Wright's crack brigades attacked the Rebel sharpshooters and drove them back toward "Silver Spring." Rodes's infantry then pitched into the fray in turn, and easily 1,000 to 1,500 casualties attested to the sharp encounter. A famous vignette captured by inveterate storyteller Henry Kyd Douglas of Jackson's and now Early's staff said much about the event. As the story went, Early quipped to Douglas at day's end, "Well, major, we haven't taken Washington, but we've scared Abe Lincoln like hell." The unimpressed junior officer, undoubtedly reflecting the army's disappointment at Early's hesitancy to capture the city, bluntly shot back, "Yes, General, but this afternoon when that Yankee line moved out against us, I think some other people were scared blue as hell's brimstone!" Nearby bystander John Breckinridge asked with a laugh, was that true? "That's true," answered a disgruntled Early, "but it won't appear in history!"[52]

The Fort Stevens affair has never attracted much attention. There were no strokes of Napoleonic-like brilliance; no grand, sweeping attacks; no massive bloodletting like Shiloh, Antietam, or Gettysburg. Hence, the battle seemingly meant little to many hardened veterans on the scene. Yet Early's coming changed the landscape. Vincent K. Tazlo wrote to friends the next day about what he found as an observer from Company H, One Hundred and Fiftieth Ohio National Guard:

> I have been today to the battlefield at Fort Stevens. Our forces have about 2 hundred killed and wounded, it is a hard sight—all the farm houses in reach of the guns of the Ft had to be burned to keep them from sheltering the rebel sharpshooters, only 2 houses escaped, but the shot and shell almost tore it [sic] in pieces and killed 15 men and 1 lieutenant in one house. I counted 15 holes made by the shot and shell in one house and the bullet holes were too numerous to count, the house is almost covered with them. I saw today what I have read so much about. I saw men of both sides buried with not more than 4 inches of dirt to cover them their hands and feet sticking out. There were a great many pools of blood and I do not see how one man can bleed so much as I saw in one pile. I saw where 32 rebs were killed by one shell they were buried on the spot. The rebel loss must have been 5 times as great as ours. The trees and fences are all cut to pieces, in one little tree not more than 2 inches through I counted 21 bullet holes and I saw large trees cut down by cannon balls. I send

you a splinter which was knocked out of a house by a shell which was sent to dislodge the rebel sharpshooters and went through the house and exploded in the rebel captain's tent, and sent him and his tent to the middle of next week.

War was hell even in so small a battle space as Fort Stevens. Jubal Early saw to that.[53]

The Confederate departure was not without controversy. Montgomery Blair's "Falkland" went up in smoke, the price paid to arsonists perhaps from Louisiana, possibly even Marylanders, or perhaps some other band of Southerners (nobody ever owned up to the desecration). Francis Preston Blair's "Silver Spring" avoided such fate, thanks to Breckinridge. The Kentuckian remonstrated personally with Early, who simply snarled back that it seemed "no use to fret about one house when we have lost so much by this proceeding." Early saw only Lexington and the younger Blair's place equated with the Virginia governor's house, if not the Virginia Military Institute, burned by Hunter. Maryland governor Augustus Bradford's country house on North Charles Street outside Baltimore also fit that category, and Johnson's raiders torched it as well. "Hard War," harsh retributive war—call it what it was—Early was one Confederate general now given to its practice, he explained at great length after the war.[54]

Early disclaimed Union claims that "Falkland" had been "burned by my orders." The fact was, he claimed, "I had nothing to do with it, and do not yet [1867] know how the burning occurred." Of course, "I believed that retaliation was fully justified by the previous acts of the enemy," yet at the time he had not wished "to incur the risk of a license on the part of my troops, and it was obviously impolitic to set the house on fire when we were retiring, as it amounted to notice of our movement." Some of his officers thought it was done by "some person in the neighborhood, who took advantage of our presence to commit the act with impunity." Early thought it might even have been "occasioned by a shell from the enemy's guns, some of which went in that direction late in the day." Or, he said, perhaps even the "act of some of my men; and a number of them had abundant provocation for the act, in the sight of their own devastated homes as they marched down the Valley on Hunter's track." Sounding somewhat lame by this point after the war—and perhaps seeking even to avoid prosecution by postwar Federal authorities—Early also cited a subsequent retaliation by Major General Benjamin Butler's burning of Confederate secretary of war James Seddon's sister-in-law's home on the Rappahannock River in tidewater Virginia. "This retaliation upon a widowed lady and her orphan children . . . was worthy of the agent selected and the cause in which he was engaged," advanced Early. But by this point, Early not only held "Beast" Butler (as he was known throughout the South) accountable, but rather the "odium of it should attach to his superiors Lincoln and Grant, he being the favourite of the former and the subordinate of the latter, and at that time, serving under his immediate orders." Jubal Early's postwar bile hid any acknowledgment of 1864 actions.

Early's orders about plundering to the contrary, he certainly turned a blind eye throughout the campaign in Maryland and as his army retired from the outskirts of Washington. They left plenty of damage at the ransacked houses of the Blairs. "Falkland" gained particular notoriety because Montgomery Blair later claimed that his own army's incompetence and poltroonery among the high command had cost him the loss of a fortune at the hands of Early's raiders. Lincoln had to personally intervene to soothe ruffled feathers in the War Department, and the younger Blair eventually became politically expendable. The rest of the Blair family viewed varying degrees of property damage and seemed more perturbed about the inability of the government to protect them from the Confederates' wanton destruction. Of course, Early would have answered that his association with the Lincoln administration made Montgomery Blair a fair target of wrath, yet Francis Preston Blair's daughter (and Montgomery's sister) Elizabeth Blair Lee recounted in her journal how camp debris littered bivouac areas on farms out beyond the Sligo Crossroads. Early's retirement again passed Grace Episcopal Church on the Seventh Street road, which would mark the final resting place eventually for seventeen of Early's dead from Fort Stevens combat. In later years, Early ostensibly sent the rector a donation for church roof repairs. Ironically, it was due to the Blairs that those dead found this suitable resting place in the parish churchyard in the first place. That was only just, perhaps, as Early's last casualty was one of his sharpshooters killed on the edge of the "Silver Spring" property. The Blair family cared for a monument over his grave until they, too, were lost to eternity as descendants sold the property for urban development in the twentieth century. [55]

Some element in Early's army perpetrated one more travesty on their return through Rockville. They carried off the courthouse records—increasingly a Confederate raiders' device across an occupied South for eliminating any local evidence of disloyal or rebellious sentiment, punishable by vindictive returning Federal authorities in their wake. By July 14, Early's fast-disappearing raiders were back across the Potomac, resting in the Big Spring area just north of Leesburg. He happily recounted after the war how "besides the money levied in Hagerstown and Frederick, which was very useful in obtaining supplies, we brought off quite a large number of beef cattle, and the cavalry obtained a large number of horses, some being also procured for the artillery." Federal pursuit proved predictably lackluster, at least in part because of a bloody cavalry delaying action in the streets of Rockville on the way out. Moreover, Early took a commanding lead of a day and a half over his pursuers when he departed overnight on July 12 and 13. Lincoln, other officials, and Grant were not pleased. Early had escaped, even if he had not taken Washington. Halleck and Wright seemed dilatory in organizing the requisite force to accomplish what the president and his chief general desired—annihilation. Still, Union soldiers were in no particular mood to double-quick chasing Early in the heat or giving battle if they caught him. A lackadaisical Wright pleaded faulty intelligence, inadequate numbers, lack of food and organized logistical support, and ignorance of what his superiors really wanted him to accomplish. So Union authorities rested on their laurels—they had pushed back the invasion, saved Washington, and now resumed daily life. There had been a scare, but they had survived. Early for his part seemed speedier in escape than he ever had in the race to capture Washington.[56]

Wright's and Hunter's men (more effectively led now by George Crook) found it difficult to concentrate and coordinate. Grant's desires for the VI Corps to return as soon as possible to Petersburg and the dislocation of Hunter's return to the theater permitted Early a certain luxury in returning to a Shenandoah sanctuary. True, there was an anxious moment for the Confederates near Purcellville in Loudon County when a small cavalry force led by Colonel William Badger Tibbitts knifed into the center of Early's marching column and cut out 80 wagons and ambulances, 117 mules and horses, and 50 or 60 prisoners. But this high point for Union pursuit was fleeting and uncoordinated.

While Rodes, Ramseur, and those involved knew all about it, it is unclear that Wright, Crook, or even Early were aware of the situation until after the fact. It was embarrassing, but Early spurred his force back behind the Shenandoah River in Clarke County and rebuffed Wright's and Crook's futile attempt to force passage. Early and Breckinridge established headquarters at nearby Berryville. Both armies were now worn out, ragged in stamina and clothing, and in great need of recuperation. Wright presumptively told Halleck at 7:30 p.m. on July 17, "I have no doubt that the enemy is full retreat for Richmond." He was similarly confident four days later when pushed by Grant, if not by Halleck, into his return to Washington en route to rejoining the army at Petersburg.[57]

Early was not finished, however. Writing his first after-action report to Lee from Leesburg on the fourteenth, Early had indicated how he would move back to the valley and drive away Yankee cavalry regarrisoning Martinsburg while also using his horsemen once more to wreck the Baltimore and Ohio Railroad westward and "also to destroy the coal mines and furnaces around Cumberland unless I get different orders." He seemed proudest of bringing off financial levy from Maryland but said nothing about any destruction left in his wake. Early was sorry that he "did not succeed in capturing Washington and releasing our prisoners at Point Lookout, but the latter was impracticable after I determined to retire from before Washington." But there was "intense excitement and alarm in Washington and Baltimore and all over the North," as the enemy greatly exaggerated the size of the invading expedition, "it being reported that you were in command, having left Beauregard at Petersburg." Finally, Early confirmed what he and Lee had known from the beginning: "Washington can never be taken by our troops unless surprised when without a force to defend it." The idea had been to rapidly effect that result. Both Early and Lee by their words and actions—even their decisions—had facilitated failure of the mission. Perhaps the retrospective wording of Lee's artillery chief Edward Porter Alexander continues to resonate most resoundingly down through the generations: "As to Early's really taking Washington with his little force, the very idea was absurd." But, was it?[58]

Could another Confederate general have had more incentive to take Washington in the dust and heat of those two July days? Would John C. Breckinridge have been more aggressive had he, not Early, been in command? Thinking of returning in triumph to the Capitol building might well have generated risk taking on his part. Alternatively, would John B. Gordon have actually taken the earthworks he so boastfully proclaimed to have mounted in the absence of defenders? Or would Longstreet, Hill, or Richard Stoddart Ewell have done any better than Early? Possibly yes; probably not! Generations have wondered about Jackson, but then that question always obtained more about Gettysburg than Fort Stevens. James C. Bresnahan raised the "what if" question in a chapter of his counterfactual scenarios and looked for the answer from the consummate Civil War tour guide and historian Edwin C. Bearss. "What if Early had been able to temporarily enter Washington?" he asked. Never shy, Bearss posited that, if Early had gotten into the city for only for a short time, the result would have exceeded the British feat in 1814. Early "would have forced Lincoln to evacuate the capital," although he added, the "rest of the campaign [the Shenandoah of 1864] would have played out as it did in 1864 with his eventual rout at Cedar Creek." Surely that was incentive enough to take action.[59]

Given Early's festering and ever-escalating hatred of the Yankee nation, the Lincoln administration's war-making policies, and the president's personal advance of emancipation, one is left wondering why Early blinked on July 11? He let slip a whole afternoon and evening for the decisive thrust. Here was Early at his weakest. Perhaps it was as simple as Early's aide, Captain William Whitehurst Old, jotted in his journal on July 11: "Troops much broken down by excessive heat, long marches, dusty roads and the exceedingly dry country through which we passed." Or maybe indeed, old Preston Blair's liquor cachet plus sylvan "Silver Spring" were just too alluring for the tired Early and his senior commanders! At any rate, Old Jube took the true answer to his grave, if he even had an explanation.[60]

5

LEE'S FORLORN HOPE
The Shenandoah Nadir

Young Lucy Rebecca Buck of "Bel Air" at Front Royal, Virginia, scribbled in her diary on July 16, 1864, "I suppose we're to be given up to the Yankees again sure enough for our army is leaving the Potomac" after its march on Washington. She wondered what it all meant—"this short and bloodless campaign in Maryland" and the return of the force to Leesburg. "General Early has an object in it, no doubt, and fully understands all he intends to do," but she wished she did, too. Indeed, Jubal Early did, as his active campaigning was not over. He had not captured Washington, but he had threatened the city and scared Abraham Lincoln and the North. For a time he was the darling of the Southern public—until the reality of only "half-a-loaf" sank in. Maybe not Washington, but at least the valley was saved, its populace protected and the harvest ensured. Early's Army of the Valley District had escaped to fight another day. That was precisely what Early had in mind, as did his commander, Robert E. Lee.[1]

Tangible results came with the herds of cattle and horses secured in Maryland and, of course, the liberated booty, especially the cash tribute extorted from towns along the way. Early's partisan friend John Warwick Daniel would enumerate what the Washington expedition truly accomplished upon Early's death in 1894. Early, Daniel claimed, had driven David Hunter's army out of the Shenandoah and kept it irrelevant for weeks. Early had immobilized Franz Sigel's force at Harpers

Ferry. Early had defeated Lew Wallace at the Monocacy. Early had forced Grant to divert two army corps from the Petersburg scene of operations. Daniel's comments (and later historians' similar observations) focused on the tactical and operational levels for the most part. But strategically, stated Daniel, Early had succeeded in shifting the "seat of war from Central and Piedmont Virginia, where it menaced to the rear of Lee, to the borderline of Northern Virginia on the Potomac." All of this was true as far as it went. Still, Daniel and others miss the fundamental fact that the strategic impact of Early's campaign held higher importance.[2]

Early's Washington Campaign had sent paroxysms of fear across the North and especially Lincoln's administration in the crucial election summer. Even the *London Times* on July 25 pronounced the Confederacy more formidable than ever. This summer of discontent anyway in Washington was worsened by Early's appearance and near miss before the city. Even Daniel and generations of apologists could not escape the obvious, however. Early had not taken Washington. He had not captured or dispersed the enemy's regime nor captured, killed, or made Abe Lincoln a refugee. He had not freed Point Lookout prisoners. All those goals had been the principal objectives in the Washington Campaign. What Early had done was to gain time and badly needed supplies for Lee, but it is tantalizing to speculate, as does Shenandoah Valley social historian John Heatwole, "if Hunter had been able to retreat down the Valley, he might have delayed Jubal Early and there probably would not have been a Confederate move on Washington [in the first place]."[3]

Nonetheless, at least some in Early's army thought he had done well. Maryland Major Eugene Blackford wrote his brother from Strasburg, Virginia, on August 15, "This corps has made the most remarkable campaign on record since [June 13]. We have marched nearly 1000 miles, fought three battles, and done pretty much as we pleased." He was talking about Monocacy, Fort Stevens, and Second Kernstown, where on July 24 the rejuvenated Army of the Valley District routed George Crook from Hunter's force. The Yankees, said Blackford, "abandoned almost everything in their flight—the country being strewed with the arms." This seemed back to normal for Jackson's old veterans. As the Marylander bragged, "We have made three invasions of Maryland—two of them of very short duration, merely to get beef cattle, and forage generally." And all that was in the space of two months. Perhaps that was what the summer campaign really amounted to in the end.[4]

Division commander Major General Stephen Ramseur, however, may have been more realistic in explaining why they had not accomplished their primary mission. Writing to his wife on that same date as Blackford to his brother, the young and newly married Ramseur told her, "Natural obstacles alone prevented our taking Washington—the heat & dust was so great that our men could not possibly march further." He suggested that "time was thus given the Enemy to get a sufficient force into his works to prevent our capturing them." This explanation became virtually dogma among future Confederate apologists. "We have, [however,] accomplished a good deal," Ramseur told his wife, "and I hope we still do good work for our cause." That was also what Early himself and his superiors, from Lee to Davis, decided at this point. In fact, the rest of the summer proved almost as irksome for the Lincoln administration and its field commanders as when the raiders had been on the capital's doorstep. Early would remain in the lower valley. He would continue to wreak havoc on the upper Potomac, targeting the Baltimore and Ohio Railroad yet again. He would even send a raiding party to practice as destructive war against the civilian populace of a Northern town as any Yankee did down South in the last year of the war.[5]

If Early and his army seemed worn out before Washington, they still had plenty of sting thereafter. At first, the general considered his job done. He announced his proposed return to the Army of Northern Virginia at the end of his official report on the Washington raid. Lee balked, however. He equivocated as late as July 23, telling President Jefferson Davis how he doubted Lincoln would allow Grant to return troops from protecting Washington as long as Early "is so close to the Potomac." In fact, Early parried uncoordinated Union moves in the lower valley until the end of July. A disaster to Ramseur's division on July 20 at Rutherford's Farm north of Winchester worried Lee that, if Early could not contain Hunter's people, the Second Corps might have to return to the main army. However, four days later, Breckinridge, under Early's direction, avenged Rutherford's Farm at Second Kernstown just south of Winchester. A more optimistic Lee now introduced to Davis how a "mounted force with long range guns might, by a secret and rapid march, penetrate the [Federal] lines south of the Potomac, and excite the alarm of the authorities at Washington." But he admitted that, if its approach "was known," then the "defenses south of the river could be manned in time to prevent it." By month's end, Lee also toyed with using the ever-quixotic Kentucky cavalier cavalryman John Hunt Morgan (recovering from wounds and pestering for suitable command while recuperating in Richmond) as a diversion in West Virginia.[6]

Early now undertook operations different from the recent past. Warning Breckinridge on August 1 that "cavalry on our front is very little to be relied on" and that he should "be constantly on the alert and ready for any emergency," Early moved to "parry and thrust" operations for the next month that wore out both his own army and Union opposition. Personal accounts and unit histories on both sides underscore almost ceaseless maneuvers and counterploys in the lower valley. But suddenly, warfare here assumed the brutal turn that already marked Union invasion and occupation elsewhere in the South. Apparently it wasn't enough for David Hunter and his lieutenants to chase Jubal Early and be chased in turn. Rather, returning to Grant's much earlier enjoinder to "eat out" the Shenandoah, Hunter (who always retained some mysterious hold over senior military members of the Union army) once again began his "pyrotechnic" antics of burning any support infrastructure helping the Confederate war effort. Of course, it was the familiar revolving door of raider and guerrilla attacks spawning Union retaliation. In this case, the borderland effort focused on railroad and canal as well as supply facilities, outposts, and wagon trains. Troop- and supply-carrying Baltimore and Ohio trains offered railroad infrastructure bridges, track, and logistical support, like locomotive roundhouses and turntables, as convenient targets for Confederate raids. Like the B&O as a coal carrier, the parallel Chesapeake and Ohio canal barges and locks also invited Rebel attention. The Federal government had transferred two army corps using the railroad to help relieve Chattanooga in the fall of 1863. And coal cars and barges were indispensable for both a burgeoning Northern economy and to fuel homes, businesses, and public buildings in the coming winter. Here was a strategic importance that governments and generals could understand. Confederate raiders had crippled the B&O and C&O periodically from 1861 on. And from 1862, Union response had often gone beyond hunting down just the raiders but also punishing nearby Confederate-sympathizing civilians. Early's tribute extraction as seen in Pennsylvania and Maryland previously and Bradley Johnson's raid that incinerated the Maryland governor's country home north of Baltimore during their recent raid suggested even the Confederacy was expanding its nonbattlefield lethality. Hunter had torched at Lexington and in the valley earlier. Both sides had little success controlling wild outriders and soldiery disintegrating into brigandage.[7]

Retribution went further when Hunter now burned a number of private dwellings in Jefferson County, West Virginia, turning families from their homes and sparing neither dwellings nor outbuildings. Early's predictable ire was again raised. Destroying the homes of Alexander R. Boteler, ex-Confederate congressman; Edmund I. Lee, distantly related to Robert E. Lee; and finally Hunter's own first cousin Andrew seemed beyond the pale. "Boydville," home of Charles J. Faulkner of Martinsburg, was spared only by Lincoln's personal intervention, although the presidential directive particularly implied the "burning of residences of prominent citizens of the Shenandoah Valley" had been "in retaliation for the burning of Governor Bradford's house in Maryland by the Confederate forces." Truthfully, Hunter was only responding to Grant's July 17 order to make "all the valley south of the Baltimore and Ohio road a desert as high up as possible." The general in chief did not intend that houses should be burned, "but every particle of provisions and stock should be removed, and the people notified to move out." This was standard practice in Tennessee, Mississippi, and other portions of the invaded Confederacy, so nothing new here. Grant finished with his famous enjoinder that Hunter should do such a thorough job that "crows flying over it for the balance of the season will have to carry their provender with them." Of course such orders sanctioned Hunter's own retributive abolitionist feelings toward his fellow slaveholding Southerners. Early determined that it was time Northern civilians should feel the same pain.[8]

Perhaps "retaliation in kind" may best describe this next phase of Early's life, one never regretted to his dying day. He explained, "I came to the conclusion it was time to open the eyes of the people of the North to this enormity, by an example in the way of retaliation." Indeed, revenge was always somewhere in Jubal's makeup, and it now surfaced with a vengeance in what has been called the "Chambersburg raid." Historian Scott Patchan boldly advances that "in so doing, Early altered the course of the war in Virginia and unleashed forces that he could not have fathomed at that time." Oddly, there was yet another twist to the story. Chambersburg lay in the rich Cumberland Valley of central Pennsylvania. This granary, stretching from the Potomac to the Susquehanna, from Hagerstown to Harrisburg, was to the Middle Atlantic states of the Union as the Shenandoah was to the Confederacy. Chambersburg's 5,256 residents had wealth. The town had warehouses and commercial enterprise, the shops of the Cumberland Valley Railroad serving the markets, as well as the headquarters of Major General Darius Couch's Department of the Susquehanna. Thus, it had military and civilian targets suitable to Early's intent. But as Patchan observes, Hunter burned houses; Early would burn an entire town. By late July, he dispatched Brigadier General John McCausland with a formidable raiding force of Virginia and Maryland cavalry and four cannon—2,800 men in all—via a circuitous route across the Potomac to Mercersburg and thence to Chambersburg. Union opposition was scattered but sufficient to raise the alarm. On the morning of July 30, the Rebels descended on Chambersburg, demanding $100,000 in gold or $500,000 in U.S. currency, avowedly as payment for Hunter's destruction of the private dwellings in Jefferson County. McCausland carried a written demand (there would be no decimal mistake this time like at Hagerstown), should municipal authorities fail to respond, he could burn Chambersburg. After accomplishing this task, the raiders were to move west to wreak havoc with the coal town of Cumberland on the B&O, destroy colliery equipment, and descend on the New Creek station and further destroy track, rolling stock, and other railroad assets. They would then rejoin Early in the valley. Meanwhile, Early's main force would demonstrate on the upper Potomac to draw attention away from McCausland.[9]

McCausland's ransoming of Chambersburg turned sour when residents, even the town fathers, failed to accede to his demands. Thinking military relief nearby, the disbelieving Pennsylvanians demurred, and so McCausland burned the town. Bradley Johnson resisted carrying out Early's orders, but enlisted men quickly found liquor and engaged in "every crime in the catalogue of infamy . . . except murder and rape," declared the irate Marylander. Two thousand residents lost their homes, and 550 buildings went up in smoke, numbering 278 houses, 271 barns, stables, and other structures. Confederate quartermasters and others extracted individual tribute from citizens to preserve their property as, said Johnson, "the grand spectacle of a national retaliation was reduced to a miserable huckstering for greenbacks." General Couch escaped by train, whatever military property was gleaned by the Confederates faded in the fiery glow of infamy on Northern soil. McCausland and company got away leaving a trail of destruction in their wake that enabled William Averell's 2,600 pursuers (who, to some commentators, had failed to prevent the burning in the first place) to leisurely follow the raiders back to the Potomac. While skirmishes occurred at Cumberland and New Creek, McCausland's expedition was spent. He netted little appreciable success in western Maryland and, to top off the experience, was finally overwhelmed by Averell while recuperating at Moorefield, West Virginia. This disaster on August 7 witnessed Averell's pursuers showing little quarter in exacting retribution for Chambersburg. Three hundred prisoners and all four artillery pieces fell into Union hands. Survivors, including McCausland and Johnson, eventually rejoined the main army in the valley at Mount Jackson "in great disorder, and much weakened." One may simply sense Early's disgust from his memoir words: "This affair had a very damaging effect upon my cavalry for the rest of the campaign." Confederate mounted superiority in the valley had ended.[10]

What had Early accomplished via McCausland's raid? "Intense satisfaction," according to Confederate ordnance chief Josiah Gorgas in Richmond. Consternation once more for the length of the Cumberland Valley, according to early raconteur of the 1864 valley campaign George Pond. Degradation of the railroad to some extent, distraction of Union generals and their troops on the Upper Potomac, continued disgruntlement in Washington over Early's apparent unbridled ability to undertake offensive action with implications even to renewed threat to the capital—those could be seen as ancillary results. Early's biographer Charles Osborne suggests the continued blurring of legitimate military action and inherently unnecessary resort to civilian destruction was highlighted by the sensational Chambersburg burning, for which Early seemed a willing contributor. Early rationalized to a Northern editor in 1882 that the burning would not have occurred had the town fathers simply obliged with the tribute. But Osborne interprets that Early took a simple swap arrangement of ransom for safety "much farther than any Confederate officer ever had or would." To Osborne, even Early, the trained and practicing lawyer, felt the "citizens of Chambersburg had no rights that he was bound to respect." A postwar, crabbed Early would write editor Edward Bok, "I would have been fully justified, by the laws of retaliation in war, in burning the town without giving the inhabitants the opportunity of redeeming it." Perhaps so, but at the time, Early simply joined Confederate raiders like John Hunt Morgan, perhaps even William Quantrill and the official Partisan Rangers, in conveying warfare from purely military to civilian targets. Jubal Early never recanted the validity of the wartime Chambersburg act. He exonerated subordinates—"I alone am responsible, as the officers engaged in it were simply executing my orders and had no discretion left them." Bradley Johnson, among others, would have disagreed. Still, said Early, "notwithstanding the lapse of time which has occurred and the result of the war, I see no reason to regret my conduct." Lee biographer Douglas Southall Freeman was less charitable to Early but not because of wanton destruction at Chambersburg. To Freeman, it all further proved that Early never controlled his cavalry as a disciplined force. What would subsequently unfold in the Shenandoah had a direct relationship, however, to his orders regarding Chambersburg. [11]

Chambersburg (to which Scott Patchan adds Early's brilliant victory at Second Kernstown) was the final blow that forced the Union high command to find a game changer. Even voters might wonder, posits Patchan, "how a Confederate army could penetrate Union defenses twice in the same month, threatening the national capital and burning a sizable Northern town." Jubal Early's army was still too potent, too great a threat to the whole capital region, to Northern politics, and was tying down too many resources better serving Grant before Petersburg. Hunter, by comparison, appeared incompetent. Unity of command in the region was nonexistent. The Union's fighting men were used up not in battle but by fruitless pursuit and maneuvers to no resolution. Even Lincoln occasionally sent Hunter communiqués suggesting concern. Early was winning, and the fall elections were drawing ever closer. The same day as Chambersburg, the Crater battle at Petersburg coughed up yet another slaughter of and disaster for Union arms and Grant's plans. August would prove the month of despair in Washington; Lincoln drew up the so-called blind memorandum that he had his cabinet sign sight unseen. This memo virtually anticipated the administration's upcoming defeat at the polls. Early, as much as anyone, was the cause. Confederate intelligence operator "Durst" at the capital reported on September 1 that, two days before, 300 to 400 garrison troops east of the Anacostia had mutinied and deserted forts in that sector of the Washington defenses. They had left with their arms and melted into southern Maryland until they secured civilian clothing. "Bitter against the government," they favored election of Democrat George B. McClellan and the peace ticket in the autumn. This informant told Richmond authorities, "Now would be a splendid opportunity for a few men to enter Washington from this side" as there wasn't a "single man in the forts south of the Eastern Branch, and only seven or eight at the [Navy Yard] bridge."[12]

Soon after Early's appearance in the Washington suburbs, President Lincoln, Secretary of War Edwin Stanton, Assistant Secretary of War Charles Dana, and Chief of Staff Henry Halleck had all cautioned Grant about the command breakdown for defending the city and region. Four distinct and separate military departments had failed since June to cooperate or coordinate destroying Jubal Early. Washington's direction was no better. Northern newspapers trumpeted how an inept War Department in Washington might not even be able to organize a "successful picnic or chowder party." Hunter's sacking was long overdue as a result of enabling Early's march virtually unopposed to the Potomac in the first place and continuing miscues thereafter. Horatio Wright, George Crook, and others were equally incapable of bringing the wily fox Early to ground. Washington deferred to its general in chief. Grant, in turn, was fixated on Petersburg, and it wasn't until everything came crashing down by the end of July that he untied the Gordian knot. Hunter finally defied movement once too often, and Grant quickly found his replacement by the first week in August. Young, energetic, and successful cavalry general Philip H. Sheridan— another of Grant's protégés from the west—would take over and combine all forces in the field against Jubal Early "with instructions to put himself south of the enemy and follow him to the death." He would command a single coherent strike force to deal with Old Jube and his valley Rebels.[13]

That sounded good, although an ever-skeptical Lincoln, with little confidence that anyone in Washington had ideas suitable to snaring Early, wired Grant, "It will neither be done nor attempted unless you watch it every day, and hour, and force it." Early, too, for his part, was skeptical about the newcomer, and Sheridan did little that first month to disabuse his foeman that here was simply another enemy general to be bested. Sheridan, of course, was feeling his way into independent command of an army, not division or corps, and only partially mounted. And this army comprised a diverse crowd of Hunter's old worn-down, invertebrate commanders lately bested easily by their opponents, combined with an irresolute Horatio Wright and his intrepid VI Corps as well as William Emory's relatively untried newcomers of XIX Corps from the Gulf department. So Early feinted, Sheridan hung back, partisan John Mosby raided his supply trains, and, according to Freeman, Early simply became overconfident, concluding Sheridan lacked initiative and boldness. Early's state of mind was "dangerous for any commander prior to actual test of his adversary," concludes Freeman. As Early phrased it, "If it was [Sheridan's] policy to produce the impression that he was too weak to fight me, he did not succeed, but if it was to convince me that he was not an energetic commander, his strategy was a complete success." As Early blustered in his memoirs, "Subsequent events have not changed my opinion." What Early may have missed was his job as Fabian actor in the political theater of 1864. A pawn to keep the Northern populace perennially apprehensive, thus influencing the last great hope of both Lee and Davis and hence the Confederacy—that is Lincoln's defeat at the polls—Jubal Early was ever the soldier: aggressive, combative, designing battlefield victory over opponents. How well he could do against the new man, Sheridan, remained to be seen.[14]

Indeed, Early may have stood at the pinnacle of his career after sixty days of independent command and activity. By comparison, Sheridan's first six weeks in theater found Early buffeting, dodging, and outflanking his vaunted opponent (much to Washington's and even Grant's consternation). An ever-fretful Lincoln wired Grant on September 12, "Sheridan and Early are facing each other at a dead lock." Could "we not pick up a regiment here and there, to the number of say ten thousand men, and quietly, but suddenly concentrate them at Sheridan's camp and enable him to make a strike?" As was typical of the commander in chief, it was a thought, not a command; "this is but a suggestion." What author Jeffrey Wert styles the "mimic war" cloaked various happenings.[15]

Grant had told Sheridan, as he had Hunter to push up the Shenandoah; "take all provisions, forage, and stock wanted for the use of your command"; and destroy that which could not be consumed. Protect, don't destroy, buildings, "but the people should be informed that so long as an army can subsist among them recurrences of these raids must be expected." Sheridan's object was to "drive the enemy south, and to do this you want to keep him always in sight. Be guided in your course by the course he takes." And so Sheridan had done so initially. Then Early, helped by the wily Lee and time's progression toward the Northern election in the fall, had intruded. Lee bolstered Early's army with reinforcements from Lieutenant General Richard Anderson's First Corps, which feinted on the line of the Orange and Alexandria east of the Blue Ridge and then closed off any flank movement by Sheridan against Early via the Luray Valley. The two contenders were more nearly equal in strength as August progressed, and Sheridan was also conscious of the onrushing political season where a damaging loss could endanger Lincoln's fortunes. Sheridan retired back to Halltown near Harpers Ferry, his soldiery baffled and his opponent content that he might bluff with another attempt north of the Potomac while Anderson "contained" Sheridan's lack of enterprise. The first two weeks in September continued such expectations, blue-clad soldiery enjoyed the bounty of the lower Shenandoah, and Early's people took time to harvest and grind their subsistence to get by.[16]

Several things beyond the new opponent's apparent caution now conspired to Early's detriment. McCausland's disaster had only reinforced Early's disgust of cavalry, not any demonstrable need for him to do something about it. Then Sheridan's deferral to the defense convinced Early that he might not need a restive Anderson, chafing under an ever-crotchety Early and anxious to return to Lee's fold. One of division commander Joseph Kershaw's brigadiers subsequently declared that, if the old man had been "less selfish and more harmonizing," he need not have lost those invaluable reinforcements. But that was after the fact and subsequent events. At the moment, Early's farewell dispatch to Anderson on September 3 implied word from Lee that he needed Kershaw's division back at Petersburg if it could be spared from the valley. Early thought Anderson's return route through Millwood, Ashby's Gap, and Front Royal would profitably "give the appearance of moving on Washington." He was so unconcerned about Sheridan that he chose that moment to undertake again one of his other missions, wrecking the B&O. Word had reached Early that John Garrett's work crews were back repairing earlier damage at Martinsburg. It seemed to Early like a good time to strike them. Mistrusting his cavalry, the old-infantryman Early turned to a combined arms expedition for reasons best known to him alone. In any event, he rashly divided his army in the face of the enemy less than 20 miles distant. Of course, to him that enemy would not pose any threat.[17]

It might have been a good time to strike, given normal circumstances and past experience. Baltimore and Washington businessmen were pressuring the administration about supply of provisions and coal for the winter via the canal and railroad. "The gas companies are already thinking to stop their works for want of coal," Halleck informed Grant on September 14. Pressure to drive Early "far enough south to secure these lines of communication from rebel raids" thus grew, and "if Sheridan is not strong enough to do this he should be re-enforced." So on the eighteenth, Early moved on Martinsburg from Bunker Hill with Gordon's division and part of Braxton's artillery battalion, preceded by Lunsford Lomax's cavalry. Breckinridge remained with Wharton and Rodes at Stephenson's Depot and Ramseur at Winchester to simply observe an apparently moribund Union army dug in east of the Opequon from Berryville to Summit Point. To all appearances, while his army pointed north and south on the valley turnpike, Early assumed that Breckinridge protected his flank and line of communications southward. The only trouble was that the railroad raid proved marginally useful (Lomax wrecked the railroad bridge over Back Creek, but no repair crews were in sight and ordnance officers merely purchased coal for their own battery forges). Averell's Union cavalry secured intelligence for Sheridan about his divided foe. What Early learned from reading telegrams at Martinsburg was that the Union general in chief had personally arrived in Charlestown to pry his subordinate off the defensive. Surely Early took alarm. Of course, Grant need not have worried. Atlanta had been captured, and Lincoln's reelection chances looked brighter. Sheridan now had intelligence of Anderson's departure and promised to "go in" (Grant's simple instruction to get on with things) on Monday, September 19. Grant left confident that he would do so. The Sabbath day of the eighteenth was devoted to preparation—Sheridan's army for the advance; an alerted Early that he needed to quickly reunite his dispersed formations.[18]

Historian Jeffrey Wert appropriately suggests that up to this point, Early "had conducted the campaign with consummate skill." Fellow commentator Scott Patchan would agree. Facing vastly superior numbers for much of the time, "he resorted to audacity," keeping his enemy off guard, constantly harassing the Baltimore and Ohio Railroad, all the while maintaining his own army in the lower valley where "it could feed itself and protect the granary to the south." If Early erred at all, Wert suggests, it was "on the side of boldness, even rashness." Yet he quotes the general's postwar rationale: "My only resource was to use my forces so as to display them at different points with great rapidity and thereby keep up the impression that they were much larger than they really were." Wert concludes that Early's "mistake, his fatal error," was the belief that Sheridan was hypercautious, almost timid. That probably lay behind Old Jube's willingness to lose Kershaw or Anderson and why he split the army for that unproductive raid on Martinsburg in mid-September, Wert advances. True, perhaps, but dismissing the value of his cavalry, underestimating his opponent, and an untimely foray as part of his ongoing original mission notwithstanding, Early may well have overestimated the resilience of his own fighting men. For three months he had worked them relentlessly and, particularly, as part of his ruse against Sheridan in August and September. However potent the residue of Stonewall's foot cavalry might have thought itself and its present commander still felt them invincible, reality was they were worn out, ill clad, poorly provisioned, and ready for collapse. Accordingly, the odds of a three-to-one mustering of a unified host under yet another practitioner of relentless war suggested that, by mid-September, the Confederates in the valley might face their ultimate test. Early had no understanding of this new man from the west. He also may have underappreciated conditions in his own army. August showed him nothing about Sheridan that would change his mind. His men would find no surcease from the operational tempo of the sparring and feinting. Thoughts of taking Washington were long gone, perhaps. Concern for survival only increased with autumn.[19]

Reality dawned on September 19 when Sheridan directed a straight-on attack up the road to Winchester from Berryville. The idea was to get on Early's line of communications—the valley turnpike. The result was a bloody, mishandled confrontation known to history as Opequon, or Third Winchester. Sheridan's original scheme became fouled in the so-called narrows of Berryville Canyon. Wright's ineptitude in handling his corps' movements and stiffening Confederate resistance allowed Early to concentrate his infantry and artillery and by midafternoon stymie the Federal advance. The carnage seemed typical; Rebel infantry was redoubtable as ever. Then, Early's previous expedition to Martinsburg came to haunt the effort. Sheridan's superior numbers bent Early's defensive line into an *L*-shaped defense of both the Berryville road and valley pike just outside Winchester city limits. On ground deemed "open for cavalry operations such as the war has not seen," declared Union division commander Wesley Merritt, Sheridan (a consummate champion of the cavalry as a shock force) sent Merritt and Averell smashing into Breckinridge and Wharton's infantry to the left of Gordon. Early had positioned his ever-diminishing army as best he could and probably should never have advanced so close and exposed to his opponent in the first place. But, then, he had not expected much from that opponent.[20]

The scene was captured by the famous artist Thor Thulstrup for the postwar L. G. Prang patriotic lithograph series. The ferocious final charge by Union horsemen was one of the celebrated Union victories of the conflict. Neither reputation nor an "indifferent line of breastworks" left over from the first year of the war (Early's words) saved the defenders. The Confederate army simply collapsed. Jackson's old veterans broke wholesale from the blows of saber and steed. One of the army's finest corps commanders, Robert Rodes, was killed. George Armstrong Custer was there, Fitzhugh Lee and Lunsford Lomax, too, as Merritt and Averell delivered the blistering cavalry attack that knifed through Confederate defenses. Early, Breckinridge, Gordon, and other senior commanders attempted without success to stop the precipitous rout. Campaign analyst Wert calculates that the "killed, wounded and missing incurred by the four infantry divisions and three artillery battalions reached nearly 30 percent," comparable to Confederate losses at Gettysburg. Battle chronicler Scott Patchan puts the figure at "nearly 4,000 irreplaceable soldiers, five guns, and perhaps as many as 15 battle flags." Sheridan lost only about 12 percent by comparison (Patchan declares the figure to be "more than 5,000 men, most of them killed and wounded"). A disgusted Early said it all in his report of October 9 to Lee: "In this fight I had already defeated the enemy's infantry, and could have continued to do so, but the enemy's very great superiority in cavalry, and the comparative inefficiency of ours turned the same against us." The next morning a crusty Early assailed Breckinridge with the enraged comment, "What do you think of the 'rights of the South in the Territories,' now?" A shocked Gordon nearby wondered at Early's impropriety; the Kentucky cavalier made no reply. Apparently Early had voiced the question on previously sensitive occasions. Nobody had a good answer then or now.[21]

Lincoln was elated when he heard the news. "God bless you all, officers and en[listed]. Strongly inclined to come up and see you," he wired Sheridan in "cipher" the next day. Ever contemptuous of Sheridan, Early could uncharitably declare in his memoirs, "When I look back to this battle, I can attribute my escape from utter annihilation to the incapacity of my opponent." While the victors sent the defeated "whirling through Winchester" (according to the army's chief of staff James Forsyth), the defeated had escaped. Sheridan's original intent was to interdict the valley retreat route south of Winchester. That mission had been entrusted to another of those daring young cavalrymen from the west, James Wilson (who by November and December would return there to help annihilate the Confederacy's last offensive against Nashville and middle Tennessee/Kentucky). At Opequon, however brilliant his opening ploy untangling the Berryville canyon egress, Wilson's subsequent ability to carry out Sheridan's intent had "deteriorated with possibly significant results," claims Wert. The latest chronicler of the battle, Scott Patchan, echoes Wert, suggesting Wilson was too cautious and intimidated by Lomax's outnumbered horsemen in the early part of the battle. If crippled in effectiveness, morale, and confidence, Early and his command got out to "fight another day." That day came only 72 hours later at Fisher's Hill, 20 miles south of Winchester on heights above Strasburg astride the valley turnpike, to which the Confederates had retired after Opequon. This should have been Early's position all along, inviting Sheridan's attack. "It was the only place where a stand could be made," Early told Lee, "with the hope of arresting Sheridan's progress." But the "perceived safety of their previously fortified position" (Early's words) fell prey once more to the fact the "position could be flanked, as is the case with every position in the Valley," Early complained. Moreover, Early's boon companion, John Breckinridge, had departed the very day of the Winchester disaster, sent back to his old department to contain other Yankee incursions into southwest Virginia.

The remnant of his command brought from Lynchburg in June, however, remained with Early. They were sorely needed when, yet again, Sheridan's troopers discovered an ever-vulnerable Confederate left flank. Early had intended further retreat the next day with his "very thin" line (less than 10,000) but had been caught, this time by George Crook and others. Sheridan's 35,000 would not be thwarted. The result was still another disaster. [22]

Both armies actually had been there before, in August. Formidable Fisher's Hill (1,365 feet above the valley floor and virtually unassailable at the east-end bluff) was anything but a single knob. Back then, success-flushed Confederates had daunted the hesitant Sheridan. Not in late September, although Sheridan still spent two days searching for Early's weakness. Historian Robert Krick thinks the Confederate fighting men were a spent force but wonders why Early could not have better positioned the jaded units. He understood the ground. Finally, about an hour or two after Early had ordered nighttime withdrawal on the twenty-second, Crook's undetected flanking movement from the shadow of Little North Mountain on the west hit Lomax and Ramseur like a sledgehammer. Opequon had thinned Early's ranks too much for the available terrain, so he simply failed to perceive Sheridan's right hook with Crook. Perhaps he should have, given the outcome at Winchester. In any case, once again it was all too much for tired, dejected, and forlorn survivors of the battlefield. The language of observers was colorful—"cyclone," yelling madmen, an avalanche of Yankees hitting thunderstruck defenders who fled "like the swine with an overdose of devils." As at Opequon, Early's artillerymen stood by their guns to the last, the infantry less so—the cavalry least of all. In Wert's quaint comment, "Old Jube had not trusted the mettle of these horsemen, and they didn't disappoint him." The evaporation of the once-proud Army of the Valley District was complete—another 1,235 in losses, 14 more artillery pieces, and perhaps the army's heart and soul, if not resiliency—now gone because of two catastrophic defeats within one week, unheard of for Jackson's old foot cavalry. About all Jubal Early could wire Lee from Mount Jackson the next day was that he was falling back on New Market, would try to check Sheridan's advance, and would Lee please send Kershaw's division "to my aid" through Swift Run Gap "at once." Early never said much after that about (in Krick's words) the "wretched afternoon at Fisher's Hill [that] mortally wounded he Army of the Valley."[23]

As Early had been Lincoln's nemesis in the summer, Phil Sheridan now became Early's nemesis in the autumn. Early merely termed it the "affair at Fisher's Hill" in his memoirs. He told Lee at the time that "my loss in men is not large," and moreover, once more he had escaped annihilation. This time it was due to darkness, a thunderstorm, and victory celebrations by the Federals that enabled bits and pieces of Early's army to escape up the turnpike to Woodstock, across fields, and over creeks, even up the sides of nearby Massanutten Mountain, in "disorderly general retreat" (Douglas Southall Freeman never could admit it was more like an abject rout). No wonder one survivor merely dropped by the wayside and composed some little ditty about old cavalry irregular John Imboden's "gone up the spout, and Old Jube Early's about played out." Survivors eventually regrouped far to the south at Waynesboro, opposite Rockfish Gap. An aroused Lee tried all methods to reinforce Early with Kershaw's 2,700 effectives and Thomas Rosser's 600-man cavalry brigade, while he and Early tried mightily to retrieve all possible types and numbers of valley reservists. Lee trusted that "one victory will put all things right." He counseled Early, "Do all in your power to invigorate your army, work more with all your concentrated strength" rather than only as separate divisions. "It will require the greatest watchfulness, the greatest promptness, and the most untiring energy" on Early's part, urged Lee. He suggested attention be paid to instruction and discipline of the good men he saw still manning the cavalry, and he believed a "kind Providence will yet overrule everything for our good."[24]

Indeed, Early may have been down, but he had not been knocked out. He may have been reduced to less than 10,000 men in total. Still, the war in the valley and Early's life turned markedly different after Fisher's Hill. He was now caught up in an interesting vortex of events that embraced the period from mid-September to mid-October. Playing into this vortex were not only a defeated Early and a victorious Sheridan but also instructions from higher headquarters for both generals. Increasingly, the civilian world intruded, as defeat and victory on the battlefield effected controversial response from citizenry that in Early's case, at least, suggests much about the impact of this particular period in his life upon the remainder of his career as a general officer and his postwar experience with the bitter gall of rationalizing his actions. Certainly at first, in late September and early October, he was unexpectedly aided by his opponent. The overconfident Sheridan and his army flushed with success (and Northern home-front accolades) felt Early was finished. He and his minions turned to what has been styled "the Burning," or implementation of Grant's orders to eat out and blacken the Shenandoah.

Surprisingly, by October 4, a seemingly rejuvenated Early and the Army of the Valley District was back at Mount Crawford, following discreetly Sheridan's trail of destruction but nonetheless following in anticipation of an opening to counterattack. Contrary to Freeman, Patchan, and others, this may not yet have signaled the end of a chapter begun at Lynchburg or the "beginning of the end of the Confederacy's domination of the Shenandoah Valley." It may seem so only in retrospect. True, unbeknownst to Early at the time, the wail of banshee criticism now surfaced, with Virginia governor William "Extra Billy" Smith leading the demand for his ouster. Smith had personally conferred with Lee on the matter and advanced in writing on October 6 that "it is of the greatest consequence to the country that General Early should be relieved." Smith said he knew Early's "military properties" and had no doubt he was "brave" and "patriotic," "but he has no other qualities for independent command, none whatever." Smith had been satisfied that "his trip to the mountains last fall, as now, would prove a failure, and said so." Early has "no heart for his men, none of the *gaudia certaminis* of the true soldier, no dash, I may say, no activity, utterly deficient in the great and essential power of rapid combination &c." Smith cited Breckinridge as the example of both a soldier he had in mind and the one he wished Lee would replace Early with. Indeed, Smith and Early had crossed swords in the past with no love lost. But Smith's attack (largely based on a subordinate officer under Early whose name he refused to disclose) struck Lee as civilian interference with his military provenance as well as a slap at his own choice for important missions.[25]

For the next few days, Lee equivocated, as the trail of letters between the two officials discloses much about the disintegrating state of affairs in the valley and Early's role. Smith quoted his informant's recounting how Early and his army left Waynesboro to follow Sheridan at 8:00 a.m. on October 1, "in the rain, and marched all day through the

hardest, coldest, and bleakest storm of the season." He would not pro-
nounce the march at that particular moment as unnecessary, but "it was
cruel and injudicious; cruel because a great many of the command are
shoeless and without blankets, and injudicious because exposure to
such weather will necessarily produce a great deal of sickness." The
quartermaster had already pronounced arrival of shoes at the very moment the march began. Warming to his topic, Smith's correspondent
pronounced, "This and other things, and the thorough knowledge that
seems to prevail throughout the army of General Early's character, have
produced the impression among the men that he has no feeling for
them, his appearance along the line of march excites no pleasure, much
less enthusiasm and cheers." No salute was given him, and "he is not
greeted at all by private or officer, but is allowed to pass and passes,
neither receiving nor taking notice." "One believed him a safe commander, and felt that they could trust to his caution," continued the
letter, "but unfortunately this has been proven a delusion and they
cannot, do not, and will not give him their confidence." These were
strong words—merely symptomatic of a malcontent or something more
sinister?

Early had been surprised at Winchester, claimed Smith's complai-
nant. He had not expected a general engagement, and "this destroyed
the confidence which the reputation for safety once gave the army in
him." Fisher's Hill was the "terrible subsequence." "General Early, having on every occasion fought his army in detail," he continued, "has
established the belief that he cannot fight it en masse." Here was "another source of weakness in the army." Moreover, since Early had taken
command of the district, "twenty-five pieces of artillery have been captured," rivaling John C. Pemberton's disastrous performance in the
Vicksburg campaign, and "Who has the folly to do Pemberton rever-
ence now"? Smith's correspondent ended his diatribe with "I know one
thing that I believe the good of the country requires that General Early
should not be kept in command of this army; that every officer with
whom I have conversed upon the subject is of the same opinion, and I
believe it is the sentiment of the army." Lee justifiably asked Smith on
October 10 for the name of the officer registering such venom as "justice to General Early requires that I should inform him of the accusations made against him and of the name of his accuser." The matter
could then be officially investigated. The supreme commander was

clearly uncomfortable and the more so upon receipt of the governor's reply two days later. [26]

Smith, however, was not deterred. Returning to the discussion on October 12, the chief magistrate of Virginia told Lee, "I had always regarded the summer campaign confided to General Early as presenting the finest opportunity for a great and brilliant success which had fallen to the lot of any of our generals. Up to this time I have regarded it from its commencement to this hour as a most disastrous failure." This was in contradistinction to Lee's pronouncement that "as far as I have been able to judge at this distance, he has conducted the military operations in the Valley well." Apparently in their interview the week before, Lee had expressed a willingness to change the commander in the Shenandoah "if a successor could be agreed upon in Richmond" but had added "that public sentiment had to be consulted, and that, if that sentiment called for a change it ought to be made whether Early was to blame or not." Smith admitted that he had not pursued that point at the time, but since then, testing of public opinion (his letter indicated limitations of such a survey) "added that that judgment called for a change in the commander of the Valley army." Reiterating six specific instances of culpability noted in his previous letter but eschewing a court-martial as solution, Smith concluded again that he was "deeply impressed with the conviction that General Early is not competent to independent command; that the good of the service, of which I am governed, requires that he should be relieved, and that such is the general sentiment of the country through which he has been operating." Softening his tone, he told Lee, "I trust that results will prove that I have done General Early injustice, and that he will adorn his name with the glory of redeeming our great Valley from a vandal foe." [27]

Two days later, Lee, in turn, clarified his position to the governor. He had meant to confine his remarks to the opinion of the army, not the public, "and to say that when a commander has in any way lost the confidence of his troops, he should be relieved without regard to cause." The opinion of the community at large was more likely to be erroneous on military matters than any other, "for the reason that the secrecy connected with their direction from possessing themselves of the facts essential to a fair and intelligent opinion." The result of operations is "usually the only test the people have of the merit of him who conducts them and their judgment is generally made up accordingly."

Somewhat condescendingly, Lee told Smith, "I think you will agree
with me that this is not as safe a guide as a knowledge of all the circumstances surrounding the officer, his resources as compared with those of
the enemy, his information as to the movements and designs of the
latter, the nature of his command, and the object he has in view." Yet,
said Lee, "You necessarily know only what others tell you, and, like
myself, are dependent for the accuracy of your information upon the
character of your informant." Thus Lee and Smith possessed different
information, and Lee "only illustrated this difference by reference to
the reverse at Winchester, which your informant alleges to have been
the result of surprise." He then cited Breckinridge himself as his source
for the facts on Winchester.[28]

Breckinridge, claimed Lee, "who was present on that occasion, informed me that in his opinion the dispositions made by General Early
to resist the enemy were judicious and successful until rendered abortive by a misfortune which he could not prevent and which might have
befallen any other commander." The Kentuckian had also spoken "in
high terms of General Early's capacity and energy as displayed in the
campaign while General B. was with him." Thus, Lee dismissed the
statement of Smith's informant as to the propriety of any movement
"when he does not profess to have known the reasons which induced his
superior to order it," alluding to the move from Waynesboro in the rain.
Lee knew not why Early moved on that day but admitted "I had directed him, as soon as he heard that the enemy was retiring or had
ceased to advance, to make a forward movement, if practicable, with a
view of inflicting such injury as he could, compelling the enemy to keep
his troops together instead of spreading them over the country to devas-
tate and plunder and to restore confidence and heart to his own command." Hence, Lee's own instructions "may have caused him to make
the movement complained of," he offered. Declining further argument,
Lee urged Smith to use the "utmost caution in deciding a matter which
involves the safety of the army and the defense of the country." In his
view, based on his information, Lee felt Early "has conducted his operations with judgment, and until his late reverse rendered very valuable
service considering the means at his disposal." He thought both he and
Smith lamented those disasters, "but I am not prepared to say that they
proceeded from such want of capacity on the part of General Early as to
warrant me in recommending his recall." If a "more competent com-

mander" could be found for the department, "I need not say that I should earnestly advise his assignment to it, my sole object being to have the services of the best man that can be found and such I am fully persuaded is the motive which actuates Your Excellency as well." He closed by thanking Smith "for the interest you manifest in our success and for the zealous support you are always ready to render to the army."[29]

Secretary of War James Seddon dutifully endorsed Lee's position, as did President Davis. The commander in chief opined that his own un-named informant, a "gallant officer, who was with General Early in all his movements until the battle of Winchester, in which he was wounded" (perhaps Fitzhugh Lee), had given him a "very favorable account of his conduct as a commander," one that "certainly differs very decidedly" from that of Smith's correspondent "as to the estimate in which General Early is held by the troops of his command." Davis observed judiciously that "with the knowledge acquired after the events it is usually easy to point out modes which would have been better than those adopted. General Early no doubt could, in many instances, show wherein he might have changed his operations to advantages, but this does not prove that another would have foreseen what he did not." Winchester and Fisher's Hill did not dictate change apparently. But as Lee biographer Douglas Southall Freeman hints, here was the first instance since the reorganization of the Army of Northern Virginia after the Seven Days Battles in 1862 that "public clamor was rising against one of his senior officers." Maybe Governor Smith was saying what "thousands were thinking."[30]

Others were looking at Early's performance. Confederate senator James L. Orr of South Carolina, supported by Benjamin H. Hill of Georgia, used that body's Military Committee to take censure a step further. Early had traveled the Winchester battlefield with flask in hand. The recent defeats resulted from too much presence of spirits at headquarters. Early had a special supply wagon and ambulance outfit-ted with colored manservants and barrels of brandy. Supporters refuted such charges; Early took time to answer the committee in no uncertain terms as to their inaccuracy, and the full Senate never acted on commit-tee investigations. As Early declared vehemently in a footnote to his postwar memoir, "There was another false report, as to my personal habits during the Valley Campaign, which obtained some circulation and credence, but which I would not notice, except for the fact that it was referred to on the floor of the Confederate Senate by two members of that body." "The utter falsehood of this report," Early railed, "was well known to all my staff and General officers, as well as to all others who associated with me." Nonetheless, tongues wagged, and aspersions were made and doubt cast upon Early, his generalship, and general conduct—all attributable to demon rum. Truth joined the dust of history, but altogether, damage had been done. Could a coup d'grace await Early in the valley?[31]

Were Lee, Seddon, and Davis in error? Was this the moment that the Confederacy would have been better served by replacing Jubal Early? And who would the proper replacement have been—Breckinridge, John B. Gordon, or someone else, like Anderson? Would it have made any difference given the momentum of events? Would Sheridan and his superior numbers have prevailed, or would some Fabian-like tactic a la George Washington bought more time in the valley? Early himself sounded defeated and worn out, perhaps despondent, when writing Lee from Port Republic on September 25. He had promised his chief a "full account of recent events." Early admitted that "my troops are very much shattered, the men very much exhausted, and many of them without shoes." He deeply regretted the state of things but assured his chief that "everything in my power has been done to avert it," continuing, "The enemy's force is very much larger than mine, being three or four to one" in comparison. When Kershaw arrived, "I shall do the best I can, and hope I may be able to check the enemy." But Early cautioned, "I cannot but be apprehensive of the result."[32]

Meanwhile, Sheridan and his men proceeded with their assigned task of destructive war. The starkness of the figures could not have been known to either side, much less the civilian victims at the time. Some $3,304,672 in 1864 dollar value of barns, mills, livestock, and crops was Wesley Merritt's estimate. Put another way, 20,397 tons of hay, 435,802 bushels of wheat, 77,176 bushels of corn, 10,918 beef cattle, 2,000 sheep, and 15,000 hogs were estimated. A committee of valley residents calculated losses at 30 dwellings, 450 barns, 31 mills, and three factories burned. They added 100 miles of fencing, 100,000 bushels of wheat, 50,000 bushels of corn, and 6,233 tons of hay destroyed. They tallied thousands of livestock foraged by the Yankee vandals, with farm implements, from McCormick reapers to threshing machines, broken up.

They felt damage in Rockingham County alone totaled $25,500,000! To Sheridan, explaining it all to the Joint Congressional Committee on the Conduct of War, on the one hand, this was normal operational "living off the country" necessitating hardships "brought on the people," but no outrages were tolerated. On the other hand, said Sheridan, these civilians cared not for loss of life and property in battle "so long as war did not come to their doors." When it did, they "earnestly prayed for its termination." He linked matters by suggesting that, just as war was punishment and death maximization of that punishment, "by reducing its advocates to poverty, end[ing] it quickly, we are on the side of humanity." Sheridan only said what other Union generals and politicians advocated throughout the war period and elsewhere than Virginia. "Uncivilized war" would be Early's characterization of what he beheld in the valley. Such other terms as "total war," "scorched earth," or "hard war" have proven but semantic variants. Destruction of "everything of potential value to guerrillas, military units, and Southern sympathies" (using the words of recent student of economic warfare Andrew P. Smith) was perhaps a natural touch point on the historical spectrum from the Carthaginian peace of Republican Rome to the warfare practices of the twentieth and twenty-first centuries. It was beyond the ken of Jubal Early's Southern generation, Chambersburg notwithstanding.[33]

It was not as indiscriminate as local legend and postwar Lost Cause mythology proclaimed, suggests consummate Early-watcher Gary W. Gallagher. There was no killing all livestock or torching all structures. Nonetheless, they "did severely damage the Valley's logistical output," and while the harshness of it all resonated well with Northern Republicans, such wholesale mayhem had the opposite effect with Democratic counterparts whether the inhumanity of it all really cost Lincoln votes or not. Sheridan (himself anxious enough about his lengthy line of communications back to the Potomac) began the retrograde movement down the valley by directing Alfred Torbert and his cavalry to confiscate and burn everything of "military significance" in a 92 mile area from Staunton to Strasburg. Between October 6 and 8, "the Burning" became as infamous to Virginians as Sherman's march through Georgia. It was the same economic warfare, logistically directed but designed to change "hearts and minds." Early never caught the immensity or import, but it reinforced his determination to make the Yankees pay.[34]

The remnants of the Army of the Valley District grimly followed along, watching, waiting, and anticipating what would become the last major battle of the 1864 Washington and Shenandoah campaigns. But as for "The Burning," a perplexed Early merely wrote Lee on October 9, "[Sheridan] has laid waste nearly all of Rockingham and Shenandoah [counties], and I will have to rely on Augusta [County] for my supplies, and they are not abundant there." Sheridan's purpose, under Grant's orders, he closed, "has been to render the Valley untenable by our troops by destroying the supplies." He missed the point that Shenandoah civilian producers of those supplies as well as Lee's army depended upon Early's army to protect that subsistence. In that, Early and the army failed utterly. Or perhaps the myriad reports of scouts and what he himself could see in person traipsing north behind the perpetrators reinforced his flaming hatred of the enemy, stoked a spirit of revenge, and clouded his judgment of a victorious, merciless opponent and his overwhelming superiority.[35]

The downfall of Third Winchester and Fisher's Hill continued on October 9, when Merritt and Custer fell upon newly arrived Brigadier General Thomas L. Rosser's Laurel Brigade, sent by Lee from Petersburg, and Lomax's horsemen at Tom's Brook just south of Strasburg. It was a bad omen. Fitzhugh Lee had fallen wounded at Winchester, and Rosser was 26 miles out of supporting distance from Early's main army—both impediments to Confederate success. They lost 11 cannon and their baggage train. The resulting rout was called the "Woodstock Races" and effectively demoralized Early's mounted arm for the rest of the campaign, just when the army commander needed it. Old Jube was planning a mighty blow. Hearing about the Tom's Brook breakdown from Early, a none-too-patient Lee counseled on October 12 not to send his cavalry "too far from your main body, or allow them to hazard too much."[36]

In fact, Lee may well have miscalculated or presumed Union intentions. Longstreet and others, including Lee, talked of Sheridan surrendering strength that the Lincoln administration might counter Confederate Sterling Price's threat beyond the Mississippi. Of course, even Sheridan felt constrained to send the VI Corps back to Grant now that Early seemed defeated. Lee admitted that "it is impossible at this distance to give definite instructions" and that Early should proceed under the principle "of not retaining with you more troops than you can use to

advantage in any position the enemy may take and send the rest to me."
Chiding, and not always gently, the senior leader told his almost wor-
shipful subordinate, "I have weakened myself very much to strengthen
you," and that was done with the expectation of enabling Early to gain
success so that all or part of the reinforced Army of the Valley District
got to Petersburg. Lee then soothed Early by suggesting he retained his
confidence. He encouraged him to not be discouraged, as "I rely upon
your judgment and ability, and the hearty co-operation of your officers
and men" still to secure success, though "great circumspection must be
used in your operations." All of this came at the time that Governor
Smith and others cried out for Early's relief from command.[37]

One local scion of a Shenandoah family, convalescing after Third
Winchester, made the observation that Early and his army "had just
enough grit left in it" to make a bold attack on Sheridan, "which came
near being an overwhelming success." Staffer Randolph Barton referred to Early's "Hail Mary" throw of the dice at Cedar Creek, just
north of Strasburg near Middletown on the Valley Road back to Winchester. The date was October 19, a month to the day after the Winchester disaster. "If we can only thoroughly whip Sheridan, the effect
throughout the whole country, & on the election, will be most encouraging," noted Winchester Confederate Mary Greenhow Lee. She also
noted, "We know our army cannot stay here, as there is nothing for
them to eat." But "it would be such comfort to see them again before
the long dreary winter set in." For a time, Early tried to oblige his local
supporters. He pleased oppressed Shenandoah civilians when slamming
into Sheridan's somnolent encamped army and routing it on that foggy
October morn. His battle plan was impeccable, its initial execution
striking. Then it fell apart.[38]

Sheridan had gone to Washington for consultation. Wright had been
left in charge. Poor reconnaissance, overconfidence that the enemy was
finished, and flat weariness with traipsing up and down the valley now
proved costly to the Federals, too. Gordon and cartographer Jedidiah
Hotchkiss had climbed atop Signal Knob on nearby Massanutten
Mountain and had a bird's-eye view of Sheridan's slumbering encampment below. Early's arthritis prevented the arduous scout. Returning,
the pair gave the excited army commander information that led Early to
embrace a daring plan. Outnumbered three to one, he would mount a
daring assault—a three-column converging maneuver protected on the

flanks by cavalry and designed to rout the Yankees and redeem Winchester and the lower valley. The key lay with rolling up Sheridan's exposed left flank, exploiting that same flank to get cavalry onto the Federal's line of retreat north of Middletown, and trapping survivors. Early lacked the resources for a prolonged stand-up fight. He continued to underestimate Sheridan's now-superior mounted force. It would be all about surprise—surprise for Early's 21,000 soldiery against the 38,000 unsuspecting Federals.[39]

Events went as planned for the Confederates on a foggy, damp Shenandoah morning. Crook's VIII Corps and Emory's XIX Corps collapsed; Wright's VI Corps provided the sole ray of hope. By noon, Early's men had the enemy's camps (along with army headquarters at the Belle Grove mansion); Sheridan's artillery and wagon train and much of Sheridan's infantry could be seen skedaddling northward on the valley pike. At some particular moment occurred one of those fatal pauses so typical of Early's style and conduct of a battle. After 150 years, the details still remain unclear.

Historian Keith Bohannon comes closest to explaining what went wrong for Confederate and Early's fortunes, turning upon either the "fatal halt" versus "bad conduct" of the tactical battle of Cedar Creek. One of those confrontations between Early and Gordon at the crucial moment, not the actions of the enemy, determined the course of events. What seems apparent is that some portion of Early's victory-flushed but overburdened, famished, poorly clothed, and disorganized soldiery at some point that morning turned away from finishing off Yankee resistance and fell to plundering Sheridan's camps. Early later claimed that it became apparent "that it would not do to press my troops further." They "had been up all night" moving to the attack and "were very much jaded." He continued, "In pressing over rough ground to attack the enemy in the early morning, their own ranks had been much disordered and it had required time to reform them." He alluded to the thinning of the ranks by the plundering. Moreover, in victory could be found the confusion, intermixing of commands, imprecision of a battlefield enshrouded in smoke and fog, and perhaps an army commander transiting from elation that he had at last bested a lesser mortal, Sheridan, to an irresolute one fearing that it was his legions now absenting themselves from battlefield duty for the lure of camp plunder. Yet this excuse hid something else that day.[40]

At first, Early had been elated, and a staffer heard him muttering something about the "sun of Middletown, the sun of Middletown," alluding to Napoleon's famous victory at Austerlitz. Then, at some point, Early met Gordon, who urged completing the rout if there was to be any Austerlitz. To Early, however, it was finished, noted Gordon years later. "This is glory enough for one day," this was the nineteenth of the month and precisely one month before "we were going in the opposite direction." Yet the Georgian held no sense that the battle had ended, the Federals conclusively routed. Gordon advanced, "One more blow to strike, and then there will not be left an organized company of infantry in Sheridan's army." There was still Wright's now-rallying VI Corps. An unimpressed, possibly disbelieving Early merely grunted, "No use in that," as "they will go directly." Pointing out just who faced them and that the VI Corps "will not go unless we drive it from the field," Gordon cautioned as memories of his previous unfruitful consultations with Early on other battlefields welled up. "Yes, it will go, directly," opined Early. Perhaps at midmorning it seemed so.[41]

Frankly, Confederate victory, cohesion on the battlefield, and Early's control of the situation all disintegrated as the day advanced. Sheridan rode from Winchester 20 miles away (captured in Buchanan Read's famous poem). By his fiery zeal and appearance, he gathered his defeated army on the buttress of VI Corps' resolution and seized the initiative. The uninspiring but dependable Horatio Wright made that possible. By contrast, Early, in Freeman's words, "thought the wreck of his Divisions by absentees began to sap [his] soldierly vigor." His "state of mind changed subtly," observed Freeman, "and progressively from one of concern." Object of that concern became the thing that had beaten him at Winchester and Fisher's Hill—Federal cavalry massed on the flanks (unprotected by the feeble Confederate horsemen that remained) and sent in with consummate precision by Sheridan in the late afternoon. The thinned ranks of Gordon, Kershaw, Ramseur, and others broke under Sheridan's combined arms pressure and evaporated southward, losing booty, captured artillery, supplies, and all semblance of an organized force. "They would not listen to entreaties, threats or appeals of any kind," bemoaned Early later, "a terror of the enemy's cavalry had seized them, and there was no holding them." "My men ran without sufficient cause," he told Lee from New Market two days later. After the war, Early asserted blatantly, "could 500 men have been rallied, at either [Cedar Creek or Hupp's Hill to the immediate south] who would have stood by me, I am satisfied that all my artillery and wagons and the greater part of the captured artillery could have been saved, as the enemy's pursuit was very feeble." Delusional on Early's part, perhaps, or not, his Army of the Valley District simply had had enough of this part of the war.[42]

Estimated losses in this climactic battle in the Shenandoah Valley amounted to 5,672 Federals and 2,910 Confederates. Sheridan claimed Early lost more than 23 artillery pieces and 1,600 prisoners as well as relinquishing those captured from him. Lincoln told a victory crowd at the White House on October 21, "We may as well consider how fortunate it was for the Secesh that Sheridan was a very little man [in height]. If he had been a large man, there is no knowing what he would have done with them." And the next day, the president effusively wrote Little Phil, "With great pleasure I tender to you and your brave army, the thanks of the Nation, and my own personal admiration and gratitude, for the month's operations in the Shenandoah Valley; and especially for the splendid work of October 19." This event surely solidified the election and began the death knell of the rebellion. Lincoln's nemesis had been erased.[43]

No doubt, the detachment of Lomax's cavalry to guard prisoners and ensure safekeeping of captured equipment for transit south, thus denying a reconnaissance element for the army commander, Early's fatal delay before wavering Federal lines north of Middletown and (Freeman's words) a "certain relaxation of grip after the action was joined" may be seen as keys to the disaster. Discounting Sheridan's performance, modern analysis flows toward what Thomas Lewis concludes as but one commander holding the secret. That commander was not the fighter John B. Gordon who had engineered the victory but rather the army commander. Perhaps it was his arthritis acting up in the dews and damps, perhaps his petulant irascibility faced with Gordon's rising fortunes, or possibly a sudden flush of overconfidence itself that accompanied Jubal Early's performance at Cedar Creek. Perhaps fatigue and depression overtook even his personal, leisurely ride to take charge after Gordon and others had effected initial success. Whether or not Gordon's "clear vision of the battlefield" (Lewis's words) was replaced by Early's "limited, badly flawed one" and Gordon's "implacable drive" supplanted by Early's "certain temerity," no doubt the crucial moment of Cedar Creek found Early wanting as it had at Gettysburg, the Wilderness, Fort Stevens, and even Third Winchester. To hospital steward and now assistant surgeon William J. Jones of the Fifty-First Virginia in Wharton's division, Gordon was the hero of the morning; Early was the villain of the afternoon. Or perhaps there was always a flaw in Jubal Early—like so many, better at divisional command and below than corps and above.[44]

On the other hand, there may have been more truth in Early's view at the time than accorded by historians. "The state of things was distressing and mortifying beyond measure," Early told Lee in his October 21 official report. He continued:

> We had within our grasp a glorious victory, and lost it by the uncontrollable propensity of our men for plunder, in the first place, and the subsequent panic among those who had kept their places, which was without sufficient cause, for I believe that the enemy had only made the movement against us as a demonstration, hoping to protect his stores, &c., at Winchester, and that the rout of our troops was a surprise to him.

Here was Early's bane, going back to the beginning of the war in northern Virginia—breakdown in discipline and plundering as a result. Early told Lee he had tried his best to instruct subordinate officers against this danger, to no avail because "almost all our good officers of that kind had been killed, wounded, or captured." It was "mortifying to me, general, to have to make these explanations of my reverses," pleading no lack of effort or faithful labor and certainly sparing no effort "to expose my person and set an example to my men." Knowing "that I shall have to endure censure from those who do not understand my position and difficulties," and still willing "to make renewed efforts," Early recognized the inevitable. If Lee thought "that the interests of the service would be promoted by a change of commanders, I beg you will have no hesitation in making the change," he entreated. The interests of the service outweighed "any mere personal considerations," Early continued, and if required, he was willing "to surrender my command into other hands."[45]

Of the late battle, however, the disgusted comment appearing in Jedediah Hotckiss's journal entry for that fateful Wednesday was more revealing. Lee and Early never read it at the time or later, perhaps, or

Hotchkiss never shared it with them: "This was one of the most brilliant victories of the war turned into one of the most disgraceful defeats, and all owing to the delay in pressing the enemy after we got to Middle-town; as General Early said, 'The Yankees got whipped and we got scared.'" Shades of Henry Kyd Douglas's comment upon leaving "Silver Spring" outside Washington three months before? Apparently both he and Hotchkiss harbored the same thought. Early had a knack for equiv-ocating and losing a victory. Moreover, Lomax trying but failing to do anything significant for Early at Cedar Creek conjured detachment of Bradley Johnson on the Baltimore–Point Lookout raid in that same July. The presence of good cavalry—however dismissive Early was of such—could have been of great use. There were those gnawing words in his report about the reverses—"they are due to no want of effort on my part, though it may be that I have not the capacity or judgment to prevent them. I have labored faithfully to gain success, and I have not failed to expose my person and to set an example to my men." Such sentiments stood juxtaposed with accomplishment. Early was not far off when he told Lee, "I think it is not entirely without compensating benefits." The Union's VI Corps had been prevented from returning to Grant, and (perhaps fallaciously) "Sheridan's forces are now so scat-tered that he will not be able to send Grant any efficient aid for some time," as "he will be afraid to trust the Eighth and Nineteenth Corps." Historian of the XIX Corps Richard B. Irwin commented just two years before Early's death,

> Early may be said to have accomplished the ultimate object of his attack at Cedar Creek, yet at fearful cost, for although all thought of transferring any part of Sheridan's force to the James was for the moment given up, on the other hand Early had completed the de-struction of his prestige, had suffered an irreparable diminution of numbers, and had seen his army almost shaken to pieces.

There would always be various ways of viewing Jubal Early and his performance.[46]

Still, Lee did not replace him. He did withdraw most of the valley army once post–Cedar Creek sparring with Sheridan ceased and tasked Early merely to keep an eye on Union movements as the active cam-paigning season shut down. Early dutifully pursued that requirement, reorganized fragments of commands left to him, and drew what few reinforcements he could gain from Breckinridge in southwest Virginia. Sheridan withdrew closer to his base of supplies, and Early's 2,000 odd remnants went into winter quarters between Rockfish Gap and Staunton. The valley war, the threat to the upper Potomac, and any thought of taking Washington was over. Partisans, guerrillas, and brigands began to surface in its stead. Like elsewhere across the embattled South, they had been there all along but in less prominence. This was not Early's kind of war. Nor was the firestorm of controversy unleashed by certain elements in the lower valley about recent disasters befalling the Army of the Valley District. The virus of discontent likewise echoing across the Confederacy could be found, too, in the wake of the Shenandoah defeat.

Murmurs from the ranks of Early's defeated force surfaced soon after Cedar Creek. Assistant surgeon William Jones of the Fifty-First Virginia wrote a Dr. B. P. Morriss of Amherst Court House, Virginia, on October 28 of his dissatisfaction with the general and "until a change in commanders is made" not to expect much from the valley. Men "may be ever so brave," but they would not fight unless they had good leadership. Early is "no doubt a brave man and a good Commander but present operations in the valley" proved him incapable of leading the army. Early "nominally commands the army," observed Jones, "but personal observations" justified the contention "that John Barleycorn occupies a conspicuous portion on Jubal's staff." "There will never be anything but defeat and disaster" until Early was divested of command, was one Augusta County malcontent's comment to President Davis as he impugned Early's leadership qualities for commanding rank and file and asserted "too free use of ardent spirits both by officers high and low" was the root cause of the army's difficulties. Early took umbrage, defending his performance to the Senate Military Committee in Richmond. Biographer Charles Osborne explores the controversy and exonerates Early, but the damage was done at the time. People of the lower valley and probably much of his diminished command thought the general no longer capable of inspiring sacrifice and dedication. On the other hand, there were those, like ex-governor John Letcher (whose Lexington residence had fallen prey to Hunter's hellions), who from Richmond contended the valley force was better than ever and who thought "General Early a good officer" and still capable of putting "his revilers to shame."[47]

Early's personal pillorying of his shrunken command on October 22 did not help. Professor Gallagher, in turn, criticizes "Early's lack of judgment when it came to building morale," as shown in this address, which directly questioned his soldiers' courage and steadfastness at Cedar Creek. A victory that "would have been one of the most brilliant and decisive of the war" had instead slipped away because "many of you, including some commissioned officers, yielded to a disgraceful propensity for plunder, & deserted your colours to appropriate to yourselves the abandoned property of the enemy." Of course, as shown in his battle report of the day before, herein lay the root cause for his defeat, so Early's rant to the troops is explicable, if a striking example of intemperately poor leadership. The immediate result, said one of those pilloried, was that Early had made sweeping accusations "thus endeavoring to shift responsibility, which rightly rests upon him alone." Coming so soon on the heels of bitter defeat after all the lofty expectations spawned among the rank and file since June and July, even August, victories, those closest to the scene may well have been correct. A time for change at the top, reorganization below, and rejuvenation of freshening, more inspiring leadership throughout beckoned the valley army. Yet Early stayed around for the next four and a half months.[48]

Professor Aaron Sheehan-Dean's examination of Virginia soldiers in the Shenandoah campaign suggests that at least some of Early's men rallied, did not blame their commander, and dutifully soldiered on after the trio of defeats. However, one suspects it was not out of any sense of loyalty to Early by either soldier or civilian in the valley that dictated feelings and actions. Rather a complex allegiance to defending home against vile Yankees, lingering flickers of Confederate identity, and the grim determination born of fatalism—for fighting and dying would continue even in the valley—drove remnants of resistance in the wake of Early-induced disasters. Sheehan-Dean suggests the remainder of the fall and the onset of winter may have had less to do with Early in the valley, but "rather, the military losses in late fall and the barn and mill burning campaign led by Sheridan fired the hatred of Confederates for Federals to a higher temperature, producing a sullen sheen of bitterness and mistrust that lasted well into the postwar years." Such explanation tells us as much about a defeated, dejected, and embittered lieutenant general who had contributed his fair share to those very conditions and why Jubal Anderson Early would be as he was in the postwar years. The cause for much of the defeat and suffering could conveniently transfer blame to an enemy that perpetrated crimes against humanity. Early could conveniently cloak his personal failures and bitterness in the mantle of deeds of a "vile mercenary army, burning our towns, destroying our crops, desolating our country and killing our people" (the words of one Virginia artillerist who served with him) in the Shenandoah nadir.[49]

Early's consultations with Lee about his shrunken command and the "difficulties of my position in the Valley" after Cedar Creek confirmed that his chief had left him there "to produce the impression that the force was much larger than it really was" and to do the best he could with meager resources. Of course, this was merely a continuation of what Lee had intended all along. A besieged Lee could offer little else, and basically, he never could after the Washington raid. Early's illuminating letter to Lee on the last day of January 1865 told much about his perceived continuing role and mission. He offered the observation "beyond all doubt" that a considerable portion of Union general George H. Thomas's Army of the Cumberland had gone from middle Tennessee to reinforce Grant and William T. Sherman, by this point marching through the Carolinas after destroying John B. Hood's Army of Tennessee before Nashville the previous month. Thomas was a disloyal Virginian, Early felt, and as with Sheridan accorded him short shrift. More enlightening, however, Early asked Lee to get the secretary of war "to revoke the exemption granted [John] McNeill's company from the act abolishing partisan rangers." Early wanted McNeill and others like him to "cut the [Baltimore and Ohio] railroad to impede the passage of troops over it," and this had been thwarted by the refusal of these companies to acknowledge [Harry Gilmor's] authority. Here was Early's typical dislike for the irregular soldier, Early's typical aversion to undisciplined, independent cavalry, but he was not alone. All over the shrinking Confederacy, commanders like him—Nathan Bedford Forrest, for example—wanted these freebooters tucked back under regular authority and command. Early's words only echoed general sentiments: "The fact is that all those independent organizations, not excepting [John] Mosby's, are injurious to us, and the occasional dashes they make do not compensate for the disorganization and dissatisfaction produced among the other troops." Frankly, it had been that way from the onset of the Partisan Ranger Act of 1862. Lee sent Early's request on to the War Department.[50]

Departure of John Breckinridge to become the Confederacy's last secretary of war on February 20, 1865, opened Early's final chance for meaningful service when Lee gave him command of a department of southwestern Virginia and eastern Tennessee as well as the Valley District. It was an empty portfolio, and everyone should have recognized it—the Confederacy was clearly in its death throes. When the eastern war concluded at Appomattox in April, Jubal Early would not be there. His meaningful contribution to the Confederacy had come to an abrupt end a month before on March 2, 1865, at Waynesboro when Sheridan led 10,000 cavalry to obliterate Early's remaining screening force in the valley. In fact, Waynesboro was merely a small impediment en route to wrecking the Virginia Central Railroad and James River and Kanawha Canal before reaching Grant to lead the spring offensive. Early explained to Lee that he "did not intend making my final stand on this ground," yet if his forlorn hope would stand in fight, he could hold until dark, Early offered. He would then cross the South River and take a blocking position in Rockfish Gap, "for I had done more difficult things than that during the war." Both Early and his men could not hold, Early fleeing over the mountains, with a corporal's guard eventually reporting at Lee's headquarters in mid-March. Later, Early claimed his Waynesboro action "diverted Sheridan from Lynchburg, which he could have captured without difficulty, had he followed Hunter's route and not jumped at the bait unwillingly offered him by the capture of my force at the former place." Somehow, Early's continuous carping at an inferior foe and misperception of real strategic intent dogged him to the end. Lee thought he might still return Early for service in the Shenandoah. Gordon had already supplanted him in charge of the Second Corps and taken the remnants back to the main army at Petersburg. With memories of defeat and devastation, aspersions to Early professionally and privately continued to surround his reputation, and a public howl rose against any such return. The end of March found Early trying to assist with reorganization in southwestern Virginia. A telegram (and subsequent fuller letter, both dated March 30) from Lee then terminated "my military career," he noted in his memoirs.[51]

The ever-courtly and fatherly leader of the Army of Northern Virginia patiently explained the situation to his loyal subordinate. Resource allocation now was a priority, and "it is essential that we should have the cheerful and hearty support of the people, and the full confidence of the soldiers without which our efforts would be embarrassed and our means of resistance weakened." Lee had concluded reluctantly that Early "could not command the united and willing co-operation which is so essential to success." His "reverses in the Valley, of which the public and the army judge chiefly by the results," had impaired Early's influence with both sectors and "would add greatly to difficulties" attending military operations in southwest Virginia. Lee retained confidence in Early's "ability, zeal, and devotion to the cause," he said, and thanked him "for the fidelity and energy with which you have always supported my efforts, and for the courage and devotion you have ever manifested in the services of the country." In the words of Douglas Southall Freeman, "To this fate had fallen 'Old Jube' of Manassas and of Williamsburg, of Cedar Mountain and of Sharpsburg, of Salem Church and of Monocacy." Remembered would be the Jubal Early, if not of Fort Stevens and Second Kernstown, then Gettysburg, the Wilderness, and most assuredly Third Winchester, Fisher's Hill, Cedar Creek, and Waynesboro. Early, Stonewall's anointed successor, was now blamed for occassioning "the burning" in some southern circles. As Gary Gallagher quotes George Mooney of the Fifth Virginia, "Oh what a difference between Jackson's Army & the *fire* he put into us & the *will* to fight & how it all *dried up* under Early!" Just the opposite would have attended passage down the Shenandoah Valley en route to Washington in the summer.[52]

Lost in public vituperation (and this was natural for a people in defeat) was the Jubal Early who had helped Lee's defense of Richmond by tying down sizable Federal forces to defend Washington—"the equivalent of a Federal Corps, or, roughly, as many Federals as he had infantry in any single engagement of the campaign," proclaims Freeman. Early and his Army of the Valley District gained Lee at least six months reprieve, if not quite ensuring the Shenandoah harvest so needed by soldiery and people of the eastern Confederacy. As Gallagher adds, while Early's campaign "represented a sound trade-off for the Confederacy that, over a period of four months, met Lee's logistical goals and created a sizeable second front, his efforts ultimately took on the aspect of an unmitigated disaster." In the end, Early's very success proved his undoing. Outnumbered and outgeneraled in independent command, his collapse in a mere 30 days between September 19 and October 19 ensured a Northern Union party victory and reelection of Lincoln, wrecked the Shenandoah granary and its human resources, and helped destroy Lee's army as a fighting force. Such unintended consequences were not in Early's plans, obviously, nor was the prosecution of the war to its bitter end on Lincoln's and Grant's terms of destructive war. The tragedy of the Confederacy was the tragedy of Jubal Early and vice versa.[53]

Lee's dismissal came at a low point for Jubal Early. Battling pneumonia at the time, Early retired to his Rocky Mount home. Springtime found him unbowed and still determined, if cognizant of his fate:

> I was not embraced in the terms of General Lee's surrender [Appomattox] or that of General [Joseph E.] Johnston [at Durham Station], and as the order relieving me from command had also relieved me from all embarrassment as to the troops which had been under me [included in surrender terms], as soon as I was in condition to travel, I started on horseback for the Trans-Mississippi Department to join the army of General [Edward] Kirby Smith, should it hold out.

Early had the "hope of at least meeting an honorable death while fighting under the flag of my country." Smith surrendered before Early reached him. But "without giving a parole, after a long, weary and dangerous ride from Virginia to Texas, I finally succeeded in leaving the country." A new chapter beckoned for this unrepentant Rebel. At first it would prove just as ominous as the last.[54]

6

UNREPENTANT APOSTLE OF THE LOST CAUSE

Notwithstanding historian Emory Thomas's observation that Jubal Early (like others) was an example of a "man 'made' by war," one could argue that it was the postwar period that vaulted the backwater lawyer to even greater fame. Like Stonewall Jackson, Nathan Bedford Forrest, John C. Pemberton, and Josiah Gorgas as "living examples of the military aristocracy of merit" spawned in the war, Thomas admits only Early, within three years of leaving his status of "struggling lawyer in a back-water region of Virginia," led an "independent command to the very gates of Washington." Yet within six to nine months thereafter, rocketlike, a humbled, even humiliated, Lieutenant General Early had been sent packing by a superior enemy and a commanding officer acutely sensitive to public pressure during the dying days of their experiment in rebellion. It would remain to be seen how either Lee or Early recovered in the aftershocks of that experiment. Thomas's fellow historian Gary Gallagher observes that Early at least "emerged from the war an ardent Confederate nationalist without a country."[1]

To the victor go the spoils. A defeated and embittered Jubal Early did not want to stay around for that after Appomattox. "I cannot live under the same Government with the Yankee," he told P. G. T. Beauregard in the fall of 1865. He would go voluntarily into exile "rather than submit to the rule of our enemies." "Bitter sorrow" attended seeing "our Country prostrate at the feet of our detested foes," he continued. If the opportunity ever arose again "for giving that glorious old battle flag to the breeze," he flared, "I shall hasten to range myself under its folds." Two years later, he would still wail about "infernal demons in Washington" promulgating unrestrained power and sorrow upon the South, vowing that, if the fight were ever rejoined, he thought he could "scalp a Yankee woman and child without winking my eyes." Perhaps, as Gallagher asserts, Early more generally feared prosecution for the burning of Chambersburg. Nonetheless, the fiery, still-combative fighter laid down the purpose of his remaining years. Early's fight, however, waged under the old Rebel flag, would now be with attitude and words, not arms. For the next 30 years, he tried exile and redemption but never reclusion! He had moved from a prewar provisional constitutional Unionist to Southern nationalist combatant and now to a postwar unrepentant racist yearning for the might-have-been and dedicated to turning back the clock while redeeming a memory of how the war could have turned out otherwise. Never reconciled to fate, Jubal Early became an exponent, even a founding father, of the Lost Cause movement explaining the Civil War. He fairly personified the later caricature of an unreconciled Rebel breathing, "Forget, Hell!" He would become the epitome of a Confederate in the attic![2]

Early had found no Confederate cause to cling to when he reached Texas immediately after the war. So with like minds, he rode on into Mexico and made his way to Havana, Cuba, and eventually to Canada. There, in Toronto, he began his quest for exoneration, penning his memoir of the final year of the war—making a case that he had performed capably against enormous odds, mainly numerical—especially against Sheridan's legions. This theme would become a staple not only from Early but also of Lost Cause gospel, gleaned from Lee's own final statement to his troops at the end about succumbing to "overwhelming resources and numbers." Lee after Appomattox sought out numerous correspondents among his old subordinates verifying his impression so as to demonstrate to the world the "odds against which we fought." No doubt true, the argument (still advanced today) hid significant blemishes that Jubal Early never admitted. Of course, his own personal mission would remain for eternity—"to transmit, if possible, the truth to posterity, and do justice to our brave Soldiers." He wore gray suits the rest of his life and sported civilian accessories that reflected Confederana. Former antagonist George Crook recorded, upon encountering him in 1890, that Early was enfeebled and stooped "but as bitter and violent as an adder."[3]

The road assigned to a postwar Jubal Early was exceedingly rocky at first. Despite various benefactors easing his passage through Texas to Mexico, he had to get there by ship through the Caribbean, hoping that the French puppet government of Archduke Ferdinand Maximilian would provoke a war with the United States, to which Early might contribute his skills. In this, Early was disappointed. Tensions between France and the United States over Mexico had now abated. He used the three months below the border penning a remembrance of the Shenandoah Valley campaign and the last year of the war but could not find a publisher. So Early left Mexico unrequited. Lack of resources plagued his travels at every turn, although he drew upon family and friends for survival. Meanwhile, the whole period in exile provided time for collecting research materials and commencing unflagging correspondence with others preparatory to publishing what he considered the correct version of war history. His 130-page campaign history, *A Memoir of the Last Year of the War for Independence, in the Confederate States of America*, finally surfaced in pamphlet form in 1866. Printed for $211 from his sparse funds by Lovell and Gibson in Toronto (and reprinted a year later), Early dedicated the piece to the memory of the "Heroic Dead, who fell fighting for Liberty, Right and Justice." Indeed, here was the "first book-length reminiscence by a major military figure of either side of the Civil War," says Gallagher. Like its author, it showed little willingness to forgive much less to forget. In fact, it contained the foundations for the Lost Cause school of Southern apologists who largely shaped even national thinking on the Civil War for the next century. The South, claimed Early, had fought not to preserve slavery but rather the legality and constitutionality of secession. And Early also introduced both the blame game and the numbers game to postwar thinking. Northern elements caused war, and only supremacy of overwhelming Northern resources defeated the valorous South with its superior principles, leaders, fighting men, and, of course, its heroic women. A victimized South bore the cross of destruction and postwar humiliation. These themes became a staple of Jubal Early's interpretation of what went awry between 1861 and 1865.[4]

Apparently Early also embarked upon an apologia for slavery and the American South during his Canadian period. Set down between

1865 and 1870, it would not be published "till passion having cooled and prejudice abated" and then only by a niece two decades after Early's death. Yet passages from the unpublished version would creep into speeches and pronouncements of his elder years. Its title, *Heritage of the South,* could only be truly appreciated from its subtitle that purported to be a history of the introduction of slavery, its establishment in colonial times, and effect upon American politics—subjects upon which Early was no authority but definitely had feelings. If "many white southerners muffled their opinions about the 'positive good' of slavery after the war," says Gallagher, Early was not one of them. His work set slavery in an evolution from ancient to modern worlds. It was an economic necessity to the Founding Republic's economic and social identity, he advanced. Early veered off into "religious cant," racial profiling, and mainly the political correctness of caste and class as essential to maintaining an ordered society in the South and perpetuation of the power of a white Southern minority. This was from an Early who never invested in slaves although always possessing a "negro servant," according to the niece who eventually took the tract to print. If Jubal Early was little different from many Americans of his time, his subsequent influence in the making of a Southern mindset suggests much for his mark on history.[5]

Early followed events back home from afar. He could look across the Canadian border at the American fort "at which the cursed old flag, which always reminds me of a barber's pole, untwisted and ironed out, is always flying." Tough words for a man who had once served and fought under, while swearing allegiance to, that symbol. He saw Reconstruction as a political and social abomination. Scathing in denunciation of Lincoln, successor Andrew Johnson was a "miserable, cowardly renegade" and traitor to his Southern origins, Early seethed. Ulysses S. Grant, the next president, was a "man of too little sense and too little character to be anything else than a mere tool in the hands of others." When the national government sought the letter Robert E. Lee had sent relieving Early, the victim of said action told requesting authorities "that the original letter is in my possession, beyond the reach of provost marshals and agents of the Freedmen's Bureau, or even [judge advocate general Henry] Holt with his Bureau of Military Justice and suborners of perjury." He informed former subordinate brigadier Thomas Rosser by letter from Canada on May 10, 1866, that his hatred of the "infernal Yankees" was only increasing and that he would not speak to any if he met them. "War to the death," was his mantra.[6]

At this time in life, Jubal Early still hoped to "have another chance at them," vowing to be in if war ever broke out between the United States and any other country. Woe to any Confederates on the national side, as he suggested that former colleagues might take up arms against, rather than submit to, the "cowardly fiends who rule in Washington." Only age and ill health prevented him from leading western Indians—"20,000 or 30,000 Commanches and Apaches"—eastward across the Plains states and the Mississippi so that they might leave a trail behind them "that would not be erased in this century." Hatred at a distance blinded Early to reality. Even his memoir fell flat to Southerners suffering the degradation of postwar Reconstruction and in stark contrast with Robert L. Dabney's almost simultaneous appearance of a more uplifting paean to Stonewall Jackson's valley success two years before Early's defeats.[7]

It was fellow Confederate leader Fitzhugh Lee who once observed that, when Jubal Early had drawn his sword for war, he discarded the scabbard "and was never afterward able to find it." Indeed, Early pecked away at preparing memoir reflections—always in pursuit of the truth by his own definition. He communicated with friends and relatives about the state of things, fuming about a new wave in Virginia politics, and President Johnson's terms for embracing top Confederate leaders back into the fold of the Union. Fellow expatriate John Breckinridge also sojourned north of the border, so Early had a soul mate. Together they watched Robert E. Lee try to pave the way for reconciliation but never felt constrained to precisely follow his example. New animosities began to surface, some directly from personality, some by the political economics of a new South based on railroads, commerce, and industry. A falling out with distant common-law wife Julia McCreary in Rocky Mount after years of separation (which typically for Early appeared to result from her violation of his honor and trust), the unceasing financial cares "for a pensioner on the bounty of those whose means are limited" (relatives and friends), a lack of means for earning his own way in a foreign country, and even some primeval urge to return home all apparently conditioned Early's exile by the spring of 1869. Conditions had eased for his return, as Johnson's pardoning had rendered moot an already-dormant indictment of Early, Breckinridge, and others for treason. Thus, lessening of fears about prosecution for war crimes like Chambersburg played a role.

Frankly, Early was aging. Canada was too cold and damp for his health, while irritation about Virginia politics over wartime debt and public education gnawed at him. Reconstruction, better styled national unification, spawned problems for friends and kinsmen and beckoned for a solution. The slipping away of antebellum and wartime memories of honor, former ways, and institutions as well as the changing demographics of politics and race festered through the correspondence between Early and others. Early was restive, afraid that time and events were passing him by, and that no fruitful existence might attend further life outside Virginia. At some point, he even thought it would have been preferable to have been killed on the battlefield and spared the indignities of his postwar existence. An arthritic human wistfully desiring home surroundings closer to those he venerated, like Lee, the stirring of need for exoneration of his own performance in the final death throes of the Confederacy—whatever welled up in Jubal Early's heart and mind, he returned to the Old Dominion by early summer 1869. Never accepting pardon, his new base of operations would be Lynchburg, where he turned once more to a modest law practice; a sparse bachelor lifestyle; and an old-boy coterie for swapping stories, hard liquor, and tobacco chewing, as well as befriending a cranky Jubal! One Richmond newspaper enthused how Early commanded "our admiration for his undying pluck" and was a "Confederate and Virginian to the backbone." The general had "hung out after nearly everybody else had succumbed." Jubal Early was still a fighter, no denying it. [8]

The twilight of Early's life would encompass tilting at new windmills and enemies largely through refighting the Civil War and reinterpreting, if not rewriting, history. His remaining years would not be flattering to the old veteran who once stood at Robert E. Lee's right hand, a chosen instrument for securing victory. Just as then, Early would never reflect an old soldier, defeated and fading away. He personally feuded not only with any Yankee purporting to tell the story other than as Early remembered. He also took on old mates—D. H. Hill, James Longstreet, John Mosby, James L. Kemper, John B. Gordon, and, most of all, William "Extra Billy" Mahone. Virginia-centric, Early tried to corner all attention to the Confederate cause, eastern war theater, and heroes from the Old Dominion. Yet Early the individual would never accommodate the new era and at one and the same time would reflect key features of the Reconstruction—the Gilded Age South transitioning to a New South of Populist-Progressive–era Jim Crow. The defeated South necessarily faced both forward and back. Unpurged of its heritage like victorious powers systematically accomplished in occupied Germany, Japan, and Austria after the Second World War, the American South after the Civil War was buffeted by new demographics and economic, social, and political revolution yet clung to old ways, customs, thoughts, and actions. This postwar image seemed incarnate in a Jubal Early battling for tradition and honor, a certain recidivism trying to refight old battles against the unstoppable march of time. It was he who reflected Mississippi novelist William Faulkner in his revealing comment about how, for every generation of fourteen-year-old Southern boys, it would always not yet be three o'clock on the third afternoon at Gettysburg. Pickett's charge could always be stopped before it started. It did not happen, nor would it ever. Certainly this was the way Jubal Early saw it, fighting old battles to counter, even perhaps roll back, the relentless ocean waves of the new.[9]

Early—the antebellum soldier turned country lawyer and then separatist general—now found new fields to conquer. He attached his name to money-making schemes, such as the Louisiana lottery (partnering with his old commander from 1861 P. G. T. Beauregard), that may or may not have helped the people of the South recover from privation. Traveling back and forth from Lynchburg to New Orleans by train relentlessly from 1877 to 1893 certainly provided wherewithal—$5,000–$10,000 progressively over the years, plus $250 monthly expenses. There never seemed to be a question of moral values—gambling, possibly graft and corruption, attending the effort in Early's mind. The lottery was controversial, especially in Southern religious circles. But cloaked in the righteous mantel of a recovering Southern people and the all-too-explicable human search for easy wealth, exoneration by the presence of respected leaders like Beauregard and Early overcame opponents. The aging warriors must have cut a striking pose before two ticket drums—Early in Confederate gray suit, Beauregard garbed in black. In the end, all that was a mere backdrop to a new mission, a new life eulogizing the old and involving region and cause. Early would find a place in history not from politics, economic gain, or pietistic acquiescence to change. No, his new life witnessed almost total immersion in a crusade based on the old, his military period as a senior Confederate general. It would reflect him at his best (and worst)— combining the tenacious, combative soldier with the legal drapery of impeccable attention to detail, firm advocacy, and pursuit of fact and truth, naturally as he saw such. Through moral and philosophical certainty and combat with new foes (and former comrades like Mahone and Longstreet) over events long past but transgressions more recent, Jubal Early "generally displayed himself at his most contentious, self-serving, vindictive, and defective," offers his biographer Charles Osborne. But he added quickly that Early was "not to be deflected, silenced or overcome." As another historian, Gaines Foster, observes, Early evidenced the "prototypical unreconstructed Rebel."[10]

Like so many veterans on both sides, Early became defender of what he knew best, set in new raiment. Militant defender of the South's Lost Cause in juxtaposition to the Victorious Cause of the Union, he now became its patron of history and paragon of virtue, not blemish. By focusing principally upon the South's experiment with self-determination; force of arms; and throw of the political, economic, and social dice for independence, Early reflected true believer but also self-promotional, diehard conservative/traditionalist. In more vernacular terms, Early reflected bias toward virtually everything and all who did not fit his paradigm. His speeches and correspondence reflect a crabbed man and spirit, crippled as much by perspective as ailment. A zealot, he became a rallying point for portraying the Southern side of the war (racist and rebellious as it truly was to all but the most unrepentant Southerners), for rebuilding pride and hope in a defeated people to face the challenges of a New World dominated by Northern Republican radicals, commercial and industrializing wealth, emancipated hordes (not merely given freedom but also citizenship), and a history written by victors with their own bias. Early was not alone in this—others, such as Tennessean S. A. Cunningham, banded in pursuit of explaining the Lost Cause. Yet others may not have seemed quite so rabid. Educators, propagandists, keepers of the true word, passionate exponents of a civil religion with saints (and cleansed of sinners), this band of brothers who experienced the fiery ordeal sought an only temporarily interrupted stream of Southern history, based on honor, country, religion, and demographics. Thus they rationalized their existence as survivors.[11]

Early's brand of the New Faith centered upon the sacred soil of Virginia. Although hardly from the First Families of Virginia (FFV) class, to Early, his state reflected the South's honor; tradition; leadership; intolerance of apostasy; belief in only one God whose only begotten Son, the new Christ, was immortalized by Robert E. Lee (perhaps in the legacy of George Washington and the state's founding fathers). Ironically, this creed would become almost mystical in the hands of a religious agnostic like Jubal Early. Nonetheless, led by one of Lee's inner circle, Early, with the help of many others, spread its appeal across the American South (and, avowedly, to many in the North), seeking to forget what actually caused the catastrophe that had prostrated the land by their own hand; cost over a half-million lives and countless resources, real and monetary, to the country in general; and perhaps sacrificed a generation of young manhood alone to the South. This was a peculiar atonement, but it did offer surcease, succor, and rejuvenation. In a way, the explanation for every former Confederate of that era lay in the trinity of his own individual life. Rather than a continuum of Southern history for most, like Jubal Early, their heritage was more compartmentalized—antebellum, bellum, and postbellum incantations mirrored and memorialized for family and community. In Early's predicament, he chose to become a "cardinal" of the new faith, a preacher of a past useful for the present and for all eternity.

It helped, of course, that Robert E. Lee conveniently died on October 12, 1870. Lee's death immediately provided opportunities—a catalyst for cultism, banding of a brotherhood for cooperation and for corporate self-pity, and introduction of alternate history. Led by Early, this project moved to enshrine Lee through monuments and tribute. True to the heritage of a disputatious people, however, the opportunity also opened for division, dispute, and conflict. Early quickly joined the vanguard of such disputants as to where Lee's remains should be enshrined—Richmond or Lexington, Virginia. Martyrdom for the fallen leader opened vistas beyond what Early had seen as personal memoir portraying what he had or had not done in his final year fighting for his beloved chieftain. Moving deftly from memoir interpretation to writing, speaking, and eventually arguing almost continuously, Early became apostle of a cause that was neither defeated nor annihilated by events on the battlefield in his view. When he told a Montgomery, Alabama, audience half in jest that Lee's Army of Northern Virginia never had been defeated but "simply wore itself out whipping the enemy," this was his article of faith. His litany recited a South overwhelmed by enemy power, resources, unchivalrous practices, and mongrel hordes in the ranks. Once laid down as gospel, this New Testament religion became mired in internal interpretive controversy to which Early took second fiddle to no other preacher. Forgotten or conveniently overlooked was displeasure with Lee as accomodationist—conciliatory, humbled servant of fate whose sense of duty retired him to an inconspicuous postwar position reviving education as the way forward. Lee never penned memoirs or passionately pronounced on much of anything. In 1867, he wrote authors E. A. Pollard and, some ten months later, Albert Taylor Bledsoe that he had little desire to "recall events of the late war" and that he had yet to read anything that had been published on the subject. Lee left that chore (opportunity?) to others, and they would be legion. Moreover, Jubal Early, in the words of historian Caroline Janney, became "most dogmatic in his efforts to seize control of Lee's memory."[12]

Perhaps control best explains Early's approach to most everything relating to Confederate memory. If his dismissal by Lee in 1865 troubled him, Early did not show it. Or perhaps his ardent admiration and desire to honor his former chief was a subliminal urge to make right his performance as some betrayal of Lee's trust. Disparate efforts to memorialize Lee remained inchoate until 1873, when the merger of nascent stirrings of veterans, true believers in the Lost Cause, and organizing abilities of Early and others anointed their so-called Southern Historical Society in Richmond with the ashes and dust of the Confederate past. The society, essentially founded and led by Early, became something of his personal platform. So much so that legend has it that one old soldier, Robert N. Stiles, declared earnestly that nobody ever took up a pen to write about the conflict "without the fear of Jubal Early before his eyes." At the birthing meeting held at White Sulphur Springs, West Virginia, in August, 54 (largely Virginians, although eleven other states were represented) heard Jubal proclaim the war plan for a united group. Decrying Yankee histories of the war as fabrications, Early advanced that a yet-to-be-written Southern history "devolves upon the survivors of those who participated in that war, to furnish the authentic materials of history." We must "vindicate that cause," he boomed, we must "rekindle and strengthen the faith and spirit of the

living," we must "do justice to the memory of our fallen comrades."
History written by enemies should be an anathema, and Appomattox
had not ended the duty of Lee's soldiers to use memory to instill truth.
Exoneration from images and charges of treason and rebellion would
henceforth ride with the new mission just as *vindication* became the
watchword of the movement. The new society and its meetings, publications, and speeches would provide the weapons. Early would make
good use of them all. [13]

Unfortunately, so much of Old Jube's crusade also seemed to be
belligerent encounters with others over historical interpretation. Oddly,
Gettysburg, not the abortive Washington campaign or his performance
in the Shenandoah, provided the grist for such sparring. But the dyspepsia among Southern veterans also centered on performance in battle, conduct of Lee's lieutenants, application of resources, valor, legitimacy of cause and action, as well as the refocus of the war's causation,
constitutionalism, crimes of Reconstruction, and white supremacy that
ranged through the pages of the Lost Cause organ *Southern Historical
Review* and similar publications. Ever-stoked by Early and old soldiers
whose aging minds shunted facts and remembrance into passionate
myths and legends, battle was joined on literary and speech platforms.
Issues included why Gettysburg was lost—Longstreet's tardiness on the
second day, not Ewell's/Early's hesitation on the first as the answer.
Perhaps it was the postwar embrace of Republicanism, even friendship
with erstwhile enemy Ulysses S. Grant by former lieutenants like Georgian John B. Gordon, that so irked Early and his coterie. But fellow
Virginian John Mosby also went over, earning Early's ill-tempered comment in 1878 that ranger Mosby's "idea was that the highest motive that
can influence a soldier is the desire for plunder, and whose *post bellum*
history is in accordance with his war experience—still fighting for
plunder." Early's venomous tongue nearly prompted a duel with
William Mahone. The wonder is that it did not do so with countless
others. [14]

Jubal Early joined the pantheon of Confederate immortals on March
2, 1894. True to form and given to legend creation, four years before he
had returned from a New Orleans trip to find his office building compromised by fire, condemned by authorities, and in danger of imminent
collapse. Seeking to find something of value and helped by several
African American assistants, he was seated at his desk when the walls

came tumbling down. Arriving firemen and Lynchburg townsfolk thought demise (perhaps wishing for it) had finally come for the cantankerous old soldier. When the dust cleared, however, Jubal was still seated in his chair, his white campaign hat still atop his head, and his beard whitened by falling plaster, but descended several floors into the rubble. "Uh, I didn't know there were that many bricks between me and hell," he announced unconcernedly. Looking up at one of his rescuers, old friend and mayor Robert Yancey, the unperturbed Early demanded, "Hey, Bob! Blast my hat to hell, I didn't know you were up there, boy! Damn it, you go get me a julep." Old Jube wasn't quite ready to see if Jehovah or Lucifer was his true maker. [15]

Finally, on February 15, 1894, the aged Early suffered a bad fall coming out of the Lynchburg post office, tumbling down granite steps to the sidewalk. Seemingly unhurt and unbowed by the experience, Early subsequently insisted on his regimen of leaving his abode provided by relatives for his daily trip downtown on business. Obviously, as the days passed, however, Jubal Early was no longer himself, languishing housebound, visited by old friends, and surrounded by solicitous messages from across the nation. Late on the evening of March 2, Early died, clasping the hand of his old friend, Lynchburg editor and now Virginia senator in Washington John Warwick Daniel. Local obituaries mentioned his worth at death of perhaps $200,000 or $300,000 (largely from lottery salary), his sole battle defeat at Cedar Creek, and "envious colleagues" seeking to defame his service while leaving it to the "colorless and dispassionate pen of history" to render final judgment. He was a rough diamond, observed the four-column commentary, citing an "exclusive and repellent exterior" hiding a "warm, sympathetic heart" waxing in an un-Early-like way, "even as the eagle that soars with an unwinking eye nearest the sun wears beneath his wing the softest down." [16]

Early's funeral befitted a lieutenant general of the Confederacy. Flags flew at half-staff (ironically, perhaps the "barber-pole banner" he so despised) for three mid- to late-afternoon hours paralleling the funeral hours in Lynchburg (and perchance replicating some Good Friday symbolism?). Cannons boomed at five-minute intervals to total 36 firings. A marching procession in the city included Virginia Military Institute cadets, local militiamen (but certainly not black units, about whom Early always had strong feelings), more than 300 Confederate veterans, reversed boots in the stirrups of the general's mount, flags, and his draped casket drawn by four black horses. A typically brief Episcopal funeral service in St. Paul's Church was highlighted by the Reverend T. M. Carson, a veteran of the 1864 Valley campaign who told the congregation how he had personally seen Early's forces "retiring before the almost countless numbers of the enemy" (Early's gospel that he would have appreciated) and the tragic figure of the beaten general "bowed almost to the saddle" (which Early most surely would not). Pathos attends funerals, and Carson waxed eloquently about how the view of the Early of Cedar Creek was also "one of the most noble pictures he had seen during the war—bent under the storm, but unconquered and unconquerable!" Somehow, it must have seemed strange for the sardonic unbeliever to be buried by established church ritual. The graveside service at Spring Hill Cemetery was equally brief but profound. A final salute, "Taps," a mourner—one of Jubal's "noblest and bravest followers"—delivering a farewell kiss on the cold brow of the dead, and then the casket was closed and lowered. Jubal Early was delivered to the ages. Or was he?[17]

7

OLD JUBE AND AMERICAN MEMORY
Explaining Jubal Early

A mid-1990s British television production of *Oliver's Travels* had the intriguing subtitle of *Looking for Aristotle*. Starring Alan Bates, Susan Cusack, and Michael Byrne, writer Alan Plater and director Giles Foster wove a delightful story of an ex-humanities professor from Wales and a female policewoman on suspension who together set out on an odyssey to find a missing crossword puzzle compiler. The combination of tale and travel provided viewers with scenery and anomaly as the pair end up at Scapa Flow in the Orkney Islands, more famous as the graveyard for the German kaiser's World War I scuttled High Seas Fleet. Aristotle, of course, was the crossword compiler, and finding him mixed exhilaration with letdown. For the pair, the process of looking for Aristotle was perhaps more pleasing than actually finding him. Could it be the same in searching for and possibly locating Jubal Early?

In the end, how are we to explain this Confederate general? Contemporaries and historians have tried. Lee called him his "bad old man." Army of Northern Virginia Second Corps subordinates saw him as plain looking but "every inch a soldier" as well as "one of the great curiosities of the war," his face like a full moon and a voice like a "cracked Chinese fiddle" emitting a "long drawl and accompanied by an outpouring of oaths." Careless of appearance in camp or field—a soldier's soldier—"as brave as he is homely, and as homely a man as any man you ever saw." Early's friend and U.S. senator John Warwick Daniel eulogized at his funeral, "Virginia holds the dust of many a faithful son, but not of one whom loved her more, who fought for her better, or would have died for her more willingly." While Early himself might have caviled at such gush (especially from one who, at times, seemed to flirt unconscionably with reconciliation), he surely would have smiled at much of what Daniel said, much of what he did, derived from being a native son. True, Early graduated West Point and served in the regular army, but he left that for country law. And we often overlook the fact that the Southern Confederacy of planter and slave mostly comprised hard-working farmers and middle professionals who bought into their peculiar version of the "American dream." It is there in the Jubal Anderson Early of Franklin County, Virginia, that we must begin and end any explanation of this notable Confederate general, apologist, and cantankerous nineteenth-century character.

John Esten Cooke, sometime veteran of J. E. B. Stuart's cavalry and Southern literary figure in his own right, conveyed the impression of an antebellum Early. Speaking of Early as this "Whig Submissionist" or opponent of secession, Cooke suggested a "gentleman of resolute courage and military experience" who fought advocates of the secession ordinance "with unyielding persistence, aiming by his hard-hitting argument, his kindling eloquence and his parliamentary skill" the direction "his judgment approved." Cooke refers at that point to Early more as politician than soldier but, once the gauntlet was thrown for withdrawal, "put on a gray coat, took to the field, and fought from the beginning to the very end of the war with a courage and persistence surpassed by no Southerner who took part in the conflict." True, these were Cooke's words in 1867 and immediately preceded a fuller paean to Early's accomplishments against all odds that would become standard grist in postwar ex-Confederate expulgation. Yet obviously the prewar Jubal Early of relative obscurity would transition to a wartime Early whose fate was determined by conditions beyond his control. [1]

Cooke claimed that, while many in and out of the army "doubted the soundness of his judgment," none ever questioned the "tough fibre of his courage." Everything about him was "bold, straightforward, masculine and incisive." Combativeness was one of his great traits. Even Lee admitted Early had led a forlorn hope toward the end of the war and that such hope rarely succeeded, said Cooke. But turning back to the man, Cooke claimed what he most remembered about Early was "that

sometimes cynical humour, and the force and vigour of his conversation." His voice was not pleasing "but his 'talk' was excellent," his intellect was "evidently strong, combative, aggressive in all domains of
thought, his utterance direct, hard-hitting, and telling." Cooke waxed
eloquently about Early's forceful speech, strong will, sustained energy,
and the "native vigour of his faculties." He repeated that Early was
"sarcastic and critical" and criticized in return a "man of rough address,
irascible temperament, and as wholly careless whom he offended." His
enemies might call into question his brains and judgment; "what they
could not call in question, however, was his 'zeal, fidelity and devotion.'" And, of course, Cooke pointed to the words and judgment of Lee
in that regard.[2]

Even his erstwhile opponent, Union cavalry general William Woods
Averell, declared, "There can be no question of Early's fearful energy
and dauntless courage." During the war, Early's contemporaries followed his moves with interest and enthusiasm. War department official
Roberrt Kean noted in his diary the day the general stood before the
gates of Washington, "Early, Breckinridge, Rodes, Gordon and Ramseur are men to dare and do almost anything." At the same time, reading in Northern newspapers of Early's third try at invasion that might
prove "the charm" of ultimate victory, Jason Phillips in *Diehard Rebels*
recounts, "Confederates enjoyed weeks of good rumors and fantastic
predictions." Still, there were naysayers at the same time; Confederate
government officials could be as fickle about Early as the public. Ordnance chief Josiah Gorgas was a superb example. While declaring in his
journal on August 6 that the "burning of Chambersburgh [*sic*]by Early
gives intense satisfaction," two weeks before he had carped, "The only
good [Early] has done [on his advance to Washington] is to arouse the
waning enthusiasm at the North & drawn a few additional recruits to
their Standard—he will lose a good many stragglers on his way back to
the valley." By October, Gorgas noted Early's defeats, his loss of eighty
cannon since May, "then comes the old Story—our left gave way—a
total rout ensued, the men behaving disgracefully & scattering into the
woods." As a result of Cedar Creek, "it is time to let him retire!" Then
there was that young woman visiting at "Bloomfield" in Clarke County
after Early's return from Washington who had wondered about Early's
objective at the time. She was not alone then or later. And second
guessing Jubal Early could be a lifetime pursuit.[3]

Perhaps it was simply as Lee's artillerist/staffer Brigadier E. Porter Alexander later judged: "Early proved himself a remarkable corps commander. His greatest quality perhaps was the fearlessness with which he fought against all odds & discouragements." Alexander had his own post-hoc axe to grind. "I have always thought that there was a much better play that he sending of Early on the raid to Washington," he opined. "That play was pure bluff," and retrospectively Alexander noted in 1864, "We had seen enough of Grant already to judge that he was *not* easily bluffed." Better to have sent Early to reinforce Johnston north of Atlanta; "it would not have been bluff at all, but the very strongest play on the whole military board." If successfully countering Sherman, then Early might have returned with a large part of the Army of Tennessee to reinforce Lee. With the advantage of interior lines before Richmond/Petersburg, "first class play would have required that we should utilize our one single advantage." Even later, when Early was back in the valley, said Alexander, "There was no reasonable hope of Early's accomplishing any valuable result with any force we could possibly send him." It seemed to Alexander, then, that after the middle of July 1864, Confederate policy should have been to play the Petersburg and Atlanta armies as one. Lee should have taken Early's corps in person to defeat a vulnerable Sherman and then return to deal with a presumably benign Grant. Such were the pipe dreams of retrospect, wholly unrealistic given Confederate fixation on the east, the impossible logistics in a twilight Confederacy, and the vagaries of confronting Sherman. Alexander was implicitly critiquing the Davis/Lee conduct of the war, not the operational abilities of Jubal Early.[4]

Enlightening, too, are thoughts from four other senior leaders—James Longstreet, John Mosby, John B. Gordon, and William Mahone—all Early antagonists at some stage. They suggest perhaps an inevitable evolution between war and postwar views of Early. Lee may have been too courtly or even paternal about his flock to go beyond labeling Early his "bad old man." Others were less courteous as postwar friction with Early helped shape a stereotype as time passed. Stubborn, difficult to work with, opinionated, perhaps more ambitious in the eyes of peers than his surviving writings suggest, Early must be considered in light of these peer impressions as well as official reports when all were supposed to cooperate for the good of the cause. Maybe it was the cause (in postwar capitals that enflamed the senses as aging men tried to explain defeat and their own role). They do illumine the three faces, the three stages, of Jubal Early himself. Certainly all four Confederate leaders encountered Early during the war: one as peer (Longstreet), a second as long-time subordinate (Gordon), a third less so but a postwar political rival (Mahone), and the fourth as an irregular collaborator (Mosby). Three of them restrained themselves until Early was dead. So much of the impression left stems from their postwar retrospections that supplant any solidarity of wartime bands of brothers even when bitter rivalries attended command in that conflict.

James Longstreet became the lightning rod for rationalizing failures and misdeeds of others in the eastern conflict. He especially incurred Early's postwar wrath in the battle for Lee's remembrance. But his acquiescence to Lee's style of reunion, the fact he became a hated Republican or lackey of the victors, and his foot-dragging at Gettysburg made him a target for the vitriolic Early cabal. Longstreet proved no competition, as ably shown in William Piston's able biography. If Longstreet ignored Early's slander, offers Piston, he miscalculated Early's words, which "took on great power and the ring of authority because he told Southerners exactly what they wanted to hear." Piston suggests, if Lee's warhorse thought "Early's mediocre war record and his wartime unpopularity" a detriment, then the conscious choice of a "second battle" about Gettysburg for going to a new mat proved Early was at his best (and worst as a crabbed and guilt-ridden old man). About the most revealing comments that Longstreet left for posterity about Early's character and conduct came in his own 1895 memoirs when speaking of his antagonist at Gettysburg. He dismissed Early, "who advised the battle *from the other end of the line from his command*, which should have given warning that it did not come from the heart of a true soldier." More tellingly, Longstreet pronounced of Early's own performance on the first day of that struggle, "There was a man on the left of the line who did not dare to make the battle win. He knew where it was, had viewed it from its earliest formation, had orders for his part in it, but so withheld part of his command from it as to make co-operative concert of action impracticable." This man—obviously Early—"had a pruriency for the honors of the field of Mars, was eloquent, before the fires of the bivouac and his chief, of the glory of war's gory shield; but when its envied laurels were dipping to the grasp, when the heavy field called for bloody work, he found the placid horizon, far and away beyond the cavalry, more lovely and inviting." What Longstreet was loath to advance publicly while Early lived he delivered posthumously. Early "wanted command of the Second Corps, and, succeeding to it, held the honored position until General Lee found, at last, that he must dismiss him from field service."[5]

Another object of Early's scorn was northern Virginia partisan ranger John Singleton Mosby, also a Republican turncoat during Reconstruction. Mosby probably encountered Early first in the formative stages of the Washington expedition when the general had petitioned the partisan ranger for a diversion into Maryland collaterally with his own movements. The resultant activity south of Frederick on the railroad may not have been much to Early, who always harbored doubts as to the reliability and performance not just of cavalry but particularly the partisan ranger variety. Still, Mosby did his part. Furthermore, he protected his own corner of the Confederacy from both armies trooping through and disrupting local tranquility and economics. Mosby's major mistake came in the postwar period and hence Early's vitriol. As was typical of so many veterans' feuds, Mosby returned the sentiment, and by the unveiling of Lee's monument in Richmond in 1894, he informed a correspondent "that I would be given the cold shoulder if I went, and probably that old fraud—Jubal Early—who assumes to be a sort of administrator of the Confederate Army, would, as he generally does on such occasions, make some insulting allusions to 'men who have deserted since the war'—meaning those who have voted the Republican ticket." He went on to explain to Aristides Monteiro (an old college chum from the University of Virginia, now [later] a doctor) the position taken by many ex-Confederates but seldom voiced (perhaps fearing the aging warrior's wrath) about Early: "The fact is that old Early himself was the first man after the war who deserted our people." At first chance after learning of Appomattox, observed Mosby, "he took to his heels and ran away to Canada instead of doing as I did—staying with our people—taking all the chances—and helping them to recover self-government." Here was a point of view that tells us much about how Old Jube was regarded by some peers in later life.[6]

In the end, John B. Gordon, as brigade and division commander, and William Mahone (hardly an Early intimate but occasional associate), through a quip echoing Gordon, may provide the most revealing peer impressions of Jubal Early. Neither the inspiring, fiery Georgian who went on to the U.S. Senate after the war nor Early's fellow yeoman Virginian also turned postwar politician held their fire on what they thought of Early. It was Gordon, in his own 1903 memoirs, who provided telling comment on his brushes with his superior and the differences of opinion at Gettysburg, Rappahannock Bridge, the Wilderness, and Cedar Creek. They point to chinks in Early the commander, although not necessarily the soldier. Gordon himself pronounced Early an "able strategist and one of the coolest and most imperturbable of men under fire and in extremity." In the same breath, Gordon noted that Early possessed "certain characteristics which militated against his achieving the greatest successes." Likening Early to Union general George B. McClellan, Gordon advanced that Early "lacked what I shall term official courage, or what is known as the courage of one's convictions." Lee and Grant, even Jackson, had it, said Gordon, although his own rather opaque description remains distant to twenty-first-century eyes. The possessor of the courage he was trying to describe was bold "but sees with quick, keen vision the weak and strong points in the adversary, measures with unerring judgment his own strength and resources, and then, with utmost faith in the result, devotes all to its attainment—and wins." Equally anti-Longstreet for this reason, perhaps, Gordon pronounced bluntly, "General Early possessed other characteristics peculiarly his own, which were the parents of more or less trouble to him and to those under him: namely, his indisposition to act upon suggestions submitted by subordinates and his distrust of the accuracy of report by scouts, than whom there were no more intelligent, reliable, and trustworthy men in the army."[7]

Mahone, whose postwar political and business practices hardly endeared him to Early, soon engaged in verbal pugilism once they both found their footing in Reconstruction Virginia. Mahone made the mistake of collaborating with a sycophantic Northern veteran, which caught Early's eagle eye and began another of the veteran's competitions about Confederate memory that soon degenerated into name calling, questions of personal honor, and other abuses that must have titillated readers of such tracts as the New York–published *Historical* magazine. Mahone suggested than the did not like to fight under Early because the latter "was always hesitating whether to fight or not; he would ride up and down his lines, from fifteen to twenty minutes, debating whether or not to begin; whereas the battle was to be lost or won, meanwhile." Here were words worthy of duel, and Early was up to it. His rejoinder caused Mahone to modify his words, declaring Early "brave enough and untiring as an officer" but adhering to his position that Early was disputatious to the point of even arguing with himself (Braxton Bragg–like) as to what to do. Delay was the consequence when the battle might be fought and victory gained. Such were the personal depths to which Jubal Early and the others stooped in trying to revisit scenes long past. Mahone reflected what Gordon would say later. As Jubal Early took such to be serious aspersion "on my conduct and judgment as a military commander," such contemporary impressions paint a portrait of the controversial Early. [8]

Preeminent Southern historian of his generation, Virginia newsman and publisher Douglas Southall Freeman had this candid assessment of Jubal Early. Freeman himself had grown up in Lynchburg and dimly remembered a fearful, stooped old general. As Lee's biographer and also of his "lieutenants," Freeman decided that he was "unmarried, snarling and stooped, respected as a soldier but never widely popular as a man." Candidly, Early's "sharp tongue is so critical of others that men refuse to see his excellences as a soldier." He also underscored public indictment of Early in the Shenandoah: "Early had retreated from Washington when it had seemed within his grasp; he had been routed at Winchester, routed at Fisher's Hill, routed at Cedar Creek." "That could only mean incompetence, mismanagement and the loss of the confidence of his officers and men," in the minds of the people, said Freeman. Yet this foremost student of Lee's lieutenants could still conclude that, while after the war contemporaries correctly said the third day at Gettysburg marked the "high water mark" of the Confederacy (on the "just determination of military values" alone), "if proximity to White House, to Capitol and to Treasury be considered strategically the greatest advance, then the honor of it fell a year and a week after Pickett's charge to that strange, bitter, and devoted man, Jubal A. Early, former Commonwealth's Attorney of Franklin County, Virginia." Here was the towering testament to Early by one who knew and appreciated what he had accomplished. [9]

One student of Jubal Early, Thomas Schott, concludes that if Early wasn't remembered for his role in creating the Lost Cause mythology, "he would be almost as renowned as one of the finest upper echelon commanders in the Army of Northern Virginia." Arguably, he posits, that of Lee's subordinates, only Jackson and Longstreet "surpassed him in ability." Early's foremost biographer Charles Osborne intones that everything in his military career before the summer of '64 was a "build-up to his last campaign." And so First and Second Bull Run, Williamsburg, Fredericksburg, and Salem Church appear as such. But so, too, were the missteps at Gettysburg, Rappahannock Bridge, and the Wilderness. Perhaps these were lost opportunities rather than mistakes and presaged Early's performance from Fort Stevens to Waynesboro. Of course, the first flight occurred when Early was a subordinate, not an independent field general. And the final performance did include singular victories, albeit minor in comparison. [10]

Osborne utilizes the almost ebullient observations of University of North Carolina graduate student Terry Moss to refute any majority opinion that "seemingly condemns [Early] as a failure." Together, they rebut a widely entertained opinion that Early's efforts between June and October "placed a lien on future operations" and "made wasteful use of precious resources." Certainly the naysayers overlook the fact that everything flowed from Richmond and Lee's strategic instruction, sanction, and provision of means. But Osborne and Moss rather suggest that Early's summer operations "did yield considerable military benefits for the Confederate cause." They cite the "rescue of Lynchburg" and "clearing the Valley" from Hunter, "capture of Federal depots at Martinsburg and Harpers Ferry" for replenishing "increasingly impoverished commissaries of the Confederacy," advance upon Washington that "rattled and immobilized" Federal military and civilian officials, and the retardation effect that Early's summer raid had on the "momentum of Grant's offensive in eastern Virginia." [11]

Osborne and Moss continue with the post-Washington phase of Early's contributions, decidedly more controversial, in fact. This pair concur that, through the end of 1864, Early achieved Lee's objective of "siphoning [Union] troops away from Petersburg." Of course, they did so, too, for Confederate resources. But in trying to paint a more favorable picture, they claim that Union casualties in the valley "denied to Grant" the equivalent of an infantry corps (14,500), while costing Lee and Early only 10,000 men. Again, of course, Lee could ill afford even those numbers; Grant very much could. Finally, say Osborne and Moss, though weakened by desertion, attrition, and transfer, Early's valley army diverted sizeable Union resources, thus "exerting a palpable influence on the overall military situation." Essentially a position echoed by recent strategic scholar Donald Stoker, by implication, Old Jube's time and luck simply ran out after he basically ensured Lee and the Confederacy a fully half-year's dispensation. We might always ask, was this necessarily true? Still, it casts more favorably upon Early's place in history.[12]

Certainly, as far as early summer events, Early did rescue Lynchburg from Hunter's possible capture. Yet would Hunter's seizure of that invaluable transportation and supply center "have forced Lee's evacuation of Richmond months before it finally took place"? That is plausible, and both Osborne and Moss, possibly others, would agree. There follows the equally plausible explanation that the subsequent "clearing of the Valley" in late June and much of July took Hunter "completely from the sphere of operations, neutralizing his force and impairing his true usefulness." Yet Hunter's troops eventually returned to the theater and became part of Sheridan's ravaging horde (no matter how wobbly their performance). Hunter was destined by Washington to get back into the Shenandoah at some point. His absence, of course, held more potentially fatal consequences for the Union than how the "clearing operation made possible the undisturbed harvest of much of the upper Valley's grain." Harvesting, milling, and transporting to Lee and elsewhere to the Confederacy's benefit gained only temporary reprieve given Early's failure in midsummer to capture the nation's capital and the advent of a new practitioner of Grant's mandated scorched-earth policy, over which Early would have marginal influence due to marked failure on the battlefield. If Early was merely a forlorn hope by this time, the whole game in the Shenandoah became one of who could race first to the finish— harvesting or destroying the rich resources (animal and vegetable)— while at the same time somehow affecting Northern elections that could predict the future for war and peace. Here Jubal Early played a pivotal role as instrument for both sides, so it may be said that the fate of two nations and his own rode on events over which he had some control.

At that moment, Mary Greenhow Lee of Winchester captured the essence of explaining Jubal Early to posterity. "If we can only thoroughly whip Sheridan, the effect throughout the whole country, & on the [Northern] election, will be the most encouraging, we know our army cannot stay here, as there is nothing for them to eat, but it will be such a comfort to see them once more, before the winter, the long dreary winter sets in," she penned in her journal on Wednesday night, October 19, 1864. The sun of Middletown (Cedar Creek) had risen and set with a crash that day. Jubal Early's fate, nay even that of the Confederacy, had been affected by Philip Henry Sheridan. Mary Lee was unaware of the result. In the concluding words of George E. Pond, associate editor of the influential turn-of-the-century professional *Army and Navy Journal* and himself a veteran of the events embracing the pair, "When [Sheridan] entered the [Shenandoah] Valley, it was wholly under Confederate control; he left it with Confederate power there wholly broken." All that Early had accomplished before—from West Point days to his reluctant secessionism, his steady rise to senior Confederate command from Manassas through the Overland campaign, and his zenith before Fort Stevens at Washington, even the brilliant Fabian-like actions thereafter (worthy emulation of George Washington nearly a century before)—everything was swept away in the autumn breezes by Philip Sheridan. After that, everything in Jubal Early's life was the bitter gall of defeat, the seeking of redemption perhaps through virulent anti-Yankeeism and rewriting the history of an experiment in rebellion as he saw it. Perhaps it might have been better if Early's death, not Lee's, had come in 1870. All that Early accomplished in the last quarter century before his own demise simply gave us a Confederate in the attic and little else to explain. The image of slanted Virginia preeminence in the late war; old veterans wrangling; bigotry and false memory; and the crippled portrait of a beleaguered, unremorseful old general whose real story and contribution was stopped short by the very truth that he sought so long to reject—the overwhelming application of Union power of war in the machine age—traced to his stillborn effort and Sheridan's florid legions. All that Jubal Early sought to reject about Union victory was true, and explaining his role as victim and defeated in that saga has left a legacy for historians. [13]

Nonetheless it may be time to place Jubal Early's wine in other vessels. We may continue to have new topics and interpretations along with the traditional portraits. Bruce Levine's tracing of the social revolution that transformed the South repeats the words of a Louisiana captain (also quoted by student of the war Joseph Glathaar) about how the Cedar Creek reversal of Rebel fortunes was "one of the most shameful and disgraceful stampedes on record" and equal to the First

Manassas spectacle only with "men in gray now doing the running." Somehow this picture vindicates Early's pillorying of the boys in the ranks for failing him that day rather than the reverse, as has been the conclusion of many historians. And Stephanie McCurry's ferreting out an obscure Early broadside to Shenandoah soldiers' wives in November after Cedar Creek—one that ensured these beleaguered civilians that "wheat and corn purchased for them by county welfare committees would not be subject to impressments by Confederate federal agents as it had been previously"—plays to the influence of military wives in domestic "politics of subsistence and its public expression"(the focus of her work) but also to portraying Jubal Early in a softer light. Moreover, Nina Silber's placement of Early front and center for the Lee redemption and makeover after the war indeed served important (nay vital) roles then and now. We need to understand either the fact that Civil War and Reconstruction were but a single epoch for America or that there were two distinct periods to contemporaries. Early serves as a useful tool for either approach. The Early of Silber and like-minded historians led the assault in making Lee the "noble white commander whose unblemished character could serve as a positive reflection of the white South in the postwar years." Thus Early helped Lee "serve a variety of political ideological and regional agendas."[14]

The search for a more useful Jubal Early takes other twists when one further plumbs the depths. Newer accounts of the military story attribute motive and result, weakness and self-determination in explaining his generalship. And well they might in this year of the sesquicentennial of his personal rise and fall. But when Yael Sternhell interprets the world of movement in the Confederate South through routes taken by armies, refugees, and flotsam/jetsam destabilized and dislocated by war, his brief mention of Early (and not even in connection with the Shenandoah) merely tweaks the surface of new breath for using official sources. Early's impact (through his leadership position) whether moving to Gettysburg, Washington, or in the northern Shenandoah fairly begs for better clarifying of his presence and attitudes, much less employment of his forces in an ever-evolving Civil War home front or civilian story. The vehicles of Second Corps, Army of the Valley District, regular and irregular raider cavalry, and his logistical train all feed to fleshing out Early's passing across the pages of history. In essence, Early's actions after Lynchburg fed Confederate hopes, hearts, and minds in the valley and elsewhere but also provided the lightning rod for Federal response—not a counterpoise battle army alone but orders borne by Hunter and Sheridan. Those orders ultimately turned the world upside down for both loyal Confederate as well as Union-disposed black and white civilians whom Early was supposed to protect as wards of some Confederate state and whose confidence he ultimately lost when he could not do so—hence, his relief by Lee in the end. Here, then, Early can be reinterpreted not merely as himself but rather as an instrument of something transcending an evolution in war itself. That suggests new interest in defining destruction in the Civil War and transformation of Southern landscapes as suggested by recent works of Yael Sternhell, Megan Nelson, Lisa Brady, and Andrew Smith.[15]

Beside the figure cloaked in the mantle of traditional Civil War history stands another Jubal Early. This was the Early who became a man hardened and burdened by war. Not necessarily the battlefield, mind you, but rather the Confederate version of what historian Charles Royster termed "destructive war." Royster finds personification of this new mode of conflict that enveloped civilians as well as soldiers in Stonewall Jackson and William T. Sherman. In so doing, he delivers only a glancing blow at the Confederate manifestation by neglecting Jubal Early (unless Early be judged a disciple or acolyte of Jackson, which is not apparent). But it was Early, not Jackson, who delivered a Confederate version of destructive war in 1863 and 1864. Perhaps it stemmed from what Early thought he saw of Yankee depredations in Fredericksburg, or perhaps his conversion was completed subsequently. At any rate, his response took two forms—extortion and destruction. Extortion of Union civilian capital translated to ransoming Gettysburg, York, Hagerstown, Middletown, and Frederick. It manifested itself for subordinates in not rigidly enforcing his orders against foraging and pillage when hungry and thirsty ranks desecrated such properties as Unionist Southerner John De Sellum's at Gaithersburg, Maryland. And it may well have translated in some fashion to a confiscation and reenslavement of blacks found in Pennsylvania in June and July 1863, although in the convoluted thinking of law and war and humanity—liberated or free or refugee labor was fair game for confiscation (contraband or property recovery) in the name of military economics.[16]

Still, there was an even nastier side to the evolving Early. Witness the destruction of Congressman Thaddeus Stevens's Caledonia iron-

works community, the callous indifference to the fate of Francis Preston Blair's lovely "Silver Spring" or son Montgomery's "Falkland," or
even Maryland governor Augustus W. Bradford's country house north
of Baltimore. Early's direct crowning achievement in his version of
destructive war against an enemy came with Chambersburg, over which
he seemingly gloated in later years. Here was the avenger Early merg-
ing with the extortionist Early—a vindictive figure who was merely a
prelude to the venomous postwar old general. Prosecutor for perceived
wrongs; prejudiced against "nonsubmissionist" nonbelievers in the new
Confederacy; hypocritical about foraging, straggling, and robbery by his
command, Jubal Early cannot escape the judgment of time for his own
Sherman-like tactics that might equate Chambersburg, if not his extortion of Yankee capital, with marching from Atlanta to the sea after
burning Atlanta and evicting its citizens, as well as the mystery of who
torched Columbia, South Carolina. Perhaps Jubal Early was "as
thoroughgoing as Sherman in their representations of war hurtling
along its career, blind to moral dicta," to capture Royster's apt charac-
terization. [17]

In a way, the eminent exponent of the western theater of the Civil
War as the decisive one, Richard M. McMurry, has established what
should be a new curiosity, if not some sort of new paradigm, for thinking about the whole epoch. Counterfactualism underpins McMurry's
"fourth battle of Winchester" work published in 2002. The key point
comes at the moment of Rebel victory at Cedar Creek. Jubal Early is
killed by a shell fragment, his loyal subordinates John B. Gordon, Stephen Ramseur, and Willie Pegram also rendered hors de combat. Joseph B. Kershaw succeeds Early in this hypothetical suggestion.
McMurry omits Sheridan from any return to the gates of Washington,
which might have been unnecessary by McMurry merely playing the
"what if" card three months earlier when Early appeared before Washington. One could stop with the victorious dusty veterans poised to take
the capital in mid-July. Capture of the city, dispersal of the Union
government, or death or maiming of Lincoln would have rendered the
valley defeats, capture of Atlanta, and Lincoln's reelection all moot. A
"Conferate States of America" might have joined a rump United States
plus Canada and Mexico on the North American continent. Early, not
Lee or Jackson or anyone else, would assume the pinnacle of the Confederate pantheon. It was not to be, although Jubal Early will always

remain useful as much for the factual as any counterfactual history of Civil War and modern America. Was it bachelorhood, arthritis, ambition, or some fatal flaw of indecision cloaking overconfidence in Early's wartime character that then necessitated his curmudgeonly, even SOB, postwar portrait? We may never know, and probably we don't need to![18]

Jubal Early was a man of strong convictions—native Virginians disloyal to the Confederacy, soldiers should remain single until after the war, straggling and pillaging were an abomination, draft dodging was akin to treason. However arguable Gary Gallagher's portrait of "patriotic submission," Early was after the war what historian Jason Phillips aptly and more politely terms a "diehard." History is filled with them. Unfortunately, perhaps, Early's least-endearing traits emerge from his bitterness and his postwar support of an unvanquished, racially rancid region—a blight on the escutcheon of America's past. There can be no escaping his self-serving explanations for defeat, his unrelenting condemnation of the victors, and an unremitting and unflagging crusade to create something heroic and mythic from the ashes of a failed experiment in rebellion. But of all of us studying and searching for "the Jubal Early," Gallagher makes the strongest case for a key link in the man's transformation forged by the experience of war. Federal armies "exhibited behavior that differed markedly from Early's model of fair treatment of an enemy's population and property," he cogently observes. "Every Federal transgression," by Early's definition, "against the sanctity of property and the stable social and racial order of the antebellum years strengthened his [Confederate] national identity and nourished his loathing of the North and northerners," in Gallagher's words. We might safely add the humiliation of defeat on valley battlefields and the degrading treatment from his own people in the winter of 1864–1865 after Waynesboro surely had an effect. Even his chosen route to avoid a new submission to the victors in early Reconstruction impacted a certain country hauteur that marked Jubal Early. But was his a transformation from Virginia state loyalty to a new Confederate national loyalty as Gallagher contends (both a wartime and postwar experience)? Or, still more, was Early's peculiar approach a result of a unique prism superimposed upon his distinct personality already conditioned by a painful malady but heretofore cloaked by professional success, battlefield victory, accolades of the public, and patronage from a beloved superior?

From the lofty perch of achievement to the depths of defeat was a human phenomenon that tore to the inner soul of a man of honor and dedication. And was Gallagher's choice of words *forced emancipation* by Yankees (more appropriate than *confiscation*, *liberation*, or *humanitarian intervention*) of the institution of slavery part of such transformation that only added to Early's postwar burden? Early "seldom resorted to anti-northern cant during the antebellum years" (Gallagher's words), yet his rabid Yankee-baiting hatred was hardly muffled thereafter.[19]

That said, however, from the unquenched brands and coals that seemingly continue to attend Lost Cause followers, Early may have unwittingly provided American memory with a useful cross to bear and rather some unshakable truths. Early as symbol, sword, and shield for the American South's Confederate period—one of fiery trial, purging of a caste and class based on race, agricultural economics, and aggrieved sense of honor—also yields a figure for integrating the formula of a New South. This South was not just one of commerce, business, and industry but also segregation and human discrimination in mockery of the sacred documents that Americans even today hold dear. Early thus provides utility for remembrance and memory. A healthy laugh at Old Jube's expense because of his Ichabod Crane–like appearance and demeanor will remind us of the archetypical American who confronted the likes of Dickens, de Tocqueville, and others in antebellum America. And we surely need that to offset the Southern stuffiness of Lee, Jackson, the Johnstons, and Beauregard in their high-collared gray uniforms of the rebellion period. We do indeed need the unreconstructed, acerbic, prejudiced, feuding, and crabbed Early to remind us of who we really are—lurking just beneath the surface of a preachy, savior of mankind, exemplar of God's chosen people from a city on the hill.

The Jubal Early we choose to remember is surely not the starched, formal oil portrait in the Virginia Historical Society—except perhaps the dark, piercing eyes; bald pate; and slight frown. On the other hand, despite the gold sash, tightly buttoned frock coat, and sword appropriately adorning the martial figure, this is a portrait of a man in pain. Much of Jubal's life was painful. He was physically in his grave by the time his cherished Virginia entered perhaps the most painful period in its long history. The Old Dominion's discriminatory Jim Crow constitution of 1902 opened that period. Early's spirit could be seen in its enactment. The constitution, with voting restrictions and school segregation among its provisions, stood until 1971, mocking the community that provided George Mason, Thomas Jefferson, and Patrick Henry to the founding fathers pantheon. Happily, Old Jube's signature was not upon this document as it had been on the Old Dominion's secession declaration in 1861. His ghost, however, now supplanted his person in supplying tone—both a dubious distinction.

On the other hand, do we have any good reason not to still accept historian Frank Vandiver's 1960 conclusion that Early "deserves an honored place in the ranks of Confederate generals?" He was a good administrator, Vandiver claims, although "with some lapses concerning the mounted army." He was a "natural leader, a quick and generally sound tactician, a good strategist," perhaps arguable assertions given continued microscopic dissection by Civil War buffs and professionals. His 1864 Valley campaign, states Vandiver, "did more than most diversions to form a pattern in war" as "what he did in the Shenandoah certainly prolonged the conflict through the winter of 1864." Finally, suggests the renowned Rice University scholar, had Early "been able to brush past the militia at Washington's battlements, he might have altered the course of history." On this point, posterity can only marvel at the campaign that could have changed the war but admit that it most assuredly did so anyway![20]

Jubal Early fired one additional solid shot of that campaign—the "raid on Washington"—13 years before his death. His letter to Washington's *National Republican* in early August 1881 (reprinted by the *New York Times* on August 6 to capture a wider Northern audience), proves informative from several perspectives. Similar to what can be found in his memoir, even the *Autobiographical Sketch*, his letter pointed to three principal themes—the force he claimed to have had at the time, why no assault was made on the national capital, and the burning of Postmaster General Montgomery Blair's "Falkland" mansion. It was vintage, unapologetic Early, reflecting much of what he had spent so much time, ink, and words rationalizing since Appomattox. From a corps numbering 17,079 in aggregate before the commencement of the spring campaign to 9,000 when detached to save Lynchburg, Early claimed, the force he appeared with before Washington (counting returned stragglers, previously wounded, and accretion of Breckinridge's men from Lynchburg) numbered perhaps 12,000. But dispersed cavalry and only 40 pieces of artillery (nine batteries with no more than two to four guns apiece) all suggested inadequacy to Early, who used this to set the stage for rationalizing his second point—why he did not directly attack Washington's defenses. Of course, he then noted his inability to place Rodes's division in battle line (his whole command having marched "fully fifteen miles in very hot, dry weather and over exceedingly dusty roads, and was, of course very much exhausted, many of the men having fallen by the way from heat and exhaustion"). He referred then to intelligence from a local wayside sympathizer (citing "nothing but earthworks" but feebly manned by perhaps 20,000 defenders—still enough to spook Early because "knowing that earthworks in the then state of the science of war were impregnable against my force, and not feeling very much encouraged by the information given me"). With customary bravado, he told his informant that, if that was all the enemy had in opposition, then "we would not mind that." Given the "tall talking" of most Confederates as to their numbers and intent, claimed the general, any of his men taken prisoner over the course of the campaign "contributed in no small part to the bewilderment of [my] opponents and the success of my efforts to baffle him for so long a period."

Early now further clouded the issue of whether Lee had expected and issued direct orders for him to actually capture Washington. However varied subsequent interpretations of words in actual 1864 dispatches reflecting the two men's understanding of what was to be done have been, 17 years later, Early stated for *National Republican* (hence *Times* readers, too) that it had never been Lee's idea, or any order but Early's own decision, that he should or could capture Washington. Lee had thought "threatening" not "capturing" the enemy capital was all that was possible. Furthermore, said Early, his taking the place had depended upon Grant's response with reinforcements. Because that had occurred by the night of July 11, the issue was rendered moot, so that he subsequently made "mere demonstrations to amuse the enemy" until escape could be made that next night. Early then closed out his arguments by turning attention to the practice of destructive war as had occurred before Washington. Having found "Silver Spring" abandoned by the Blairs ("if Mr. Blair had been at home his property and his privacy would have been respected as was that of all citizens who remained in their homes"), Early claimed to have placed a guard over the place, recovered and returned stolen personal property, but made no pretense to denying that Blair beef cattle as well as the herds of other citizenry was confiscated because his soldiery had been reduced to living off the country. Early seemed proud that the Blair mansion had not been confiscated as a hospital and that he had spared destruction of the place because father and son had opposed the "policy pursued by some Federal commanders in the south in the destruction of private property and imprisonment of non-combatant citizens." Similarly, he placed protection over son Montgomery's "Falkland" so that that destruction was done "without my authority." He reiterated his own practice of levying tribute and ordering the burning of Chambersburg as retaliation. All these acts were in accordance with the laws of war, concluded Early, closing that "if I had ordered the burning of Blair's house I would not now seek to evade responsibility." So ended Early's testament to his missed opportunity to change history, that moment that would have vaulted him to the pinnacle of Confederate fame and glory.[21]

More stories and anecdotes will probably always surface about "Old Jube," possibly the character in the most colorless tapestry of blood and gore, suffering and destruction, in American history. There is reputably a recipe out there for General Early's "Stonewall Punch" "because of its effects on the imbiber were like hitting a stone wall." Well, if Old Jube was not the imbiber contemporaries said he was, he certainly hit his share of stone walls in life and career. His twelve-ounce schooner glass filled with cracked ice, sugar, bourbon, hard cider, and Virginia Concord red wine was obviously not because of any linkage to a lemon-sucking Stonewall Jackson. In a male-dominated world (civilian and the army), Early's disdain for women was legendary. Scornful of John B. Gordon's wife in camp, he was known to exclaim, "I wish the Yankees would capture Mrs. Gordon and hold her till the war is over." But he was forced to eat his words on more than one occasion, admitting not only that her husband fought better when she was around but also that if the army "would keep us as she does, I'd never issue another order against straggling."

This author's favorite anecdote will forever remain the disrespectful tale of Jubal Early and his opposite—the dour Calvinist Cromwell of the Confederacy and his superior officer, Stonewall Jackson. The tale is familiar to the point of banality and told before in this book. Why had Stonewall seen so many stragglers in the rear of Early's marching column? Retorted Old Jube, so typical that one can almost hear the profanity as he penned it, "Probably because he rode in rear of my division." Here was the penultimate Jubal Early—irreverent, practical, businesslike, and perhaps harboring arthritic pain that may ultimately best explain Early's attitudes, actions, and crosses to bear across the years between then and now.[22]

Visual memorials to Jubal Early's presence in history vary from period photographs and manuscripts in various archives to street and highway names (especially in Virginia) to a statue in front of the Franklin County, Virginia, courthouse, as well as quasi-humorous allusions to his first name or contractions thereof. A citizen group in his native Rocky Mount, Franklin County, Virginia, seeks to restore and preserve his boyhood home.[23] In the end, his uniqueness—even his standing as the last unrepentant rebel in the attic—may yet be appreciated best by something so prosaic that even he might look down (or up) from the afterlife and chuckle or swear in appreciation. As unlikely as it seems, a humble ferryboat named for him plies the crossing where he returned victorious from his chance to change the world. The sole such craft still rippling the Potomac River at White's Ferry upstream from Washington, DC, the *General Jubal A. Early* carries great symbolism. Here is where Early retired from the aborted pinnacle of wartime success, his brink of immortality. Like Old Jube, the ferryboat is an anachronism—a symbol of the past—fighting to preserve the past, undefeated and unbowed before the march of time, the elements, interstate highway bridges, and forgetful obscurity. For Confederate Lieutenant General Jubal Early and the ferryboat *General Jubal A. Early*, the banners will not be furled by Appomattox. Faulkner-like, it will always not yet be midafternoon on a hot, smoke-filled July day at Gettysburg. The guns are laid, brigades in place behind rail fences, everyone waiting for the word to attack. "It hasn't happened yet, it hasn't even begun yet but there is still time for it not to begin" are Faulkner's immortal words. For Jubal Early—the general, his cause, and his ferryboat namesake in the twenty-first century—there is still time for it not to begin.

In the end, history will inevitably focus on Jubal Early, the Confederate general. Just as inevitably, students of the Civil War will make the comparison between "Old Jube" and the "Mighty Stonewall," much as Gary Gallagher did in his 1997 essay on that subject. As with Gallagher, arguments will be cast anew with the Shenandoah Valley the logical juncture point for comparison. Yet, such comparative points can be made at any time after Jackson's death in May 1863. Gettysburg and the Overland campaign of the following spring provide ample moments for "what ifs"—either implied in Faulkner's words, or unceasingly in the wistful phrase "if only Jackson had lived." Here again, the Shenandoah campaigns of 1862 and 1864 seem most logical and Gallagher hones in accordingly to suggest that the two soldiers performed quite similarly given contextual differences in time, force composition, nature of their opponents, and so forth. Yet, even then, Gallagher and a host of others miss the point. The critical moment of strategic mass for comparison lay with the Washington campaign and no other. Only there could either Jackson or Early through boldness and determination have changed the war in an afternoon.

We might be tempted to conclude that at Washington and nowhere else really, Early proved to be no Jackson. Surely, Stonewall would not have held back, would not have shrunk from opportunity on those two stifling days before Fort Stevens in northwest D.C. He would have taken the initiative, pressed through the poorly manned fort line, captured the city, and dispersed the Lincoln regime, even captured or killed Lincoln himself. Stonewall Jackson would have changed the war in a single afternoon sings the stuff of hope and myth. Jackson being human too would have suffered the heat, the dust, the 400 miles since Richmond. His "foot soldiers" of '64 were not those of '62 and maybe he would have known it and also sought the cooler climes of "Silver Spring," rest and mere rattling of Washington nerves. We shall never know. Jackson, like Early, might well have blinked also! And, after 150 years, except for the aficionados, does it really matter?[24]

BIBLIOGRAPHY

PRIMARY SOURCES

Manuscripts

Allan, William. "Reminiscences," Southern Historical Collection, University of North Carolina Library, Chapel Hill, North Carolina (SHC/UNC), n.d.
Daniel, J. W. papers, University of Virginia, Charlottesville, Virginia.
Gordon–Blackford papers, Maryland Historical Society, Baltimore, Maryland.
Greer, George diary, U.S. Army Heritage Center, Carlisle, Pennsylvania.
Jones, William J. Correspondence, Museum Quality Americana, copy, author's research files, Fort Ward Museum and Park, Alexandria, Virginia.
Lee, Edmund Jennings papers, Duke University, Durham, North Carolina.
Miscellaneous papers, Montgomery County Historical Society, Rockville, Maryland.
Ramseur, Stephen papers, Southern Historical Society, University of North Carolina, Chapel Hill, North Carolina.
White, Lewis collection, Joseph and Sharon Scopin, Darnestown, Maryland.

Jubal Early Papers

College of William and Mary, Swem Library, Williamsburg, Virginia.
Duke University, William R. Perkins Library, Durham, North Carolina.
Huntington Library, San Marino, California.
Library of Congress, Washington, DC.
New York Historical Society, New York, New York.
U.S. Military Academy, West Point, New York.
Virginia Historical Society, Richmond, Virginia.
Miscellaneous Research files, Monocacy National Battlefield Visitor Center, Frederick, Maryland.

Books

Alexander, Edward Porter. *Fighting for the Confederacy: The Personal Recollections of General Edward Porter Alexander.* Edited by Gary W. Gallagher. Chapel Hill: University of North Carolina Press, 1989.

Basler, Roy P., Marion Delores Pratt, and Lloyd A. Dunlap, eds. *Collected Works: The Abraham Lincoln Association, Springfield, Illinois.* New Brunswick, NJ: Rutgers University Press, 1953.

Buck, Lucy Rebecca. *Sad Earth, Sweet Heaven: The Diary of Lucy Rebecca Buck during the War between the States, Front Royal, Virginia, December 25, 1861–April 15, 1865.* Edited by William P. Buck. Birmingham, AL: Cornerstone, 1973.

Colt, Margaretta Barton. *Defend the Valley: A Shenandoah Family in the Civil War.* New York: Oxford University Press, 1994.

Cooke, John Esten. *Wearing of the Gray: Being Personal Portraits, Scenes, and Adventures of the War.* Edited by Philip Van Doren Stern. Bloomington: Indiana University Press, 1959.

Crist, Lynda Lasswell, Mary Seaton Dix, and Kenneth H. Williams, eds. *The Papers of Jefferson Davis.* Vol. 9. Baton Rouge: Louisiana State University Press, 1997.

Crist, Lynda Lasswell, Kenneth H. Williams, and Peggy L. Dillard, eds. *The Papers of Jefferson Davis.* Vol. 10. Baton Rouge: Louisiana State University Press, 1999.

Douglas, Henry Kyd. *I Rode with Stonewall, Being Chiefly the War Experiences of the Youngest Member of Jackson's Staff from the John Brown Raid to the Hanging of Mrs. Surratt* Chapel Hill: University of North Carolina Press, 1940.

Dowdey, Clifford, and Louis H. Manarin, eds. *The Wartime Papers of R. E. Lee.* Boston: Little, Brown, 1961.

Early, Jubal A. *Autobiographical Sketch and Narrative of the War between the States.* Philadelphia: J. B. Lippincott, 1912.

———. *A Memoir of the Last Year of the War for Independences, in the Confederate States of America: Containing an Account of His Commands in the Years 1864 and 1865.* Columbia: University of South Carolina Press, 2001.

Eby, Cecil D., Jr., ed. *A Virginia Yankee in the Civil War: The Diaries of David Hunter Strother.* Chapel Hill: University of North Carolina Press, 1961.

Goode, John. *Recollections of a Lifetime.* New York: Neale Publishing, 1906.

Gordon, John B. *Reminiscences of the Civil War.* New York: C. Scribner's Sons, 1903.

Hewitt, Jane B., ed. *Supplement to the Official Records of the Union and Confederate Armies.* 100 vols. Wilmington, NC: Broadfoot Publishing, 1994–1999.

Hotchkiss, Jedidiah. *Make Me a Map of the Valley; The Civil War Journal of Stonewall Jackson's Topographer.* Edited by Archie P. McDonald. Dallas: Southern Methodist University Press, 1973.

Hyde, Thomas W. *Following the Greek Cross or Memories of the Sixth Army Corps.* Boston: Houghton Mifflin, 1894.

Kean, Robert Garlick Hill. *Inside the Confederate Government: The Diary of Robert Garlick Hill Kean, Head of the Bureau of War.* Edited by Edward Younger. New York: Oxford University Press, 1957.

Laas, Virginia Jeans, ed. *Wartime Washington: The Civil War Letters of Elizabeth Blair Lee.* Urbana: University of Illinois Press, 1991.

Longstreet, James. *From Manassas to Appomattox: Memoirs of the Civil War in America.* New York: Da Capo Press, 1992.

Mahon, Michael G., ed. *Winchester Divided: The Civil War Diaries of Julia Chase and Laura Lee.* Mechanicsburg, PA: Stackpole Books, 2002.

Nichols, George W. *A Soldier's Story of His Regiment (61st Georgia): And Incidentally of the Lawton–Gordon–Evans Brigade, Army of Northern Virginia* Tuscaloosa: University of Alabama Press, 2011.

Opie, John Newton. *A Rebel Cavalryman with Lee, Stuart and Jackson.* Chicago: W. B. Conkey, 1899.

Scopin, Joseph, compiler/editor. *As I Remember; the Lewis Cass White Collection.* Darnestown, MD, Scopin Design, 2014.

Sheeran, James B. *Confederate Chaplain.* Edited by Joseph T. Durkin. Milwaukee, Wi: Bruce Publishing, 1960.

Sorrel, G. Moxley. *Recollections of a Confederate Staff Officer.* New York: Neale Publishing, 1905.

Stephens, Robert Grier, comp./ed. *Intrepid Warrior: Clement Anselm Evans, Confederate General from Georgia: Life, Letters, and Diaries of the War Years.* Dayton, OH: Morningside, 1992.

Stiles, Robert N. *Four Years under Marse Robert.* New York: Neale Publishing, 1903.

Strader, Eloise C., ed. *The Civil War Journal of Mary Greenhow Lee (Mrs. Hugh Holmes Lee) of Winchester, Virginia.* Winchester, VA: Winchester–Frederick County Historical Society, 2011.

U.S. War Department. *The War of the Rebellion: A Compilation of the Official Records of the Union and Confederate Armies.* 128 vols. Washington, DC: Government Printing Office, 1880–1901.

Wiggins, Sarah Woolfolk, ed. *The Journals of Josiah Gorgas, 1857–1878.* Tuscaloosa: University of Alabama Press, 1995.

Worsham, John H. *One of Jackson's Foot Cavalry,* edited by James Robertson, Jr. and Bell Irvin Wiley. Jackson, TN: McCowat-Mercer Press, 1964.

SECONDARY SOURCES

Books

Anders, Curt. *Henry Halleck's War: A Fresh Look at Lincoln's Controversial General-in-Chief.* Carmel: Guild Press of Indiana, 1999.

Ashdown, Paul, and Edward Caudill. *The Myth of Nathan Bedford Forrest.* Lanham, MD: Rowman and Littlefield, 2005.

Blight, David W. *Race and Reunion: The Civil War in American Memory.* Cambridge, MA: Belknap Press of Harvard University Press, 2001.

Brady, Lisa M. *War upon the Land: Military Strategy and the Transformation of Southern Landscapes during the American Civil War.* Athens: University of Georgia Press, 2012.

Bresnahan, James C., ed. *Revisioning the Civil War: Historians on Counter-Factual Scenarios.* Jefferson, NC: McFarland, 2006.

Browning, Robert M., Jr. *Forrest: The Confederacy's Relentless Warrior.* Washington, DC: Brassey's, 2004.

Bushong, Millard Kessler. *Old Jube: A Biography of General Jubal A. Early.* Boyce, VA: Carr Publishing, 1955.

Coddington, Edwin B. *The Gettysburg Campaign: A Study in Command.* New York: Scribner's, 1968.

Collins, Darrell L. *Major General Robert E. Rodes of the Army of Northern Virginia.* El Dorado, CA: Savas Beatie, 2008.

Cooling, Benjamin Franklin. *Counter-Thrust: From the Peninsula to the Antietam.* Lincoln: University of Nebraska Press, 2007.

———. *The Day Lincoln Was Almost Shot: the Fort Stevens Story.* Lanham, MD: Scarecrow Press, 2013.

———. *Jubal Early's Raid on Washington.* Tuscaloosa: University of Alabama Press, 2007.

———. *Monocacy: The Battle That Saved Washington.* Shippensburg, PA: White Mane Publishing, 2000.

———. *Symbol, Sword and Shield; Defending Washinghyon During the Civil War.* Shippensburg, PA: White Mane Publishing, 1991.

Cooling, Benjamin Franklin, and Walton B. Owen. *Mr. Lincoln's Forts; A Guide to the Civil War Defenses of Washington*. Lanham, MD: Scarecrow Press, 2010.

Dabney, R. L. *Life and Campaigns of Lieut.-Gen. Thomas J. Jackson* New York: Blelock, 1866.

Davis, William C. *Breckinridge: Statesman, Soldier, Symbol*. Baton Rouge: Louisiana State University Press, 1974.

Duncan, Richard R. *Lee's Endangered Left: The Civil War in Western Virginia, Spring of 1864*. Baton Rouge: Louisiana State University Press, 1998.

Early, Jubal A. *The Heritage of the South: A History of the Introduction of Slavery, Its Establishment from Colonial Times and Final Effect upon the Politics of the United States*. Lynchburg, VA: Press of Brown-Morrison, 1915.

Faust, Drew Gilpin. *This Republic of Suffering: Death and the American Civil War*. New York: Random House, 2008.

Fishel, Edwin C. *The Secret War for the Union: The Untold Story of Military Intelligence in the Civil War*. Boston: Houghton Mifflin, 1996.

Flood, Charles Bracelen. *1864: Lincoln at the Gates of History*. New York: Simon and Schuster, 2009.

Foster, Gaines M. *Ghosts of the Confederacy: Defeat, the Lost Cause, and the Emergence of the New South, 1865–1913*. New York: Oxford University Press, 1987.

Freeman, Douglas Southall. *Lee's Lieutenants: A Study in Command*. 3 vols. New York: C. Scribner's Sons, 1942–1944.

Gallagher, Gary W. *Becoming Confederates: Paths to a New National Loyalty*. Athens: University of Georgia Press, 2013.

———, ed. *The Shenandoah Valley Campaign of 1864*. Chapel Hill: University of North Carolina Press, 2006.

Goodwin, Doris Kearns. *Team of Rivals: The Political Genius of Abraham Lincoln*. New York: Simon and Schuster, 2005.

Gordon, Lesley J., and John C. Inscoe, eds. *Inside the Confederate Nation: Essays in Honor of Emory M. Thomas*. Baton Rouge: Louisiana State University Press, 2005.

Greater Chambersburg Chamber of Commerce. *Southern Revenge! Civil War History of Chambersburg, Pennsylvania*. Chambersburg, PA: Greater Chambersburg Chamber of Commerce, 1989.

Gordon, Paul and Rita. *A Playground of the Civil War; Frederick County Maryland*. Frederick, MD: The Heritage Partnership, 1994.

Hale, Laura Virginia. *Four Valiant Years in the Lower Shenandoah Valley, 1861–1865*. Strasburg, VA: Shenandoah Publishing House, 1968.

Harris, William C. *Lincoln's Last Months*. Cambridge, MA: Belknap Press of Harvard University Press, 2004.

Harsh, Joseph L. *Confederate Tide Rising: Robert E. Lee and the Making of Southern Strategy, 1861–1862*. Kent, OH: Kent State University Press, 1998.

———. *Sounding the Shallows: A Confederate Companion for the Maryland Campaign of 1862*. Kent, OH: Kent State University Press, 2000.

———. *Taken at the Flood: Robert E. Lee and Confederate Strategy in the Maryland Campaign of 1862*. Kent, OH: Kent State University Press, 1999.

Hasselberger, Fritz. *Confederate Retaliation: McCausland's 1864 Raid*. Shippensburg, PA: Burd Street Press, 2000.

Irwin, Richard B. *History of the Nineteenth Army Corps*. New York: G. P. Putnam's Sons, 1892.

Janney, Caroline E. *Remembering the Civil War: Reunion and the Limits of Reconciliation*. Chapel Hill: University of North Carolina Press, 2013.

Jones, Virgil Carrington. *Ranger Mosby*. Chapel Hill: University of North Carolina Press, 1944.

Judge, Joseph. *Season of Fire; The Confederate Strike on Washington*. Berryville, VA: Rockbridge Publishing Company, 1994.

Kennedy, Frances H., ed. *The Civil War Battlefield Guide*. 2nd ed. Boston: Houghton Mifflin, 1998.

Leech, Margaret. *Reveille in Washington, 1860–1865*. New York: Harper and Brothers, 1941.

Leepson, Marc. *Desperate Engagement; How a Little-Known Civil War Battle Saved Washington, D.C., and Changed American History*. New York: St. Martin's Press, 2007.

Levine, Bruce. *The Fall of the House of Dixie: The Civil War and the Social Revolution That Transformed the South*. New York: Random House, 2013.

Lewis, David J. *Frederick War Claim: Evidence and Argument in Support of Bill to Refund Ransom Paid by the Town of Frederick during the Civil War, to Save Said Town, and the Union Military Supplies from Destruction*. Frederick, MD: Historical Society of Frederick County, 1912.

Lewis, Thomas A. *The Guns of Cedar Creek*. New York: Harper and Row, 1988.

Lewis, Thomas A., and the editors of Time-Life Books. *The Shenandoah in Flames: The Valley Campaign of 1864*. Alexandria, VA: Time-Life Books, 1987.

Long, David E. *The Jewel of Liberty: Abraham Lincoln's Re-Election and the End of Slavery*. Mechanicsburg, PA: Stackpole Books, 1994.

Mahon, Michael G. *The Shenandoah Valley, 1861–1865: The Destruction of the Granary of the Confederacy*. Mechanicsburg, PA: Stackpole Books, 1999.

Martin, Samuel J. *The Road to Glory: Confederate General Richard S. Ewell*. Indianapolis: Guild Press of Indiana, 1991.

McCurry, Stephanie. *Confederate Reckoning: Power and Politics in the Civil War South*. Cambridge, MA: Harvard University Press, 2010.

McMurry, Richard M. *The Fourth Battle of Winchester: Toward a New Civil War Paradigm*. Kent, OH: Kent State University Press, 2002.

Murfin, James V. *The Gleam of Bayonets: The Battle of Antietam and the Maryland Campaign of 1862*. New York: T. Yoseloff, 1965.

Neff, John R. *Honoring the Civil War Dead: Commemoration and the Problem of Reconciliation*. Lawrence: University Press of Kansas, 2005.

Nelson, Megan Kate. *Ruin Nation: Destruction and the American Civil War*. Athens: University of Georgia Press, 2012.

Nye, Wilbur S. *Here Come the Rebels!* Baton Rouge: Louisiana State University Press, 1965.

Osborne, Charles C. *Jubal: The Life and Times of General Jubal A. Early, CSA, Defender of the Lost Cause*. Chapel Hill, NC: Algonquin Books of Chapel Hill, 1992.

Palmer, Michael A. *Lee Moves North: Robert E. Lee on the Offensive from Antietam to Gettysburg to Bristoe Station*. New York: John Wiley and Sons, 1998.

Patchan, Scott C. *The Last Battle of Winchester: Phil Sheridan, Jubal Early, and the Shenandoah Valley Campaign, August 7–September 19, 1864*. El Dorado Hills, CA: Savas Beatie, 2013.

———. *Shenandoah Summer: The 1864 Valley Campaign*. Lincoln: University of Nebraska Press, 2007.

Phanz, Donald C. *Richard S. Ewell: A Soldier's Life*. Chapel Hill: University of North Carolina Press, 1998.

Phillips, Edward H. *The Shenandoah Valley in 1864: An Episode in the History of Warfare*. Charleston, SC: Military College of South Caolina, 1965.

Phillips, Jason. *Diehard Rebels: The Confederate Culture of Invincibility*. Athens: University of Georgia Press, 2007.

Piston, William Garrett. *Lee's Tarnished Lieutenant: James Longstreet and His Place in Southern History*. Athens: University of Georgia Press, 1987.

Pond, George E. *The Shenandoah Valley in 1864*. New York: C. Scribner's Sons, 1883.

Ray, Fred L. *Shock Troops of the Confederacy: The Sharpshooter Battalions of the Army of Northern Virginia*. Asheville, NC: CFS Press, 2006.

Royster, Charles. *The Destructive War: William Tecumseh Sherman, Stonewall Jackson, and the Americans*. New York: Knopf, 1991.

Scharf, J. Thomas. *History of Western Maryland: Being a History of Frederick, Montgomery, Carroll, Washington, Allegany, and Garrett Counties from the Earliest Period to the Present Day, Including Biographical Sketches of Their Representative Men*. 2 vols. Baltimore: Regional Publishing, 1968.

Sears, Stephen W. *Landscape Turned Red: The Battle of Antietam*. New York: Ticknor and Fields, 1983.

Simpson, John A. *S. A. Cunningham and the Confederate Heritage*. Athens: University of Georgia Press, 1994.

Smith, Andrew F. *Starving the South: How the North Won the Civil War*. New York: St. Martin's Press, 2011.

Spaulding, Brett W. *Last Chance for Victory: Jubal Early's 1864 Maryland Invasion*. Gettysburg, PA: Thomas Publications, 2010.

Spielvogel, J. Christian. *Interpreting Sacred Ground: The Rhetoric of National Civil War Parks and Battlefields*. Tuscaloosa: University of Alabama Press, 2013.

Stackpole, Edward J. *From Cedar Mountain to Antietam: August–September, 1862*. Harrisburg, PA: Stackpole Boohs, 1959.

Stephens, Gail. *Shadow of Shiloh: Major General Lew Wallace in the Civil War*. Indianapolis: Indiana Historical Society Press, 2010.

Sternhell, Yael A. *Routes of War: The World of Movement in the Confederate South*. Cambridge, MA: Harvard University Press, 2012.

Stoker, Donald. *The Grand Design: Strategy and the U.S. Civil War*. New York: Oxford University Press, 2010.

Tanner, Robert G. *Retreat to Victory? Confederate Strategy Reconsidered*. Wilmington, DE: Scholarly Resources, 2001.

Taylor, Paul. *He Hath Loosed the Fateful Lightning: The Battle of Ox Hill (Chantilly), September 1, 1862*. Shippensburg, PA: White Mane Books, 2003.

Thomas, Emory M. *The Confederacy as a Revolutionary Experience*. Columbia: University of South Carolina Press, 1991.

Towns, W. Stuart. *Enduring Legacy: Rhetoric and Ritual of the Lost Cause*. Tuscaloosa: University of Alabama Press, 2012.

Vandiver, Frank. *Jubal's Raid: General Early's Famous Attack on Washington in 1864*. New York: McGraw-Hill, 1960.

Walker, Gary C. *Hunter's Fiery Raid through Virginia Valleys*. Gretna, LA: Pelican, 2008.

Waugh, John C. *Reelecting Lincoln: The Battle for the 1864 Presidency*. New York: Crown, 1997.

Welker, David A. *Tempest at Ox Hill: The Battle of Chantilly*. New York: Da Capo Press, 2002.

Wert, Jeffrey D. *From Winchester to Cedar Creek: The Shenandoah Campaign of 1864*. New York: Simon and Schuster, 1987.

Whitmore, Nancy F., and Timothy Cannon. *Frederick: A Pictorial History*. Norfolk, VA: Donning, 1981.

Williams, Kenneth P. *Lincoln Finds a General: A Military Study of the Civil War*. New York: Macmillan, 1949–1959.

Williams, T. Harry. *The Military Leadership of the North and South* [Harmon Lecture Number Two]. Colorado Springs, CO: U.S. Air Force Academy, 1960.

———. *P. G. T. Beauregard: Napoleon in Gray*. Baton Rouge: Louisiana State University Press, 1955.

Wilson, Charles Reagan. *Baptized in Blood: The Religion of the Lost Cause, 1865–1920*. Athens: University of Georgia Press, 2009.

Winkle, Kenneth J. *Lincoln's Citadel: The Civil War in Washington, DC*. New York: W. W. Norton, 2013.

Wood, W. J. *Civil War Generalship: The Art of Command*. Westport, CT: Greenwood, 1997.

Woodworth, Steven E., ed. *Grant's Lieutenants: From Chattanooga to Appomattox*. Lawrence: University Press of Kansas, 2008.

Worthington, Glenn H. *Fighting For Time or The Battle That Saved Washington and Mayhap the Union*. Baltimore: Day Printing Company, 1932.

Articles and Essays

Blair, William Alan. "Early, Jubal." In *The Encyclopedia of the Confederacy*, edited by Richard N. Current. New York: Simon and Schuster, 1993.

"Burning of the Blair House," Confederate Veteran, volume 19, (July 1911), 336.

Cooling, Benjamin Franklin. "Chasing 'Old Jube': David Hunter, Lewis Wallace, and Horatio Wright." In *Grant's Lieutenants: From Chattanooga to Appomattox*, edited by Steven E. Woodworth, 133–54. Lawrence: University Press of Kansas, 2008.

Delaplaine, Edward S. "General Early's Levy on Frederick." In *To Commemorate the One Hundredth Anniversary of the Battle of Monocacy: "The Battle That Saved Washington,"* 42–55. Frederick, MD: Frederick Civil War Centennial, 1964.

Feis, William B. "'Grant's Relief Man': Edward O. C. Ord." In *Grant's Lieutenants: From Chattanooga to Appomattox*, edited by Steven E. Woodworth, 173–94. Lawrence: University Press of Kansas, 2008.

Early, Jubal. "The Advance of Washington in 1864," 310-311. Southern Historical Society Papers, volume 9.

———, "The Raid on Washing Genl. Early Again Tells His Story." New York Times, August 6, 1881.

Gallagher, Gary W. "From Antebellum Unionist to Lost Cause Warrior: The Personal Journey of Jubal A. Early." In *New Perspectives on the Civil War: Myths and Realities of the National Conflict*, edited by John Y. Simon and Michael E. Stevens, 93–118. Madison, WI: Madison House, 1998.

———. "Jubal Early vs. Stonewall Jackson," *Columbiad* 1 (Spring 1997), 20–33.

"General Jubal Anderson Early 1816–1894: 'Lee's Bad Old Man,'" http://www.jubalearly.org/jubal.html.

Green, Alvin. "Burning of the Blair House." National Tribune, August 16, 1900.

Hess, Earl J. "Franz Sigel." In *Grant's Lieutenants: From Chattanooga to Appomattox*, edited by Steven E. Woodworth, 85–103. Lawrence: University Press of Kansas, 2008.

Nash, Steven E. "'In the Right Place and at the Right Time': Philip H. Sheridan." In *Grant's Lieutenants: From Chattanooga to Appomattox*, edited by Steven E. Woodworth, 155–71. Lawrence: University Press of Kansas, 2008.

Power, J. Tracy. "Jubal A. Early (1816–1894)." *Encyclopedia Virginia.* http://www.encyclopediavirginia.org/Early_Jubal_A_1816-1894.

Schott, Thomas E. "Jubal Early: Confederate in the Attic." In *Lee and His Generals: Essays in Honor of T. Harry Williams*, edited by Lawrence Lee Hewitt and Thomas E. Shott, 229–50. Knoxville: University of Tennessee Press, 2012.

Seilheimer, George O. "The Historical Basis of Whittier's 'Barbara Fritchie.'" In *Battles and Leaders of the Civil War; Being for the Most Part Contributions by Union and Confederate Officers*, edited by R. U. Johnson and C. C. Buel. Vol. II, 618–19. New York: Century Company, 1887.

Silber, Nina. "When Charles Francis Adams Met Robert E. Lee: A Southern Gentleman in History and Memory." In *Inside the Confederate Nation: Essays in Honor of Emory M. Thomas*, edited by Lesley J. Gordon and John C. Inscoe, 349–60. Baton Rouge: Louisiana State University Press, 2005.

NOTES

PREFACE

1. T. Harry Williams, *The Military Leadership of the North and the South* [Harmon Memorial Lecture, No. 2] (Colorado Springs, CO: U.S. Air Force Academy, 1960), 16.

2. Matt Atkinson and Brad Gottfried, "Surveying the Experts," in *Revisioning the Civil War: Historians on Counter-Factual Scenarios*, ed. James C. Bresnahan (Jefferson, NC: McFarland, 2006), 221–22.

3. See Paul Ashdown and Edward Caudill, *The Myth of Nathan Bedford Forrest* (Lanham, MD: Rowman & Littlefield, 2005).

I. MOLDING A PIEDMONT SOLDIER, LAWYER/RELUCTANT SECESSIONIST

1. Thomas E. Schott, "Jubal Early: Confederate in the Attic," in Lawrence Lee Hewitt and Thomas E. Schott, editors. *Lee and His Generals* (Knoxville: University of Tennessee Press, 2012), p. 230; Jubal Anderson Early, *Narrative of the War between the States* (Philadelphia: J. B. Lippincott, 1912), *Autobiographical Sketch* n.p.; Millard Kessler Bushong, *Old Jube: A Biography of General Jubal A. Early* (Boyce, VA: Carr Publishing, 1955), chap. 1; and Charles C. Osborne, *Jubal: The Life and Times of General Jubal A. Early, CSA, Defender of the Lost Cause* (Chapel Hill, NC: Algonquin Books of Chapel Hill, 1992), chap. 1, 475.

2. See various letters in 1833 from family to Early, Folder Correspondence 1847–48, 1861, Box 16, Jubal Early Papers, Manuscript Division, Library of Congress, Washington, DC, hereinafter cited LC.

3. Osborne, *Jubal*, citing Letter, Jubal A. Early to his father, November 8, 1835, volume 1, Jubal Early Papers, LC; Edward J. Stackpole, *From Cedar Mountain to Antietam, August–September, 1862* (Harrisburg, PA: Stackpole, 1959), 100.

4. Gary W. Gallagher, *Becoming Confederates: Paths to a New National Loyalty* (Athens: University of Georgia Press, 2013), 60–61.

5. Early, *Autobiographical Sketch and Narrative*, "autobiographical sketch," n.p.; Bushong, *Old Jube*, 16–19; Osborne, *Jubal*, 13, 19–21.

6. Early, *Autobiographical Sketch and Narrative*, "autobiographical sketch," n.p.; Bushong, *Old Jube*, 19–21; Osborne, *Jubal*, 22–25.

7. Early, *Autobiographical Sketch and Narrative*, "autobiographical sketch," n.p.; Bushong, *Old Jube*, 22–23; Osborne, *Jubal*, 25–26; Gallagher, *Becoming Confederates*, 61.

8. Early, *Autobiographical Sketch and Narrative*, "autobiographical sketch," n.p.; Bushong, *Old Jube*, 22–24; Osborne, *Jubal*, 26–30.

9. Early, *Autobiographical Sketch and Narrative*, "autobiographical sketch," n.p.; Bushong, *Old Jube*, 23–24, based on Early Scrapbook, Early Papers, LC.

10. Early, *Autobiographical Sketch and Narrative*, "autobiographical sketch," n.p.

11. Early's life in this period can be traced in his correspondence, for example with L. Woods, November 13, 1838, and April 22, 1839, Folder, Correspondence 1847–1848, 1861, Box 16, Early Papers, LC.

12. Early, *Autobiographical Sketch and Narrative*, "autobiographical sketch," n.p.; Bushong, *Old Jube*, 24; Osborne, *Jubal*, 31–33.

13. Early, *Autobiographical Sketch and Narrative* , "autobiographical sketch," n.p.; for a comprehensive enunciation of Early's passage in this period based on long study, see Gallagher, *Becoming Confederates*, 65–74, based largely on his essay, "From Antebellum Unionist to Lost Cause Warrior: The Personal Journey of Jubal A. Early," in *New Perspectives on the Civil War: Myths and Realities of the National Conflict*, ed. John Y. Simon and Michael E. Stevens (Madison, WI: Madison House, 1998), 93–118.

14. Gallagher, *Becoming Confederates*, 64–65.

15. Osborne, *Jubal*, 39, citing George H. Reese, ed., *Proceedings of the Virginia State Convention of 1861* (Richmond: Virginia State Library, 1965), 1:103, 152.

16. See Osborne, *Jubal*, 41–46; Bushong, *Old Jube*, 26–33.

17. Bushong, *Old Jube*, 32–34, citing *Richmond Examiner*, April 23, 1861, and April 25, 1861.

18. Bushong, *Old Jube*, 33–35, citing *Richmond Enquirer*, April 18, 1861.

19. Gallagher, *Becoming Confederates*, 57, 67–71.

20. Gallagher, *Becoming Confederates*, 72–73.

21. Osborne, *Jubal*, 52, citing Reese, *Proceedings*, 4:362; Thomas E. Schott, "Jubal Early: Confederate in the Attic," in *Lee and His Generals: Essays in Honor of T. Harry Williams*, ed. Lawrence Lee Hewitt and Thomas E. Schott (Knoxville: University of Tennessee Press, 2012), 231; John Goode, *Recollections of a Lifetime* (New York: Neale Publishing, 1906), 60; Early, *Autobiographical Sketch*, 1.

22. Quoted in Gallagher, *Becoming Confederates*, 68.

2. PROVING HIMSELF

1. Early's career may be adequately followed in his *Autobiographical Sketch and Narrative of the War between the States*, (Philadelphia: J. B. Lippincott, 1912); Millard Kessler Bushong, *Old Jube: A Biography of General Jubal A. Early* (Boyce, VA: Carr Publishing, 1955); Charles C. Osborne, *Jubal: The Life and Times of General Jubal A. Early, CSA, Defender of the Lost Cause* (Chapel Hill, NC: Algonquin Books of Chapel Hill, 1992). His comment about niggardly [tardy] promotion is quoted by Gary W. Gallagher, *Becoming Confederates: Paths to a New National Loyalty* (Athens: University of Georgia Press, 2013), 62, citing a letter from Jubal A. Early to Richard S. Ewell (ca. April 1863), James A. Walker Compiled Service Record, Microfilm Roll 257, National Archives and Records Service (NARS), Washington, DC.

2. U.S. War Department, *The War of the Rebellion: A Compilation of the Official Records of the Union and Confederate Armies* (Washington, DC: Government Printing Office, 1880–1901), 1(2):554–58 (especially 557), 806, 822, 835, 851, 858, 860, 883, 905–6, 912, hereinafter cited as *ORA*, with appropriate series, volume, part, and page numbers.

3. *ORA*, 1(2):906.

4. Osborne, *Jubal*, 59–60; Early, *Autobiographical Sketch and Narrative*, chap. 5; Edwin C. Fishel, *The Secret War for the Union: The Untold Story of Military Intelligence in the Civil War* (Boston: Houghton Mifflin, 1996), 34.

5. *ORA*, 1(2):557–58.

6. Osborne, *Jubal*, 59–60, 73–75; Early, *Autobiographical Sketch and Narrative*, 47–52.

7. General Orders Number 7, March 15, 1862, Box 16, Jubal Early Papers, Library of Congress; Early, *Autobiographical Sketch and Narrative*, 53–55; Osborne, *Jubal*, 71.

8. Ibid.

9. Osborne, *Jubal*, chap. 6; *ORA*, 1(11, pt. 1):606–9 (also 406, 541, 565, 567, 602–4), and 1(11, pt. 2):611–13; Bushong, *Old Jube*, 59–63; Early, *Autobiographical Sketch and Narrative*, 75–77.

10. *ORA*, 1(11, pt. 3):664–65; Bushong, *Old Jube*, 69–80; Osborne, *Jubal*, 90–99, 102–7; Early, *Autobiographical Sketch and Narrative*, 99, 100–2, 106–10.

11. *ORA*, 1(11, pt. 2):611–13, and 1(12, pt. 2):706–7, 712, 715–16. For background and details for Early in the Northern Virginia campaign, see, for instance, Benjamin Franklin Cooling, *Counter-Thrust: From the Peninsula to the Antietam* (Lincoln: University of Nebraska Press, 2007), chaps. 1–5; Edward J. Stackpole, *From Cedar Mountain to Antietam* (Harrisburg, PA: Stackpole, 1959), 36, 59, 64, 67, 70, 97–99, 172–73, 190–91; Joseph L. Harsh, *Confederate Tide Rising: Robert E. Lee and the Making of Southern Strategy, 1861–1862* (Kent, OH: Kent State University Press, 1998), 131, 149; David A. Welker, *Tempest at Ox Hill: The Battle of Chantilly* (New York: Da Capo Press, 2002), 158–62; Paul Taylor, *He Hath Loosed the Fateful Lightning: The Battle of Ox Hill (Chantilly), September 1, 1862* (Shippensburg, PA: White Mane Books, 2003), 63, 68, 72, 84.

12. Early, *Autobiographical Sketch and Narrative*, 134–35; Osborne, *Jubal*, 117. On Lee's missed opportunity, see Michael A. Palmer, *Lee Moves North: Robert E. Lee on the Offensive from Antietam to Gettysburg to Bristoe Station* (New York: John Wiley and Sons, 1998), 5–14.

13. Osborne, *Jubal*, 119, citing Henry Kyd Douglas, *I Rode with Stonewall, Being Chiefly the War Experiences of the Youngest Member of Jackson's Staff from the John Brown Raid to the Hanging of Mrs. Surratt* (Chapel Hill: University of North Carolina Press, 1940), 152. See also Early, *Autobiographical Sketch and Narrative*, chap. 9; George O. Seilheimer, "The Historical Basis of Whittier's 'Barbara Fritchie,'" in *Battles and Leaders of the Civil War: Being for the Most Part Contributions by Union and Confederate Officers*, ed. R. U. Johnson and C. C. Buel. (New York: Century, 1887), 2:618; Joseph L. Harsh, *Taken at the Flood: Robert E. Lee and Confederate Strategy in the Maryland Campaign of 1862* (Kent, OH: Kent State University Press, 1999), 171–72.

14. Early, *Autobiographical Sketch and Narrative*, chap. 16, 117–29. Background and details for Early in the Maryland Campaign can be followed in Cooling, *Counter-Thrust*, chaps. 1–9; Harsh, *Taken at the Flood*, 42, 171–72, 321, 328, 360, 373–74, 377, 387–389, 393, 429, 457; Joseph L. Harsh, *Sounding the Shallows: A Confederate Companion for the Maryland Campaign of*

1862 (Kent, OH: Kent State University Press, 2000), 38, 64–65, 145, 180, 208, 213, 219. Details of Antietam may be found in James V. Murfin, *The Gleam of Bayonets: The Battle of Antietam and the Maryland Campaign of 1862* (New York: T. Yoseloff, 1965), 214, 231, 237–40, 293; Stephen W. Sears, *Landscape Turned Red: The Battle of Antietam* (New York: Ticknor and Fields, 1983), 214, 219–20, 224–26.

15. Bushong, *Old Jube*, 106–7, citing Daniel Harvey Hill Papers, numbers 176–81, Virginia State Library, Richmond; *Confederate Veteran*, vol. 13, no. 10, 459; Robert N. Stiles, *Four Years under Marse Robert* (New York: Neale Publishing, 1903), 190; George Greer diary, November 27, 1862, U.S. Army Military Heritage Center, Carlisle, PA.

16. Early, *Autobiographical Sketch and Narrative,* 175–76.

17. Bushong, *Old Jube*, 114, citing a letter from Jubal A. Early to D. H. Hill, August 2, 1885, Hill Papers, 176–81; Early, *Autobiographical Sketch and Narrative*, 171–78, 190–91; *ORA*, 1(21):647, 663–67.

18. *ORA*, 1(21):1099; Bushong, *Old Jube*, 115–16; Osborne, *Jubal*, 144-145.

19. *ORA*, 1(25, pt. 2):803, 810, 811; Douglas Southall Freeman, *Lee's Lieutenants: A Study in Command; vol. 2, Cedar Mountain to Chancellorsville* (New York: Charles Scribners, 1949), chapter XXXV.

20. See Fishel, *Secret War*, 392–94.

21. Osborne, *Jubal*, 146–57; Bushong, *Old Jube*, chap. 1.

22. *ORA*, 1(25, Part 2):769–70, 860–61.

23. Freeman, *Lee's Lieutenants*, vol. 2), chap. 35, 604–5, 626, 653–54, 665; Osborne, *Jubal*, 157; Fishel, *Secret War*, 395; *ORA*, 1(25, pt. 1):1000–3.

24. Freeman, *Lee's Lieutenants*, vol. 2, xxviii.

3. SEARCHING FOR STONEWALL'S GHOST

1. U.S. War Department, *War of the Rebellion: Official Records of the Union and Confederate Armies* (Washington, DC: Government Printing Office, 1880–1901), 1(25, pt. 2):814, 840, hereinafter cited as *ORA*, with appropriate series, volume, part, and page numbers; Jubal A. Early, *Autobiographical Sketch and Narrative of the War between the States* (Philadelphia: J. B. Lippincott, 1912), 237–38.

2. Millard Kessler Bushong, *Old Jube: A Biography of General Jubal A. Early* (Boyce, VA: Carr Publishing, 1955), chaps. 13–17; Charles C. Osborne, *Jubal: The Life and Times of General Jubal A. Early, CSA, Defender of the Lost Cause* (Chapel Hill, NC: Algonquin Books of Chapel Hill, 1992), chaps. 11–16; Early, *Autobiographical Sketch and Narrative*, chaps. 11–15.

3. Early, *Autobiographical Sketch*, 236, 249–50; Edwin B. Coddington, *The Gettysburg Campaign: A Study in Command* (New York: Charles Scribner's, 1968), 86–89; *ORA*, 1(27, pt. 3):895.

4. Coddington, *Gettysburg Campaign*, 166–68; Wilbur S. Nye, *Here Come the Rebels!* (Baton Rouge: Louisiana State University Press, 1965), 144–45.

5. Early, *Autobiographical Sketch*, 254–56; Nye, *Here Come the Rebels!* 294–95; Letter from Early to J. Fraise Richard, May 7, 1886, Jubal Early Correspondence, Library of Congress.

6. Early, *Autobiographical Sketch and Narrative*, 259–61, 264; Nye, *Here Come the Rebels!* 285–94.

7. Douglas Southall Freeman, *Lee's Lieutenants: A Study in Command*, vol. 3: chap. 7, *Gettysburg to Appomattox* (New York: C. Scribner's Sons, 1944), 28–38.

8. Freeman, *Lee's Lieutenants*, vol. 3, chap. 7; Michael A. Palmer, *Lee Moves North: Robert E. Lee on the Offensive from Antietam to Gettysburg to Bristoe Station* (New York: John Wiley and Sons, 1998), chap. 2.

9. See the colorful recounting by Freeman, *Lee's Lieutenants*, vol. 3: 93–99; Ewell's report, *ORA*, 1(27, pt. 2):445–46, and Early's, 469–70.

10. Freeman, *Lee's Lieutenants*, vol. 3: 101–5; Palmer, *Lee Moves North*, 81–84.

11. Henry Kyd Douglas, *I Rode with Stonewall, Being Chiefly the War Experiences of the Youngest Member of Jackson's Staff from the John Brown Raid to the Hanging of Mrs. Surratt* (Chapel Hill: University of North Carolina Press, 1940), 247; Coddington, *Gettysburg Campaign*, 318–19.

12. Early, *Autobiographical Sketch and Narrative*, 271; Osborne, *Jubal*, 200–202; Bushong, *Old Jube*, 146–48; Kenneth P. Williams, *Lincoln Finds a General: A Military Study of the Civil War*, vol. 2 (New York: Macmillan, 1949–1959), 690–91; Edwin C. Fishel, *The Secret War for the Union: The Untold Story of Military Intelligence in the Civil War* (Boston: Houghton Mifflin, 1996), 522–25.

13. Freeman, *Lee's Lieutenants*, vol. 3: 176–78; Coddington, *Gettysburg Campaign*, 428–40, especially 440.

14. Early, *Autobiographical Sketch and Narrative*, 285–87, 302.

15. For Early's reports, see *ORA* 1(29, pt. 1):618–26. See also Lee's commentary and maps *ORA* 1(29, pt. 1):614–17 (Rappahannock Bridge) and 830–36 (Mine Run); Early, *Autobiographical Sketch*, chaps. 27, 38, and 49. See also Freeman, *Lee's Lieutenants*, vol. 3: 264; Osborne, *Jubal*, chap. 14; Bushong, *Old Jube*, chap. 15.

16. *ORA*, 1(29, pt. 1):835; Early, *Autobiographical Sketch and Narrative*, 319, 324–25.

17. Osborne, *Jubal*, 214.

18. *ORA*, 1(29, pt. 2):876; Bushong, *Old Jube*, chap. 16; Osborne, *Jubal*, chap. 15.

19. *ORA*, 1(29, pt. 1):969–73, 1(33):43–46.

20. Freeman, *Lee's Lieutenants*, vol. 3: 325–33.

21. Freeman, *Lee's Lieutenants*, vol. 3: 368–72. The absence of Early's customary after-action reports for the so-called Overland Campaign (from the Rapidan to the James) forces reliance on reports from Ewell, Gordon, Ramseur, and others. See *ORA*, 1(36, pt. 1):1069–89; Bushong, *Old Jube*, chap. 17, especially 173–78; Osborne, *Jubal*, chap. 16, especially 232–38.

22. *ORA*, 1(51, pt. 1):244–248, and 1(51, pt. 2):1012.

23. Freeman, *Lee's Lieutenants*, vol. 3: 373–74. For the Lee–Sorrel exchange, see G. Moxley Sorrel, *Recollections of a Confederate Staff Officer* (New York: Neale Publishing, 1905), 242, 247.

24. *ORA*, 1(36, pt. 1):96–97, 1(36, pt. 2):974, 1(36, pt. 3):846, 873; Bushong, *Old Jube*, 182.

4. JUBAL'S MOMENT OF TRUTH

1. Letter, Jefferson Davis to Jubal Early, December 23, 1878, Correspondence Folder—Early, "Washington can never be taken by our troops unless surprised when without a force to defend it," 1862–1869, 1878, 1884–1898, 1915, Box 16, Jubal Early Papers, Library of Congress, Washington, DC (LC). See also William C. Davis, *Breckinridge: Statesman, Soldier, Symbol* (Baton Rouge: Louisiana State University Press, 1974), 437–38.

2. Frances H. Kennedy, ed., *The Civil War Battlefield Guide*, 2nd ed. (Boston: Houghton Mifflin, 1998), 299–303. For a fuller account of Hunter's depredations, see Gary C. Walker, *Hunter's Fiery Raid through Virginia Valleys* (Gretna, LA: Pelican, 2008); Davis, *Breckinridge*, 409–41, especially 430–32; Clifford Dowdey and Louis H. Manarin, eds., *The Wartime Papers of R. E. Lee* (Boston: Little, Brown, 1961), 767–68.

3. Davis, *Breckinridge*, 438–41, especially n. 12.

4. U.S. War Department, *The War of the Rebellion: A Compilation of the Official Records of the Union and Confederate Armies* (Washington, DC: Government Printing Office, 1880–1901), 1(32, pt. 2):541–42, 566–67, hereinafter cited *ORA*, with appropriate series, volume, part, and page numbers; Benjamin Franklin Cooling, *Jubal Early's Raid on Washington* (Tuscaloosa: University of Alabama Press, 2007), chap. 1, especially 8–9.

5. Dowdey and Manarin, *Wartime Papers*, 777–79, 780, 781, 782–83.

6. *ORA*, 1(37, pt. 1):763.

7. Lynchburg is covered well in *ORA*, 1(37, pt. 1):9–160; Davis, *Breckinridge*, 441–42; Millard Kessler Bushong, *Old Jube: A Biography of Jubal A. Early* (Boyce, VA: Carr Publishing, 1955), chap. 18; Charles C. Osborne, *Jubal: The Life and Times of General Jubal A. Early, CSA, Defender of the Lost Cause* (Chapel Hill, NC: Algonquin Books of Chapel Hill, 1992), chap. 17; and Richard R. Duncan, *Lee's Endangered Left: The Civil War in Western Virginia, Spring of 1864* (Baton Rouge: Louisiana State University Press, 1998), chaps. 8–10. On Early's dispatches, see *ORA*, 1(37, pt. 1):761–66, and 1(51, pt. 2):1020.

8. *ORA*, 1(37, pt. 1):160, 766–67; Osborne, *Life and Times*, 258–59; Jubal A. Early, *Autobiographical Sketch and Narrative of the War between the States* (Philadelphia: J. B. Lippincott, 1912), chap. 37, especially 377–79; Douglas Southall Freeman, *Lee's Lieutenants: A Study in Command*, vol. 3, *Gettysburg to Appomattox* (New York: C. Scribner's Sons, 1944), 527; Scott C. Patchan, *Shenandoah Summer: The 1864 Valley Campaign* (Lincoln: University of Nebraska Press, 2007), 39.

9. *ORA*, 1(37, pt. 1):160, 766; Cooling, *Jubal Early's Raid*, 14–17; Osborne, *Jubal*, 261–63; Early, *Autobiographical Sketch and Narrative*, 380.

10. Jubal A. Early, *A Memoir of the Last Year of the War for Independence, in the Confederate States of America: Containing an Account of the Operations of His Commands in the Years 1864 and 1865* (Columbia: University of South Carolina Press, 2001), 42–43.

11. Cooling, *Jubal Early's Raid*, 18–23; Osborne, *Jubal*, 263–65; Dowdey and Manarin, *Wartime Papers*, 814–15.

12. *ORA*, 1(37, pt. 2):769.

13. Letter, Jubal Early to Robert E. Lee, June 28, 1864, CW 1—Civil War Collection, Huntington Library, San Marino, CA.

14. *ORA*, 1(37, pt. 2):766–67.

15. *ORA*, 1(37, pt. 2):762–63. On Kane, see Lynda Lasswell Crist, Mary Seaton Dix, and Kenneth H. Williams, eds., *The Papers of Jefferson Davis* (Baton Rouge: Louisiana State University Press, 1997), 9:285; Lynda Lasswell Crist, Kenneth H. Williams, and Peggy L. Dillard, eds., *The Papers of Jefferson Davis* (Baton Rouge: Louisiana State University Press, 1999), 10:86, 285.

16. Kennedy, *Civil War Battlefield Guide*, 304; Cooling, *Jubal Early's Raid*, 17–23, 25; Early, *Autobiographical Sketch and Narrative* , 381–82; Davis, *Breckinridge*, 442–44, especially n. 25.

17. Early, *Autobiographical Sketch and Narrative*, 371; Dowdey and Manarin, *Wartime Papers*, 807, 811; Letter, Jubal Early to Robert E. Lee, June 28, 1864, Civil War Collection, Huntington Library, San Marino, CA.; Letter, Jubal Early to editor, *Richmond Sentinel*, and Correspondence of the *Baltimore Gazette*, December 14, 1874.

18. Dowdey and Manarin, *Wartime Papers*, 811; *ORA*, 1(37, pt. 1):769–70.

19. *ORA*, 1(51, pt. 2):1018–29; Cooling, *Jubal Early's Raid*, 22–24.

20. *ORA*, 1(37, pt. 1):695; Early, *Autobiographical Sketch and Narrative*, 382–383; Virgil Carrington Jones, *Ranger Mosby* (Chapel Hill: University of North Carolina Press, 1944), 185.

21. Letter, Jubal Early to Robert E. Lee, July 7, 1864, C-101, Civil War Collection, Huntington Library, San Marino, CA.

22. *ORA*, 1(37, pt. 2):591, 592; Cooling, *Jubal Early's Raid*, 27–29.

23. *ORA*, 1(37, pt. 2):58–60; Cooling, *Jubal Early's Raid*, 31–38.

24. *ORA*, 1(37, pt. 1):347; Cooling, *Jubal Early's Raid*, 40–41; Early, *Autobiographical Sketch and Narrative*, 383–85.

25. *ORA*, 1(37, pt. 2):65; Doris Kearns Goodwin, *Team of Rivals: The Political Genius of Abraham Lincoln* (New York: Simon and Schuster, 2005), especially chap. 24.

26. Materials ample for understanding Lincoln's and the nation's crucial summer include Charles Bracelen Flood, *1864: Lincoln at the Gates of History* (New York: Simon and Schuster, 2009); William C. Harris, *Lincoln's Last Months* (Cambridge, MA: Belknap Press of Harvard University Press, 2004), chap. 1; David E. Long, *The Jewel of Liberty: Abraham Lincoln's Re-Election and the End of Slavery* (Mechanicsburg, PA: Stackpole Books, 1994); John C. Waugh, *Reelecting Lincoln: The Battle for the 1864 Presidency* (New York: Crown, 1997).

27. Maryland General Highway Statewide Grid Map, Map No. C-9, January 1991, and Isaac Bond Map of Frederick County, 1858 (Baltimore, MD, 1858).

28. Edward S. Delaplaine, "General Early's Levy on Frederick," in *To Commemorate the One Hundredth Anniversary of the Battle of Monocacy: "The Battle That Saved Washington,"* ed. Frederick County Civil War Centennial (Frederick, MD: Frederick Civil War Centennial, 1964), 48–54; William Allan Journal, 29–30, Southern Historical Collection, University of North Carolina Library, Chapel Hill, NC; J. Thomas Scharf, *History of Western Maryland: Being a History of Frederick, Montgomery, Carroll, Washington, Allegany, and Garrett Counties from the Earliest Period to the Present Day, Including Biographical Sketches of Their Representative Men* (Baltimore: Regional Publishing, 1968), 288–89; Nancy F. Whitmore and Timothy Cannon, *Frederick: A Pictorial History* (Norfolk, VA: Donning, 1981), 56–57.

29. On Wallace, see Gail Stephens, *Shadow of Shiloh: Major General Lew Wallace in the Civil War* (Indianapolis: Indiana Historical Society Press, 2010), especially chaps. 15–17.

30. Paul and Rita Gordon, *A Playground of the Civil War; Frederick County Maryland* (Frederick, MD, Heritage Partnership, 1994), 167–75; William Allan, "Reminiscences" (unpublished manuscript) n. d., 29–30, South-

ern Historical Collection, University of North Carolina Library, Chapel Hill, North Carolina; Jedidiah Hotchkiss, *Make Me a Map of the Valley: The Civil War Journal of Stonewall Jackson's Topographer*, ed. Archie P. McDonald (Dallas: Southern Methodist University Press, 1973), 215; David J. Lewis, *Frederick War Claim: Evidence and Argument in Support of Bill to Refund Ransom Paid by the Town of Frederick, during the Civil War, to Save Said Town, and the Union Military Supplies from Destruction* (Frederick, MD: Historical Society of Frederick County, 1912), 3, 4, 18, 19, 20.

31. See B. Franklin Cooling, *Monocacy: The Battle That Saved Washington* (Shippensburg, PA: White Mane Publishing, 1997), for a detailed account of the battle, as well as Brett W. Spaulding's well-crafted *Last Chance for Victory: Jubal Early's 1864 Maryland Invasion* (Gettysburg, PA: Thomas Publications, 2010), chaps. 3–7. Early's account can be followed in his *Autobiographical Sketch*, 387–88; and *ORA*, 1(37, pt. 1):347–48, and Gordon's experience at 351–52.

32. *ORA*, 1(37, pt. 2):144–145; John B. Gordon, *Reminiscences of the Civil War* (New York: C. Scribner's Sons,1903), 309, 313.

33. *ORA*, 1(37, pt. 1):195; 1(37, pt. 2):127. For streets and roads at Fredrick and vicinity, see Isaac Bond's map of Frederick County (Baltimore, 1858).

34. *ORA*, 1(37, pt. 2):133–36, 138; 1(40, pt. 3):95.

35. Details can be followed in Cooling, *Jubal Early's Raid*, 102–3; Stephens, *Shadow of Shiloh*, 200.

36. De Sellum's story can be found in Cooling, *Jubal Early's Raid*, 303–4, based on John T. De Sellum, undated reminiscence, copy, 46–48, and "Farm Family in County Had 1,800 Troops as 'Guests,'" undated clipping, both Montgomery County Historical Society, Rockville, MD.

37. Details can be followed in Cooling, *Jubal Early's Raid*, as well as Benjamin Franklin Cooling III and Walton H. Owen II, *Mr. Lincoln's Forts: A Guide to the Civil War Defenses of Washington* (Lanham, MD: Scarecrow Press, 2010); and Benjamin Franklin Cooling III, *The Day Lincoln Was Almost Shot: The Fort Stevens Story* (Lanham, MD: Scarecrow Press, 2013). On Eckert, see *ORA*, 1(51, pt. 1):262.

38. On Early's vanguard, see Fred L. Ray, *Shock Troops of the Confederacy: The Sharpshooter Battalions of the Army of Northern Virginia* (Asheville, NC: CFS Press, 2006), 155, 380, n. 11.

39. Early, *Autobiographical Sketch and Narrative*, 389–90; *ORA* 1(37, pt. 1):348.

40. Gordon, *Reminiscences*, 314. For other conclusions, see, for instance, John Newton Opie, *A Rebel Cavalryman with Lee, Stuart, and Jackson* (Chicago: W. B. Conkey, 1899), 246; John H. Worsham, *One of Jackson's Foot Cavalry*, ed. James I. Robertson Jr. and Bell Irvin Wiley (Jackson, TN: McCowat-

Mercer Press, 1964), 242; George W. Nichols, *A Soldier's Story of His Regiment (61st Georgia): And Incidentally of the Lawton-Gordon-Evans Brigade, Army of Northern Virginia* (Tuscaloosa: University of Alabama Press, 2011), 173; James B. Sheeran, *Confederate Chaplain: A War Journal*, ed. Joseph T. Durkin (Milwaukee: Bruce Publishing, 1960), 95; Manly Wade Wellman, *Rebel Boast: First at Bethel—Last at Appomattox* (New York: Henry Holt, 1956), 172; Allan, "Reminiscences," 32.

41. Cooling, *Jubal Early's Raid*, 116–17, 122–23; Opie, *Rebel Cavalryman*, 246.

42. Margaret Leech, *Reveille in Washington, 1860–1865* (New York: Harper and Brothers, 1941), chap. 16; Roy P. Basler, Marion Delores Pratt, and Lloyd A. Dunlap, eds., *Collected Works: The Abraham Lincoln Association, Springfield, Illinois* (New Brunswick, NJ: Rutgers University Press, 1953), 7:437–38.

43. Curt Anders, *Henry Halleck's War: A Fresh Look at Lincoln's Controversial General-in-Chief* (Carmel: Guild Press of Indiana, 1999), 586–87; *ORA*, 1(37, pt. 2):155–58.

44. See details in Cooling, *Day Lincoln Was Almost Shot*, 132–41; Ray, *Shock Troops*, 155–61; Spaulding, *Last Chance*, chap. 10.

45. Early, *Autobiographical Sketch and Narrative*, 390–91; *ORA*, 1(37, pt. 1):348.

46. Henry Kyd Douglas, *I Rode with Stonewall, Being Chiefly the War Experiences of the Youngest Member of Jackson's Staff from the John Brown Raid to the Hanging of Mrs. Surratt* (Chapel Hill: University of North Carolina Press, 1940), 294–95; Davis, *Breckinridge*, 447–48.

47. Gordon, *Reminiscences*, 315–24, 314–18.

48. Virginia Jeans Laas, ed., *Wartime Washington: The Civil War Letters of Elizabeth Blair Lee* (Urbana: University of Illinois Press, 1991), 413, also 404–5.

49. Early, *Autobiographical Sketch and Narrative*, 392.

50. *ORA*, 1(37, pt. 1):347–49.

51. Cooling, *Day Lincoln Was Almost Shot*, chap. 8; Cooling, *Jubal Early's Raid*, chap. 5; Ray, *Shock Troops*, 161–69; Miscellaneous letters, C. C. V. Crawford to Lewis Cass White, September 17 and 25, 1900, and George D. Jewitt to Louis Cass White, May 9, 22, and 27, 1914, Lewis Cass White Collection, Sharon and Joseph Scopin, Darnestown, Maryland.

52. Douglas, *I Rode with Stonewall*, 205. For the afternoon's action that caused this exchange, see Cooling, *Day Lincoln Was Almost Shot*, chap. 8.

53. Letter, Vincent K. Tazlo to friends, July 13, 1864, author's collection.

54. See Early, *Autobiographical Sketch and Narrative*, 65–66.

55. On the controversial burning of "Falkland" and looting episodes, see Cooling, *Jubal Early's Raid*, 151–53; Letter, Jubal Early to Edmund Jennings Lee, September 26, 1872, Edmund Jennings Lee Papers, Duke University Library, Durham, NC; Jubal Early, "The Advance on Washington in 1864," *Southern Historical Society Papers*, 9, 310–11; Davis, *Breckinridge*, 449; "Burning of the Blair House," *Confederate Veteran*, vol. 19 (July 1911), 336; Alvin Green, "Burning of Blair Mansion," *National Tribune*, August 16, 1900.

56. Cooling, *Day Lincoln Was Almost Shot*, chap. 9; Cooling, *Jubal Early's Raid*, chap. 7; Patchan, *Shenandoah Summer*, chap. 2; Spaulding, *Last Chance*, 187–91; Early, *Autobiographical Sketch and Narrative*, 65.

57. *ORA*, 1(37, pt. 1):268–74; Cooling, *Jubal Early's Raid*, 188–220; Patchan, *Shenandoah Summer*, chap. 3; Jeffrey D. Wert, "The Snicker's Gap War," *Civil War Times Illustrated*, vol. 17 (July 1978), 38.

58. Gary W. Gallagher, ed., *Fighting for the Confederacy: The Personal Recollections of General Edward Porter Alexander* (Chapel Hill: University of North Carolina Press, 1989), 440; *ORA*, 1(37, pt. 1):349; Early, *Autobiographical Sketch and Narrative*, 395, especially footnote; Gordon, *Reminiscences*, 315–16.

59. James C. Bresnahan, ed., *Revisioning the Civil War: Historians on Counter-Factual Scenarios* (Jefferson, NC: McFarland, 2006), 193–94.

60. William Whitehurst Old Journal in Janet B. Hewett, ed., *Supplement to the Official Records of the Union and Confederate Armies* (Wilmington, NC: Broadfoot Publishing, 1994–1999), 7:274.

5. LEE'S FORLORN HOPE

1. Lucy Rebecca Buck, *Sad Earth, Sweet Heaven: The Diary of Lucy Rebecca Buck during the War between the States, Front Royal, Virginia, December 25, 1861–April 15, 1865*, ed. William P. Buck (Birmingham, AL: Cornerstone, 1973), 268.

2. For a concise summation of Early's accomplishments, see Charles C. Osborne, *Jubal: The Life and Times of General Jubal A. Early, CSA, Defender of the Lost Cause* (Chapel Hill, NC: Algonquin Books of Chapel Hill, 1992), 290–93, including Edward M. Daniel, ed., *Speeches and Orations of John Warwick Daniel* (Lynchburg, VA: J. P. Bell, 1911), 545–46.

3. James C. Bresnahan, ed., *Revisioning the Civil War; Historians on Counter-Factual Scenarios* (Jefferson, NC: McFarland, 2006), 194, 290–93.

4. Letter, Major Eugene Blackford to his brother, August 15, 1864, Gordon-Blackford Papers, Maryland Historical Society (MDHS), Baltimore.

5. Letter, Stephen D. Ramseur to his wife, July 15, 1864, Ramseur Papers, Southern Historical Collection, University of North Carolina (SHC/UNC) Library, Chapel Hill.

6. U.S. War Department, *The War of the Rebellion: A Compilation of the Official Records of the Union and Confederate Armies* (Washington, DC: Government Printing Office, 1880–1901), 1(37, pt. 1):349, 353–54, and 1(37, pt. 2):597, hereinafter cited *ORA*, with appropriate series, volume, part, and page numbers. Particularly insightful is Scott C. Patchan, *Shenandoah Summer: The 1864 Valley Campaign* (Lincoln: University of Nebraska Press, 2013), especially chaps. 6–13, 606 inter alia.

7. *ORA*, 1(37, pt. 2):604. On the upper Potomac situation, see Fritz Haselberger, *Confederate Retaliation: McCausland's 1864 Raid* (Shippensburg, PA: Burd Street Press, 2000), chap. 7; Millard Kessler Bushong, *Old Jube: A Biography of General Jubal A. Early* (Boyce, VA: Carr Publishing, 1955), chap. 22; Osborne, *Jubal*, chap. 20; Chambersburg Chamber of Commerce, *Southern Revenge! Civil War History of Chambersburg, Pennsylvania* (Chambersburg, PA: Greater Chambersburg Chamber of Commerce, 1989), 104–11.

8. *ORA*, 1(37, pt. 2):301, 329; Bushong, *Old Jube*, 218, citing Willis F. Evans, *History of Berkeley County, West Virginia* (Wheeling, WV, 1928), 263–64.

9. Greater Chambersburg Chamber of Commerce, *Southern Revenge*, 103–4; Patchan, *Shenandoah Summer*, 270, chap. 14.

10. Jubal A. Early, *Autobiographical Sketch and Narrative of the War between the States* (Philadelphia: J. B. Lippincott, 1912), 402–5; Osborne, *Jubal*, chap. 20; Bushong, *Old Jube*, chap. 22; Haselberger, *Confederate Retaliation*, chaps. 9–13; and Edward J. Stackpole, *Sheridan in the Shenandoah: Jubal Early's Nemesis* (Harrisburg, PA: Stackpole, 1961), 98–102.

11. Early, *Autobiographical Sketch and Narrative*, 404n; Osborne, *Jubal*, 309–10; Douglas Southall Freeman, *Lee's Lieutenants: A Study in Command*, vol. 3, *Gettysburg to Appomattox* (New York: C. Scribner's Sons, 1944), 573–76.

12. *ORA*, 1(43, pt. 2):861; Roy P. Basler, Marion Delores Pratt, and Lloyd A. Dunlap, eds., *Collected Works: The Abraham Lincoln Association, Springfield, Illinois* (New Brunswick, NJ: Rutgers University Press, 1953), 7:456n, 466n; Patchan, *Shenandoah Summer*, 311–12.

13. *ORA*, 1(37, pt. 2):194, 223, 259, 366, 374, 384, 385, 408, 414, 422; *New York Times*, July 11, 1864; *New York Herald*, July 28, 1864.

14. Early, *Autobiographical Sketch and Narrative*, 415; Freeman, *Lee's Lieutenants*, vol. 3: 576; Basler, Pratt, and Dunlap, *Collected Works*, 7:476; Patchan, *Shenandoah Summer*, 315–18.

15. Jeffrey D. Wert, *From Winchester to Cedar Creek; The Shenandoah Campaign of 1864.* (New York: Simon and Schuster, 1987), chap.3; Basler, Pratt, and Dunlap, *Collected Works*, 7:548.

16. Wert, chap. 3; Early, *Autobiographical Sketch and Narrative*, chap. 44.

17. *ORA*, 1(43, pt. 2):862; Early, *Autobiographical Sketch and Narrative*, 419; Wert, *From Winchester to Cedar Creek*, 44.

18. Early, *Autobiographical Sketch and Narrative*, 419; *ORA*, 1(43, pt. 2):83, 84.

19. Wert, *From Winchester to Cedar Creek*, 44–45; Patchan, *Shenandoah Summer*, 316–17; Freeman, *Lee's Lieutenants*, vol. 3: 576–77. In addition to Wert, pivotal studies of the Valley campaign include Stackpole, *Sheridan in the Shenandoah*, chaps. 9–14, and topographical engineer Jedediah Hotchkiss's end-of-year report, *ORA*, 1(43, pt. 1):appendix.

20. Scott C. Patchan, *The Last Battle of Winchester: Phil Sheridan, Jubal Early, and the Shenandoah Valley Campaign, August 7–September 19, 1864* (El Dorado Hills, CA: Savas Beatie, 2013) is the most thorough dissection of the battle.

21. Stackpole, *Sheridan in the Shenandoah*, chap. 9; *ORA*, 1(43, pt. 1):555; Wert, *From Winchester to Cedar Creek*, chaps. 4–6 (Early's quote, 109); Early, *Autobiographical Sketch and Narrative*, chap. 45, 425–26 especially; Patchan, *Last Battle of Winchester*, 429.

22. Patchan, *Last Battle of Winchester*, chap. 21; Wert, *From Winchester to Cedar Creek*, 106–28; William C. Davis, *Breckinridge: Statesman, Soldier, Symbol* (Baton Rouge: Louisiana State University Press, 1974), 454; Basler, Pratt, and Dunlap, *Collected Works*, 7:13.

23. *ORA*, 1(43, pt. 2):876, 878; Robert E. L. Krick, "A Stampeed of Stampeeds: The Confederate Disaster at Fisher's Hill," in *The Shenandoah Valley Campaign of 1864*, ed. Gary W. Gallagher (Chapel Hill: University of North Carolina Press, 2006), 161–99.

24. *ORA*, 1(43, pt. 2):877–81, 885, 891–92. The soldier ditty is quoted in Wert, *From Winchester to Cedar Creek*, 127; Early, *Autobiographical Sketch and Narrative*, chap. 46; Stackpole, *Sheridan in the Shenandoah*, chap. 10; Patchan, *Last Battle of Winchester*, 423–44.

25. *ORA*, 1(43, pt. 2):893–95.

26. *ORA*, 1(43, pt. 2):894–95.

27. *ORA*, 1(43, pt. 2):895–96.

28. *ORA*, 1(43, pt. 2):897.

29. *ORA*, 1(43, pt. 2):897–98.

30. Freeman, *Lee's Lieutenants*, vol. 3: 585–88; *ORA*, 1(43, pt. 1):557–59; *ORA*, 1(43, pt. 2):893.

31. See Jubal A. Early, *A Memoir of the Last Year of the War for Independence, in the Confederate States of America: Containing an Account of the Operations of His Commands in the Years 1864 and 1865* (Columbia: University of South Carolina Press, 2001), 121n; Bushong, *Old Jube*, 243–46; Osborne, *Jubal*, 352–54.

32. *ORA*, 1(43, pt. 1):558; *ORA*, 1(43, pt. 2):892–98; Freeman, *Lee's Lieutenants*, 587.

33. Andrew F. Smith, *Starving the South: How the North Won the Civil War* (New York: St. Martin's Press, 2011), 140–44, citing *Rockingham Register* as reprinted in the *Staunton Vindicator*, November 18, 1864.

34. Osborne, *Jubal*, 349–50; *ORA*, 1(43, pt. 2, 558); Edward H. Phillips, *The Shenandoah Valley in 1864: An Episode in the History of Warfare* (Charleston: The Citadel, the Military College of South Carolina, 1965), 19, 22–23; Gary W. Gallagher, "Two Generals and a Valley," in *The Shenandoah Valley Campaign of 1864*, ed. Gary W. Gallagher (Chapel Hill: University of North Carolina Press, 2006), 15; Andre M. Fleche, "Uncivilized War: The Shenandoah Valley Campaign, the Northern Democratic Press and the Election of 1864," in *The Shenandoah Valley Campaign of 1864*, ed. Gary W. Gallagher (Chapel Hill: University of North Carolina Press, 2006), 200–221; William G. Thomas, "Nothing Ought to Astonish Us: Confederate Civilians in the 1864 Shenandoah Valley Campaign," in *The Shenandoah Valley Campaign of 1864*, ed. Gary W. Gallagher (Chapel Hill: University of North Carolina Press, 2006), 222–56.

35. *ORA*, 1(43, pt. 1):560.

36. *ORA*, 1(43, pt. 2):891–92; "Tom's Brook, Virginia," in *The Civil War Battlefield Guide*, ed. Frances H. Kennedy (Boston: Houghton Mifflin, 1998), 319; William J. Miller, "Never Has There Been a More Complete Victory: The Cavalry Engagement at Tom's Brook, October 9, 1864," in *The Shenandoah Valley Campaign of 1864*, ed. Gary W. Gallagher (Chapel Hill: University of North Carolina Press, 2006), 134–99.

37. *ORA*, 1(43, pt. 2):888, 891–92.

38. Margaretta Barton Colt, *Defend the Valley: A Shenandoah Family in the Civil War* (New York: Oxford University Press, 1994), 342; Eloise C. Strader, ed., *The Civil War Journal of Mary Greenhow Lee (Mrs. Hugh Holmes Lee) of Winchester, Virginia* (Winchester, VA: Winchester–Frederick County Historical Society, 2011), 433.

39. On Cedar Creek, see Kennedy, *Civil War Battlefield Guide*, 323–25; Pond, *The Shenandoah Valley in 1864*, chap. 12; Stackpole, *Sheridan in the Shenandoah*, chaps. 11–12; Wert, *From Winchester to Cedar Creek*, chap. 11; Thomas A. Lewis, *The Guns of Cedar Creek* (New York: Harper and Row, 1988), part II.

40. *ORA*, 1(43, pt. 1):560–63, 581, 1031; Early, *Memoir of the Last Year*, 115; Keith S. Bohannon, "'The Fatal Halt' versus 'Bad Conduct': John B. Gordon, Jubal A. Early, and That Battle of Cedar Creek," in *The Shenandoah Valley Campaign of 1864*, ed. Gary W. Gallagher (Chapel Hill: University of North Carolina Press, 2006), 56–84.

41. John B. Gordon, *Reminiscences of the Civil War* (New York: C. Scribner's Sons, 1903, 341, 359; Early, *Memoir of the Last Year*, 115; Early, *Autobiographical Sketch and Narrative*, 447.

42. *ORA*, 1(43, pt. 2):901; Early, *Memoir of the Last Year*, 119; Early, *Autobiographical Sketch and Narrative*, 449; William W. Bergen, "The Other Hero of Cedar Creek: The 'Not Specially Ambitious' Horatio G. Wright," in *The Shenandoah Valley Campaign of 1864*, ed. Gary W. Gallagher (Chapel Hill: University of North Carolina Press, 2006), 84–133.

43. Basler, Pratt, and Dunlap, *Collected Works*, 7:58, 73–74.

44. Gordon, *Reminiscences*, 341, 359; Letter, William J. Jones to Dr. B. P. Morriss, October 28, 1864, copy, author's research files, Fort Ward Museum, Alexandria, VA.

45. *ORA* 1(43, pt. 1):563–64.

46. Richard B. Irwin, *History of the Nineteenth Army Corps* (New York: G. P. Putnam's Sons, 1892), 437–38; *ORA*, 1(43, pt. 1):564, 582, 1011; *ORA*, 1(43, pt. 2):901, 903–26 inter alia; Freeman, *Lee's Lieutenants*, vol. 3: 605.

47. See Osborne, *Jubal*, 381–85; Freeman, *Lee's Lieutenants*, vol. 3: 605; Letter, William J. Jones to Dr. B. P. Morriss, October 28, 1864, copy, author's files, Fort Ward Museum, Allexandria, VA.

48. Gallagher, "Two Generals and a Valley," 4–33, especially 18–19 and 25–27.

49. Aaron Sheehan-Dean, "Success Is So Blended with Defeat: Virginia Soldiers in the Shenandoah Valley," in *The Shenandoah Valley Campaign of 1864*, ed. Gary W. Gallagher (Chapel Hill: University of North Carolina Press, 2006), 257–87, especially 286–87.

50. *ORA*, 1(51, pt. 2):1060–61.

51. Freeman, *Lee's Lieutenants*, vol. 3: 635–36; Early, *Autobiographical Sketch and Narrative*, 465–69; Osborne, *Jubal*, 390–92.

52. George M. Mooney quote from Gallagher, "Two Generals and a Valley," 26, 33; Freeman, *Lee's Lieutenants*, vol. 3: 636; Early, *Autobiographical Sketch and Narrative*, 468–69.

53. Gallagher, "Two Generals and a Valley," 17, 19, 27–28.

54. Early, *Autobiographical Sketch and Narrative*, 468; Freeman, *Lee's Lieutenants*, vol. 3: 611.

6. UNREPENTANT APOSTLE OF THE LOST CAUSE

1. Gary W. Gallagher, *Becoming Confederates: Paths to a New National Loyalty* (Athens: University of Georgia Press, 2013), 80; Emory M. Thomas, *The Confederacy as a Revolutionary Experience* (Columbia: University of South Carolina Press, 1991), 110.

2. Early quoted by Gary W. Gallagher, introduction to *A Memoir of the Last Year of the War for Independence, in the Confederate States of America: Containing an Account of the Operations of His Commands in the Years 1864 and 1865*, by Jubal A. Early (Columbia: University of South Carolina Press, 2001), xi–xii; Letter, Jubal A. Early to John C. Breckinridge, March 27, 1867, quoted in Gallagher, *Becoming Confederates*, 79; see also 78–82.

3. Martin D. Schmitt, ed., "An Interview with General Jubal A. Early in 1889," *Journal of Southern History* 11 (November 1945): 548–49, 551, 558, 562, recounted in George C. Osborne, *Jubal: The Life and Times of General Jubal A. Early, CSA, Defender of the Lost Cause* (Chapel Hill, NC: Algonquin Books of Chapel Hill, 1992), 469.

4. See Gallagher, introduction, xiv; Thomas E. Schott, "Jubal Early: Confederate in the Attic," in *Lee and His Generals: Essays in Honor of T. Harry Williams*, ed. Lawrence Lee Hewitt and Thomas E. Schott (Knoxville: University of Tennessee Press, 2012), 236; Osborne, *Jubal*, 403–5; Millard Kessler Bushong, *Old Jube: A Biography of General Jubal A. Early* (Boyce, VA: Carr Publishing, 1955), 283–87.

5. See Jubal A. Early, *The Heritage of the South: A History of the Introduction of Slavery, Its Establishment from Colonial Times and Final Effect upon the Politics of the United States* (Lynchburg, VA: Press of Brown-Morrison, 1915, 7, 51–52, 78; Jubal A. Early, "Slavery," undated manuscript, J. A. Early Addresses and Papers Folder, volume 16, Jubal Early Papers, Library of Congress.

6. Early's virulent vehemence can be found in various communications in his personal papers as used in Bushong, *Old Jube*, 287–90, and Osborne, *Jubal*, 402–4.

7. Bushong, *Old Jube*, 290; R. L. Dabney, *Life and Campaigns of Lieut.-Gen. Thomas J. Jackson* (New York: Blelock, 1866).

8. *Lynchburg Daily Virginian* quoting *Richmond Examiner*, June 18, 1869. The details of Early's later life can be followed in Osborne, *Jubal*, pt. V, and Bushong, *Old Jube*, chaps. 26–28.

9. See William Faulkner, *Intruder in the Dust* (New York: Random House, 1948), 194–95.

10. Gaines Foster, *Ghosts of the Confederacy: Defeat, the Lost Cause, and the Emergence of the New South, 1865–1913* (New York: Oxford University

Press, 1987), 55; Osborne, *Jubal*, 454. On the lottery experience, see Charles Reagan Wilson, *Baptized in Blood: The Religion of the Lost Cause, 1865–1920* (Athens: University of Georgia Press, 2009), 88–90; Osborne, *Jubal*, chap. 26; and Bushong, *Old Jube*, 293, 300–302; T. Harry Williams, *P. G. T. Beauregard: Napoleon in Gray* (Baton Rouge: Louisiana State University Press, 1955), 298–300.

11. For recent literature dissecting aspects of the Lost Cause, in addition to Foster, *Ghosts of the Confederacy*, and Wilson, *Baptized in Blood*, see David W. Blight, *Race and Reunion: The Civil War in American Memory* (Cambridge, MA: Belknap Press of Harvard University Press, 2001); Caroline E. Janney, *Remembering the Civil War: Reunion and the Limits of Reconciliation* (Chapel Hill: University of North Carolina Press, 2013); John R. Neff, *Honoring the Civil War Dead: Commemoration and the Problem of Reconciliation* (Lawrence: University Press of Kansas, 2005); and John A. Simpson, *S. A. Cunningham and the Confederate Heritage* (Athens: University of Georgia Press, 1994).

12. Janney, *Remembering the Civil War*, 141; Foster, *Ghosts of the Confederacy*, 51, quoting Letter, R. E. Lee to E. A. Pollard, January 24, 1867, and Letter, R. E. Lee to A. T. Bledsoe, October 28, 1867, both in Lee Letterbook, Lee Family Papers, Alderman Library, University of Virginia, Charlottesville. For the religious overtones, see Wilson, *Baptized in Blood*. Early's comment to the Montgomery audience is recounted in Bushong, *Old Jube*, 297.

13. Janney, *Remembering the Civil War*, 142–43. See also Neff, *Honoring the Civil War Dead*, 159–62; Robert Stiles, *Four Years under Marse Robert* (Washington, DC: Neale Publishing, 1903), 188–89; J. Tracy Power, "Jubal A. Early (1816–1894)," *Encyclopedia Virginia*, accessed May 25, 2014, http://www.encyclopediavirginia.org/Early_Jubal_A_1816-1894.

14. Osborne, *Jubal*, 462–68; Bushong, *Old Jube*, quoting Letter, Jubal Early to H. B. McClellan, February 2, 1878, Jubal Early Papers, Virginia Historical Society, Richmond.

15. Variants on the tale are found in Osborne, *Jubal*, 471–72; and Bushong, *Old Jube*, 303–4.

16. Osborne, *Jubal*, 474–75, quoting *Lynchburg News*, March 6, 1894.

17. Osborne, *Jubal*, 477–78, citing Edward M. Daniel, ed., *Speeches and Orations of John Warwick Daniel* (Lynchburg, VA: J. P. Bell, 1911), 579–80.

7. OLD JUBE AND AMERICAN MEMORY

1. John Esten Cooke, *Wearing of the Gray: Being Personal Portraits, Scenes, and Adventures of the War*, ed. Philip Van Doren Stern (Bloomington: Indiana University Press, 1959), 85–101.

2. Cooke, *Wearing of the Gray*, 100–101.

3. Quoted in Laura Virginia Hale, *Four Valiant Years in the Lower Shenandoah Valley, 1861–1865* (Strasburg, VA: Shenandoah Publishing House, 1968), 382; Sarah Woolfolk Wiggins, ed., *The Journals of Josiah Gorgas, 1857–1878* (Tuscaloosa: University of Alabama Press, 1995), 122, 126, 137; Robert Garlick Hill Kean, *Inside the Confederate Government: The Diary of Robert Garlick Hill Kean, Head of the Bureau of War*, ed. Edward Younger (New York: Oxford University Press, 1957), 165; Jason Phillips, *Diehard Rebels: The Confederate Culture of Invincibility* (Athens: University of Georgia Press, 2007), 128–30; Letter, W. W. Averell to L. L. Lomax, December 20, 1894, in J. W. Daniel Papers, Small Library, University of Virginia, Charlottesville.

4. Gary W. Gallagher, ed., *Fighting for the Confederacy: The Personal Recollections of General Edward Porter Alexander* (Chapel Hill: University of North Carolina Press, 1989), 397, 440, 471.

5. James Longstreet, *From Manassas to Appomattox: Memoirs of the Civil War in America* (New York: Da Capo Press, 1992), 375–76, 402; William Garrett Piston, *Lee's Tarnished Lieutenant: James Longstreet and His Place in Southern History* (Athens: University of Georgia Press, 1987), 119–20, 118–87 inter alia.

6. Virgil Carrington Jones, *Ranger Mosby* (Chapel Hill: University of North Carolina Press, 1944), 189–90, 302, 325 n. 41.

7. John B. Gordon, *Reminiscences of the Civil War* (New York: C. Scribner's Sons, 1903), 317–19.

8. See Charles C. Osborne, *Jubal: The Life and Times of General Jubal A. Early, CSA, Defender of the Lost Cause* (Chapel Hill, NC: Algonquin Books of Chapel Hill, 1992), 462–68, also 410–11, 414–16, for a discussion of the Early–Mahone feud.

9. Douglas Southall Freeman quoted in "What Historians Say about Jubal A. Early," Jubal A. Early Preservation Trust, Inc., 1997, http://www.jubalearly.org/whatsaid.html. See also Douglas Southall Freeman, *Lee's Lieutenants: A Study in Command*, vol. 3, *Gettysburg to Appomattox* (New York: C. Scribner's Sons, 1944), xxx, 613, 770.

10. Osborne, *Jubal*, 392; Thomas E. Schott, "Jubal Early: Confederate in the Attic," in *Lee and His Generals; Essays in Honor of T. Harry Williams*, ed.

Lawrence Lee Hewitt and Thomas E. Schott (Knoxville: University of Tennessee Press, 2012), 232.

11. Osborne, *Jubal*, 392–94, citing Terry Moss, "Jubal Anderson Early, Glory to Ignominy: His Shenandoah Campaign, 1864" (master's thesis, University of North Carolina, 1981), 75–76, 85–86, 88.

12. Osborne, *Jubal*, 394; Moss, "Jubal Anderson Early," 85–86, 88.

13. Eloise C. Strader, ed., *The Civil War Journal of Mary Greenhow Lee (Mrs. Hugh Holmes Lee) of Winchester, Virginia* (Winchester, VA: Winchester–Frederick County Historical Society, 2011), 433; George E. Pond, *The Shenandoah Valley in 1864*, (New York: C. Scribner's Sons, 1883), 254.

14. Bruce Levine, *The Fall of the House of Dixie: The Civil War and the Social Revolution That Transformed the South* (New York: Random House, 2013), 230–31; Nina Silber, "When Charles Francis Adams Met Robert E. Lee: A Southern Gentleman in History and Memory," in *Inside the Confederate Nation: Essays in Honor of Emory M. Thomas*, ed. Lesley J. Gordon and John C. Inscoe (Baton Rouge: Louisiana State University Press, 2005), 354, 359; Stephanie McCurry, *Confederate Reckoning: Power and Politics in the Civil War South* (Cambridge, MA: Harvard University Press, 2010), 207, citing Broadside in McDowell Family Papers, Special Collections, Alderman Library, University of Virginia (UVA).

15. See Yael A. Sternhell, *Routes of War: The World of Movement in the Confederate South* (Cambridge, MA: Harvard University Press, 2012), 40, 138–40; Megan Kate Nelson, *Ruin Nation: Destruction and the Civil War* (Athens: University of Georgia Press, 2012), 30, 31, 32, 39, 40, 59; Lisa M. Brady, *War upon the Land: Military Strategy and the Transformation of Southern Landscapes during the American Civil War* (Athens: University of Georgia Press, 2012), 76–91; Andrew F. Smith, *Starving the South: How the North Won the Civil War* (New York: St. Martin's Press, 2011), chap. 7.

16. Charles Royster, *The Destructive War: William Tecumseh Sherman, Stonewall Jackson, and the Americans* (New York: Knopf, 1991), 38–39.

17. Royster, *Destructive War*, 362.

18. Richard M. McMurry, *The Fourth Battle of Winchester: Toward a New Civil War Paradigm* (Kent, OH: Kent State University Press, 2002), 14–19, for example.

19. On various Early positions, see Gary W. Gallagher, "Consistent Conservative: Jubal A. Early's Patriotic Submission," in *Becoming Confederates: Paths to a New National Loyalty*, ed. Gary W. Gallagher (Athens: University of Georgia Press, 2013), 69, 74–78; Phillips, *Diehard Rebels*, 183–85; Jubal A. Early, *The Heritage of the South: A History of the Introduction of Slavery, Its Establishment from Colonial Times and Final Effect upon the Politics of the United States* (Lynchburg, VA: Press of Brown-Morrison, 1915).

20. B. Franklin Cooling, "The Campaign That Could Have Changed the War—and Did," *North & South* 7 (August 2004), 12; Frank Vandiver, *Jubal's Raid: General Early's Famous Attack on Washington in 1864* (New York: McGraw-Hill, 1960), 179.

21. "The Raid on Washington: Gen. Jubal Early Again Tells His Story," *New York Times*, August 6, 1881.

22. Robert N. Stiles, *Four Years under Marse Robert* (New York: Neale Publishing, 1903), 190; "General Early's 'Stone Wall' Punch," *North and South* 24 (September 2012), 7–8; Millard Kessler Bushong, *Old Jube: A Biography of General Jubal A. Early* (Boyce, VA: Carr Publishing, 1955), 235–36.

23. Jubal A. Early Preservation Trust, Inc., P.O. Box 368, Rocky Mount, Virginia 24151; http://www.jubalearly.org/saveit.html and http://www.jubalearly.org/board.html.

24. Gary Gallagher, "Jubal Early vs. Stonewall Jackson," *Colombiad* 1 (Spring 1997), 20–23.

INDEX

ABOUT THE AUTHOR

Benjamin Franklin Cooling is professor of national security studies at the Eisenhower School, National Defense University, in Washington, DC. A prolific author of works in military, naval, and air history, specializing in the defense economic base, he has also authored Civil War studies on operations, occupation, and partisan warfare in Kentucky and Tennessee and campaigns in the national capital region, such as *Symbol, Sword and Shield; Defending Washington during the Civil War* (1991) and *Counterthrust: From the Peninsula to the Antietam* (2007), as well as four other books pertinent to Jubal Early's Washington campaign, including *Jubal Early's Raid, 1864* (2007); *Monocacy: The Battle That Saved Washington* (2000); *Mr. Lincoln's Forts: A Guide to the Civil War Defenses of Washington* (2010, Scarecrow Press), co-author; and *The Day Lincoln Was Almost Shot: The Fort Stevens Story* (2013, Scarecrow Press).

CPSIA information can be obtained at www.ICGtesting.com
Printed in the USA
BVOW03*1103210814

363480BV00002B/2/P